The Arms of the *Infinite*

The Arms of the *Infinite*

George Barker and Elizabeth Smart

CHRISTOPHER BARKER

Wilfrid Laurier University Press

WLU

We acknowledge the financial support of the Government of Canada through the Canada Book Fund for our publishing activities.

Library and Archives Canada Cataloguing in Publication

Barker, Christopher, 1943–
       The arms of the infinite : Elizabeth Smart and George Baker / Christopher Barker.

Includes index.
Issued also in electronic format.
ISBN 978-1-55458-270-9

       1. Smart, Elizabeth, 1913–1986. 2. Barker, George, 1913–1991. 3. Barker, Christopher, 1943–. 4. Authors, Canadian (English)—20th century—Biography. 5. Poets, English—20th century—Biography. I. Title.

PS8537.M37Z57 2010   C813'.54   C2010-905591-8

ISBN 978-1-55458-307-2
Electronic format.

       1. Smart, Elizabeth, 1913–1986. 2. Barker, George, 1913–1991. 3. Barker, Christopher, 1943–. 4. Authors, Canadian (English)—20th century—Biography. 5. Poets, English—20th century—Biography. I. Title.

PS8537.M37Z57 2010a   C813'.54   C2010-905592-6

Cover design by TG Design. Cover photo of Elizabeth Smart, 1948, by Michael Wickham. Text design by Catharine Bonas-Taylor.

First published by Pomona Books
PO Box 50, Hebden Bridge, West Yorkshire HX7 8WA, England, UK

Rights for this edition arranged by the Literary Agency erzaehl:perspektive, Munich/Germany (www.erzaehlperspektive.de) and in consultation with David Higham Literary, Film & TV Agents

This edition published 2010
by Wilfrid Laurier University Press
Waterloo, Ontario, Canada
www.wlupress.wlu.ca

This book is printed on FSC recycled paper and is certified Ecologo. It is made from 100% post-consumer fibre, processed chlorine free, and manufactured using biogas energy.

Printed in Canada

for G.E.B.

And also, your son does not step down out of his hammock
to be anyone's scapegoat, but to collect his own apple with
his own sin, as his son, too, will do at the proper time.

Elizabeth Smart
By Grand Central Station I Sat Down and Wept

CONTENTS

ACKNOWLEDGMENTS

Thank you to Elspeth Barker and Sebastian Barker for their kind permission to make use of passages from the letters and work of George Barker and Elizabeth Smart.

Thank you to Georgina Barker for her untiring help, advice and for her many family photographs.

Thank you also Arthur Barker, the late Ilse Barker, Graham and Olga Damant, Didy Holland-Martin, Laurence and Carol Scott, Jennifer Smart, the Coldstream Guard Archive.

INDEX OF PERSONS APPEARING

ARCHER, DAVID: Bookshop owner and patron of the arts.

BARRIE, J.M.: Author of *Peter Pan*.

BATTYE, DIANA: Socialite and psychiatrist. Married, divorced and then returned to live with Michael Asquith, the grandson of the Liberal prime minister.

BRETON, ANDRÉ: French poet, essayist and critic born in Tinchebray, Normandy. Joined the Dadaist group and co-founded the Dada magazine *Littérature* in 1919. In 1922 turned to Surrealism and in 1924 became editor of the Surrealist magazine *La Révolution Surréaliste*.

BUCHANAN, DONALD: Curator, National Gallery of Canada.

COLEMAN, EMILY HOLMES: American-born poet and novelist. Educated Wellesley College. Married Loyd Ring Colman, 1921. Moved with her son to Paris and became the society editor of the *Chicago Herald Tribune*. Married to rancher Jake Scarborough, 1940–44.

COLQUHOUN, ROBERT: Scottish artist, born in Kilmarnock. Educated Glasgow School of Art.

CRIPPS, SIR STAFFORD: Labour MP. Solicitor General, 1930. Executive head of the Labour Party, 1937. British ambassador to USSR, 1940. Lord Privy Seal and leader of the House of Commons, 1942. Minister of Aircraft Production, 1942–45. President of Board of Trade, 1945–47. Chancellor of the Exchequer, 1947–50.

CURZON, CLIFFORD: British pianist. Widely cultured with volatile temperament.

DE LA MARE, WALTER: Poet and novelist. Born in Kent and attended St. Paul's Choir School. Worked for an oil company for twenty years, during which time he started to publish poetry. Awarded Order of the Companions of Honour in 1948 and Order of Merit in 1953.

DURRELL, LAWRENCE (GEORGE): Indian-born British writer, poet and novelist.

ELIOT, T.S.: American-born British poet, critic and dramatist. Born in St. Louis, Missouri. Undergraduate at Harvard for four years, a year in Paris then three more studying philosophy at Harvard. Came to Britain to attend Merton College, Oxford, on traveling scholarship in 1911, taking up naturalization in 1927. Leonard and Virginia Woolf first published *The Waste Land* in 1922. Edited *The Criterion* from 1922 to 1939. Awarded the Nobel Prize for Literature in 1948.

EMPSON, SIR WILLIAM: English poet and critic, born in Howden, Yorkshire. Educated at Winchester and Cambridge, where he studied mathematics and literature. Professor of English literature at Tokyo, 1931–34, and at Peking, 1937–39 and 1947–1953. In the meantime with the BBC Far Eastern Service. Professor of English at Sheffield University, 1953.

FARSON, DAN: British television interviewer, writer and photographer.

FRAMPTON, MEREDITH, SIR: Painter of highly finished portraits and still lifes, sometimes with slightly surreal flavor. Only son of Sir George Frampton. Studied at Royal Academy of Arts schools from 1913. Exhibited at R.A. from 1920. Associate of the Royal Academy, 1934. Retired 1953.

GASCOYNE, DAVID: British poet and translator, championed surrealism and European literature.

GRAHAM, W.S. (WILLIAM SYDNEY): Scottish poet, born in Greenock and brought up on Clydeside. Educated at Greenock High School and worked as an engineer when a young man.

GUGGENHEIM, PEGGY: American millionaire. Patron and collector of art.

HARMSWORTH, DESMOND: Established Janus Press Publishing.

HASTINGS, GRISELL: Daughter of Lord Lammington.

HIGGINS, BRIAN: English poet from Yorkshire.

ISHERWOOD, CHRISTOPHER (WILLIAM BRADSHAW): English-born American novelist. Born in Disley, Cheshire. Educated at Repton, Cambridge, and studied medicine at King's College, London. Gave up medicine to teach English in Germany 1930–33. Best known for his works *Mr. Norris Changes Trains* and *Goodbye to Berlin*, based on his experiences in the decadence of post-slump, pre-Hitler Berlin.

JOHN, AUGUSTUS (EDWIN): Welsh painter born in Tenby. Studied at Slade School in London. Made a name for himself with his etchings, 1900–14. Later became accomplished portraitist with paintings of George Bernard Shaw, Thomas Hardy and Dylan Thomas.

JOHN, SIR CASPAR: Son of Augustus John. Educated at RN College, Dartmouth, 1916. Director General, Naval aircraft development, 1942. First Sea Lord and Chief of Naval Staff, 1960–63.

KING, MACKENZIE: Canadian Prime Minister, 1921–30, 1935–48.

MACBRYDE, ROBERT: Scottish artist, born in Ayrshire. Glasgow School of Art.

MACDONALD, MALCOLM: Colonial Secretary who in 1938 said it was Britain's aim to bring colonial self-government to all Britain's colonies.

MORAES, DOM: Indian poet, writer, editor and literary figure. Hawthornden Prize, 1958.

MORO, CÉSAR: Peruvian surrealist poet.

MORRELL, LADY OTTOLINE: Hostess and patron of the arts. Her memoirs, edited by Robert Gathorne-Hardy, appeared in two volumes in 1963 and 1974.

MUIR, EDWIN: Scottish poet, critic and novelist. Born in Orkney and later family moved to Glasgow and then he moved to London.

NIN, ANAÏS: French-born novelist. Mother was Danish, father Cuban and composer/pianist. Studied art in New York. Married bigamously to Hugh Guiler and Rupert Pole. Started the Gemor Press, 1940, and published her own works.

PAALEN, WOLFGANG: Born Vienna, 1905. Visionary thinker and painter. Joined Surrealist movement in 1935. Founded *DYN* magazine, 1944.

PEARSON, MIKE (LESTER): Canadian politician. Born in Newtonbrook, Ontario, and educated at Toronto and Oxford universities. First secretary at London office of the Canadian High Commission, 1935–39, assistant under-secretary of the state for external affairs, 1941, and ambassador in Washington, 1945–46. He was president of the UN General Assembly, 1952–53, and in 1957 was awarded the Nobel Peace Prize. Prime minister, 1963–68.

POTTS, PAUL: British-born poet and writer. Lived British Columbia, then later educated at Stonyhurst and St. Mary School, Florence. During the World War II served with the Royal Ulster Rifles and 12th Commando. In 1948 he volunteered for the army of Israel.

RIVERA, DIEGO: Mexican painter born in Guanajuato. In 1921 began a series of murals in public buildings depicting the life and history of the Mexican people. Painted a number of frescoes in the US, 1930–34. His *Man at the Crossroads* mural for the Rockefeller Center in New York was removed and put up in Mexico City because it contained an apparent portrait of Lenin. Married to Frida Kahlo.

SAINT-DENIS, MICHEL: Founded London Theatre School in 1935. Dedicated to Copeau's acting technique.

SCOTT, F.R. (FRANK): Canadian poet who studied for a time at Harvard University. Friend of the Smart family.

USTINOV, SIR PETER: British actor, writer, producer, director. Won two Oscars. Wrote autobiographies *Dear Me* and *My Russia*.

WATT, MRS. ALFRED (MADGE): Brought the Women's Institute to the UK. Having been on advisory committee of the British Columbia Department of Agriculture to assist in forming and guiding institutes, came to England and, under John Nugent Harris, founded the first Women's Institute in Anglesey. Later, on returning to Canada, she became the founder chairperson of the Associated Country Women of the World.

WHITE, ANTONIA: British novelist and translator. Educated at the Convent of the Sacred Heart, Roehampton, and St. Paul's School for Girls.

WILLIAMS, OSCAR: Ukrainian-born American poet and anthologist.

WRIGHT, DAVID: South Africa–born poet. Educated at St. John's School, Johannesburg, Northampton School for the Deaf and Oriel College, Oxford.

Elizabeth Smart, 1948
Photo by Michael Wickham

1986

⚜

I OPENED THE FRONT DOOR, saw her hand and my life changed forever. I went into the hall and in the room ahead caught a glimpse of an arm spilled out across the carpet from behind a chair. A sudden wave of panic left me dizzy with dread and I staggered into the room. There, all my worst fears lay on the floor before me. My mother was dead.

A few hours earlier, I had left her alone and stepped out into a sparkling London morning with the sound of her soft Canadian burr, reasonable and reasoning, echoing in my ears. We had been running through her worries about various members of the family and I had departed with her still languishing in bed but apparently quite healthy.

She had come to town from her cottage in Suffolk and was staying with me in my flat in Soho, as she often did when she wanted to see friends and visit her old haunts in London. As I left, I promised that when I returned we would continue where we had left off. I said I would call at the corner shop and pick up an indulgent lunch of Gauloises and pot noodles for her, and together we would nail down this worrisome world of hers.

Mum's wispy hair, still blonde despite her years, fell across her eyes. On the other side of her face and down her neck she had a livid purple bruise that left a devastated trail of some strange mechanic of death. It must have been a by-product of a sudden heart attack; a fiery comet-tail as her life sped off into the heavens. Its garish colors left me bewildered and giddy from shock.

Gasping, I sank slowly to my knees and picked up her outstretched hand, pressing it to my cheek. I knew this hand so well. I had watched these fingers knobble and crack as she kneaded the earth of her beloved garden, coaxing a dazzling array of plants and flowers into the Suffolk light. Over the years she had kissed better and caressed the knuckles of my own fingers. Mine had been disfigured from confrontation in sporting pursuits, and whenever I walked in with another bruised knee or bandaged head she would recommend the ways of the humble and sinuous dandelion that, she assured me, could crack concrete to get to the sunlight. We had often laughed as I spread my hand over hers, comparing lumpen knuckle for knuckle.

Holding it now, I was struck by how warm it was. A sudden rush of hope that she might still be alive was immediately extinguished by the popping and hissing of the old gas fire across the room. Its gentle voice confessed to me that its radiating heat had created this illusion of life.

There had been a time when she had placed this hand on my shoulder and, pulling her hair across her face with the other, asked:

"Christopher, darling, would you come if I called?"

It had worried and confused me. Why did she have to ask? But here she was, still in her old flannelette nightie, slumped low on the chair with her arms spread wide to the floor and now forever in that silent plea.

1947

TILTY MILL HOUSE WAS a solid, red-brick Victorian building with eight rooms and a Rayburn solid-fuel stove at its heart. There was no electricity. We were used to this from living in Ireland. By using candles, oil lamps and highly efficient "Tillies" (which burned methylated spirits vaporized through a cotton mantle) we had evening light. The house was girdled with a peeling white picket fence that gave way at the front to a hardened mud yard. The house stood among black wooden byres and from their depths we heard cattle stamp and low. A dense wood reared up on one side of the farmyard and Tilty Church stood looking down behind us from across a cow pasture.

As we crowded into the hallway, two closed doors followed each other on the left. Going into a room through the first door, on the right was a double-fronted cast-iron stove with a large sheet of greening copper on the carpet in front of it. A slide of soot had spilled out from its gaping bottom ash drawer and disturbed moths fluttered above in the dusty air. Running across to one of the room's two corner windows, we could see a sunny buttercup meadow and in the distance lazy summer crows were wheeling and cawing around a strip of ruined abbey wall. As my brother Bashie and me spun to our left, we pulled ourselves up on the sill and peered wide-eyed through the second window. Through it we saw a late-afternoon sun picking out the end of a three-story building and, facing us, at the very top of its end brick wall, a small clapboarded cabin with a little window in it, hanging from the roof ridge. The front wall of the building sported a huge rusting iron wheel whose rim at the bottom was submerged in the ground.

"That's a factory," I told him.

"No, darlings, that's the mill and it grinds wheat into flour to make bread." Mum had come up behind and squeezed us together in her arms.

The second room brought us to a stop as we tried to open the door. Pushing it enough to squeeze through, we stared round at four walls that were completely lined with books. On the floor was a sea of notepads, letters, magazines and old checkbooks in abandoned disarray.

"Hey, come and look at this," I heard my sister Georgina sing from somewhere beyond the hallway.

Bashie and I turned from the stacked books and squeezed through the doorway together. We barged each other down the hallway and turned into a dark corridor. A shaft of light fell across it from a half-open door. Georgina's arm pulled us into a cool stoned-floored chamber. It had empty shelves on both sides and in front of us was a large tin box with air holes all over its front door. Mum came in behind us, reached over, and turned the little butterfly catch to open it. Nestling in a geometrical cardboard tray of little cups was a burgeoning sea of huge white eggs shimmering in smart ranks to the back of the lower shelf. I had never seen so many eggs before. Mum took a scrap of paper from the top shelf that was lying in front of some other provisions.

"Mmm," she mused as she read the scrawled note. "Fred's coming round for tea to do the pumping ...," and then added, trying to sound stern, "You must never come into the pantry unless I tell you."

Pantry? Our life would now have to accommodate a lot of new words.

Looking through into the next room from a hatch door, we caught sight of a latticed window over a long shallow stone sink.

"Let's go into the kitchen!" Georgina shouted as we skipped past the back door.

The first thing that caught my eye as we entered the kitchen was not the coal-fired stove under the mantel but the rods and pistons of a massive hand pump with a black-lipped spout looping over the sink. Thrust out from the back of its vertical cranks and shafts, a long arm curved down. It had a lump of iron the size of a turnip at its end and I was first to jump up to this handle. I pushed it up as far as I could and it came crashing down in one stroke. I repeated the stroke three more times and the pressure started to build up. An iron cylinder near the floor leaked water and slowly started to wheeze. Then, with a deep coughing gurgle, a slim twist of clear cool water spiraled down from the spout and splashed into the sink. The house, we soon learned, had to be pumped up like a balloon every day to get the water running from the well below.

Bashie in the sties, Tilty, 1948
Photo by Michael Wickham

I was dizzy with happiness as we clambered up the stairs and ran into the bathroom. In it was something we had always longed for—a deep enamel tub that had two chromium-plated taps at one end. Bashie and me immediately jumped in and as we started to wrestle I realized with delight all four of us children could probably fit in it together.

Round the scrubbed kitchen table we munched through doorsteps of bread and jam with mustaches of fresh milk under our noses while Mary fed Rosie her bottle. Mum leaned with her back against the Rayburn rail and stared through the lattice window with a faraway look in her eyes. Outside, the evening sky flared a vivid crimson and Mum's smiling face was lit up from the glow. Then her chin started to tremble.

As we began our new life together, Mum was determined to record as much of it as she could. Most of her little handmade books had been devoted to the work of my father, the poet George Barker, but in one or two she had arranged snapshots and photo contact sheets of her children and her life. Now that her family had grown in number she wanted more room to spread out the story, and these weighty tomes of learning, as they buckled the shelving in the "study," seemed ideal. She took down two of the largest volumes that the house's owner, Ruthven Todd, had embossed with William Blake's name. He had half-filled both books with notes in his tidy hand, but she cut these pages out and started to stick photos in with flour-and-water paste.

Since she felt this was the beginning of a reorganization of our life, the second thing she did was to give us all a surname. Until now, she had called herself both Betty Smart and Mrs. Barker, although she had never married George. She resolved to take Barker as the family name and Elizabeth Smart later became her professional name. The "Betty" of her childhood vanished and we sadly never heard it referred to again.

As the year wore on and the summer sun kept the dusty drive and farmyard mud baked hard, the three of us explored our new home dressed in nothing more than baggy shorts held up with braces and Georgina in her light cotton frocks. Sunburned shoulders were our main worry and the soles of our feet hardened to cork as we played in the shaded stony lanes.

Unbeknownst to us, Mum was still worrying about George. Although their parting in Ireland had seemed peremptory she saw fit to write to him in London, to tell him where we were and, if he should care, to come and visit. Mindful of not having seen his new daughter yet, he traveled down from London by bus in July and arrived saying he was looking for some books he had left behind in Ireland, hoping that Mum had brought them on. For him it was a mission of curiosity and when he returned to his girlfriend in London he explained to her that he didn't think he would need to visit Tilty again. This girlfriend was only vaguely aware of where he had been, believing he had gone purely to "fetch some boxes."

He had first met Cass, a beautiful twenty-two-year-old aspiring writer, at a publisher's fund-raising party at a pub in Mayfair earlier that year. Although she had been seeing a friend of George's before she met him, after their first meeting he had assiduously won her over with his charm as he showed her around Soho. He had woven tales of his complicated love life that concerned a wife now in America and his Canadian lover (Mum) living in Ireland, claiming these relationships were over. He had carefully left out reference to any children, so when, during the next few months, Cass became pregnant they arranged for her to have an abortion, as she felt a family would be an encumbrance to their careers and relationship. She did not know that the child, if it had been born, would have been George's eighth. The termination was to become a source of much heartache between them.

After returning to Cass in London he spent the late summer with her and a coterie of poets and painters in Newlyn, Cornwall. Despite his avowal not to return to Tilty, in the autumn and through to early spring he began reappearing on a regular basis, staying for two or three days. For a while we children thought we had the beginnings of a normal family life.

Now that we were settled into our new home Mum realized she had to find work. She left us with our nanny Mary and traveled to London. While she was presenting her credentials to *House & Garden* magazine, someone had vaguely asked the picture desk if they could get hold of some photos of a large family playing together. Mum quickly offered our services as models and went to find a photographer. While she was looking in Soho drinking clubs she met an old friend called Julian Trevelyan. He put her back in touch with another old friend, Michael Wickham. He was good-looking, affable and practical. More important, he appeared separated from his wife and eager to help.

They left London the next day for Tilty in Wickham's old Riley saloon with cameras, enlargers, film and developing dishes piled up in the back seat.

That weekend, while Wickham was there photographing us, George turned up unannounced, as he was wont to do during this period. This Saturday, in January 1948, was to be his last with us for a long time. He quickly spotted he was superfluous to our needs as Wickham photographed us in our pajamas and dressing gowns playing round our little wooden table brought over from Ireland. All evening George played the gracious guest with an unruffled calm towards Wickham but on going to bed that night he picked a ferocious fight with Mum. The whole household awoke as he launched a tirade of snarling accusations of infidelity at her. He left in a huff for London the next morning and after we had silently helped him pack his bags and boxes into the taxi we chased after its disappearing tailpipe in sad and confused dismay.

As the autumn rains swept in over the woods and the dusty farmyard turned to a sticky broth of mud and dung, Georgina and I had to rein in our feral ways. We learned that we had been enrolled at the local council primary school at Thaxted. As the end of that second summer at Tilty fast drew to a close, the dreaded first day of term arrived.

We had a bus to catch every morning that stopped a mile's walk from home. Mary shooed us out the back door. Clutching my dinner money in my palm and Georgina's hand in the other, we made a run for the bus stop. After skipping over the farmyard quagmire we had three old gates to vault and then a public footpath overhung with long wet grass. If we didn't miss the bus, I usually arrived at registration in the freezing classrooms with caked mud up my legs and soaking shorts.

While in the course of becoming familiar with this new regime, Mum made a strange and alarming announcement. Granny, Mum's mother, was coming. After all those years of trailing round like gypsies we had finally settled and Granny was to travel from Canada, like visiting royalty, and confer her blessing on our picturesque abode. We had to clean the house from top to bottom and be dressed in our Sunday best for her arrival.

As the day neared, Mum became nervous. The telephone jangled occasionally to inform us of her progress. When answering one of these calls, Mum went white and immediately rang for a taxi to go to Dunmow. Michael Wickham was left to look after us in her absence and told us with a worried look that Granny had suffered a fall. As the train pulled into the station, Granny had descended the carriage to the platform, but with her failing eyesight she failed to notice the train hadn't come to a standstill.

She stepped down, hitting the platform as it sped past. Her brittle hip bones shattered and she was rushed off to hospital where, awestruck, we visited later and gazed with amazement at this ashen old lady swathed in lace and bed linen.

She left for Canada after her hospital stay and never witnessed the squalor of our happy home, much to Mum's relief. Although Michael Wickham usually left for work in London on a routine basis, he was by now her live-in lover and Granny would have found his presence difficult to understand.

Robert Colquhoun and Robert MacBryde had been introduced to Mum by a poet called Sydney Graham, who had known them from his Glasgow days at the beginning of the Second World War. Mum had the idea of asking if the Roberts would stand in loco parentis for her at Tilty while she worked in London. There was a certain amount of risk involved in this idea, for they had a reputation for moody and aggressive behavior, but Mum liked them and, as she always did, trusted her intuition.

MacBryde was small, dark and busy. He had an eye for irony, which, when combined with his Boy Scout practicality, could make him mischievous. It was told that when he first met George, whose charismatic reputation had preceded him, he carefully placed the bottom of a broken glass in his palm with the jagged edges outward. He then walked up to George and declared in his Ayrshire brogue:

"Here's something ye'll nae forget, will ye?"

Smiling, he crushed the shards into George proffered hand.

Colquhoun, conversely, was tall and taciturn, with a noble unkempt head and the predatory leanness of a laconic Gary Cooper. This sweet and charming nature, though, was also volatile, and could suddenly change, often under the influence of alcohol, and he'd unleash a thunderous temper.

The Roberts had moved from Scotland to London during the war. As outstanding students, they had met at the Glasgow School of Art and although Colquhoun was bisexual they were wholly devoted to each other. When the war came MacBryde was invalided out of military service through poor health and Colquhoun had served a time with the Royal Army Medical Corps in Glasgow. Leaving Glasgow in 1941, they had arrived in London keen to make their way in the art world, which in turn led them to the nonjudgmental and cosmopolitan world of Soho, where they met George.

The Roberts, 1952
Photo by John Deakin

They discovered that London was expensive and distracting and soon realized they would get more work done in quieter surroundings. Mum's offer would also sort them out with lodgings.

MacBryde, of the two of them, was the one who played minder to us when he came to Tilty. It was he who made us take our medicine, cook for us and shepherd us ready for school in the mornings. And tease us. At this he was a master.

"Ye'll no be coming home for tea, to see your Robbie now ye have a wee lassie?" mused MacBryde to me as he stirred a pot on the kitchen stove.

"What lassie?"

"I heard you're soft on a wee lassie called Jackie!"

I spun round and glared accusingly at Georgina.

"I *hate* girls!"

A sly triumphant grin would crack his face.

"Now there's a thing.... Ye'll be away and wed, aye tomorrow, no doot!"

He rearranged the pots on the Rayburn nonchalantly.

"I *hate* girls. I ain't never gonna git married!"

"So you'll be needing a plate for your tea yet a wee while, then?"

In the evenings, with Mum away in London, he and Colquhoun would keep us amused with a windup gramophone and a pile of scratched old 78s. His favorite was an aria with the words sweetly sung by Delia Murphy called "The Three Lovely Lasses from Banyon." MacBryde would delight us all, and especially Colquhoun, by capering and preening to the music while we children roared out the words. It would end in squeals of laughter when we all aped MacBryde's raised limp wrist, hooting out the last line in unison: "... and I shall be dressed like a *queen*!"

Apart from the windup gramophone, we had a wireless for home entertainment. It was essential for keeping up with school playground gossip on the latest episodes of *Dick Barton, Special Agent* and *Cherry Tree Cottage*. The wireless was as big as a wheelbarrow and had electrics that puzzle me even today. It required a big lead battery that partnered a thing we called an "accumulator" and its yellowing station display boasted North Reg, Belgrade, Athlone and other far-flung corners of the globe. With forehead stuck to its glazed veneer, I would pick away at its wicker front, captivated for hours.

The wireless was fun but could not compare with the excitement of a trip to the cinema. We would keep an eye out for coming attractions at the Kinema in Dunmow, so if any of our home entertainment systems were down (no needles or a flat accumulator) we had a good excuse to get pocket money from Mum and head for Dunmow.

The Kinema was at the far end of town from the Tilty road, and for your fourpenny-half from Great Eastern you were taken to the center and told by the bus conductor that this was the terminus and "All change." If you kept your head down behind the seats you could travel through town and scramble out right in front of the Kinema. It was a typical hick-town fleapit with broken seats and peeling facade and we adored it. They weren't particularly strict at the box office, but children were excluded from an "X" certificate unless they could rush the gate when the doors opened and push on through with the crowd to watch a horror film. Although the films scared us, the most frightening part of the evening was coming back. Watching the bus lights jiggle off into the dark, leaving us with a mile of slippery path past the woods was terrifying.

Another of our childhood burdens was the rationing of 1946 and 1947. We bore it without complaint, never having known a time without a ration book. It was even stricter than during the war years and life would become miserable when the strip of ration stamps for sweets had been used up before the end of the month and we had to wait for a new book.

Although the Roberts never stopped teasing us and playing practical jokes it wasn't all fun and games. Their relationship was one of constant bickering and it was usually MacBryde who started it. Mum would return on Friday evening with a party of guests and hardly had we hugged her before they all set off to The Rising Sun in Duton Hill. MacBryde would be sniping at Colquhoun even as they left.

I would lie awake in my bedroom with Bashie fast asleep in the top bunk, awaiting with dread the clatter of the returning party. After arriving back they would settle down in the living room with a preoccupied nattering and the distant murmur was briefly reassuring. I clutched at the idea that perhaps tonight it wouldn't happen. Slowly the rumble of their conversation rose in volume until, like an underground train bursting out of a tunnel, a distant door crashed open, followed by the sound of shattering glass and splintering wood. Colquhoun's bellow would bounce off the stone-flagged corridors.

"Befaaahk'n Jeeezus. You snivelling *shite*, I'll faaahking kill you."

I'd lie trembling in my bunk hoping that the thing I most feared wouldn't happen and the little latch on my bedroom door would withstand the torrent of drunken abuse and anger just outside. It always held fast and the tumult would wash on by, the sound of clattering feet on the wooden stairs signaling a troubled retreat.

Next morning the trauma of these nights would be hard to recall as MacBryde pattered around the kitchen making breakfast on the Rayburn stove. He would be singing quietly to himself, the *Banyon Girls* replaced by a troop of Irish dragoons, "… come marching down from Fife-ee-oh."

Those wild nights had their compensations. Before the house had arisen and MacBryde had started to clear up, we would comb the living room that had been the battlefield of last night's party. We'd gather up armfuls of empties to return to the pub. The Rising Sun was halfway up Duton Hill, the steepest hill in Essex, and because of this each boy racer on the council estate had a homemade, greased, state-of-the-art soapbox trolley. Ours was the envy of The Hill because Len, a local carpenter and husband of Lillian, who came to clean for Mum, had made it. He had incorporated a real car seat, a steering wheel and a hand-operated chain drive into its design. It was very heavy and never as quick as the other boys' carts, but on these occasions it made up for its failure as a racer. When we took out the car seat we could double or treble the number of empties we could pack into it. When we reached the Rising Sun, Harry Tann, the publican, would sort through our cargo, rejecting any bottles without the right brewery label. We'd come dancing home with handfuls of coins.

MacBryde's day of cleaning was often hampered by us children when, during the holidays, we would get under his feet. Gasping for peace on one such morning, he suddenly asked us if anyone knew what time it was. When we didn't, he said he would go and phone "Tim." This was something we often did for want of a working clock. Moments later he returned, full of excitement. As the speaking clock had been laboring out the time, MacBryde said he overheard two women gossiping in the background. They spoke about an airplane that had run into trouble and crash-landed near a place called Tilty Abbey, spilling a cargo of chocolate bars. Instantly we all knew exactly where that would be. The four of us tore out the door and disappeared down the drive, heading for the hills.

We spent the whole day scouring the fields and woods for the crash site. Georgina finally came out with it and told us bluntly there was no plane or chocolate, nor ever had been. We abandoned the dream and trudged home. On our return we were greeted by a chorus of concerned inquiry from both Roberts, Colquhoun joining in the jape now he had had a whole day's recovery from his hangover. MacBryde, with a glint in his eye, casually inquired as he put the teapot on the table:

"So, ye didn't find the wee plane? Now there's a shame! I ken I saw smoke away over yon woods ..."

And for a second my ears pricked up. Just in time, I caught MacBryde's twinkle and Georgina's furrowed brow.

"Oh no you don't. Ain't nothing there. Hah hah, can't catch me out twice!" I cried.

Although the Roberts were wild and, at times, heavy drinkers, they stuck to their side of the bargain with Mum. Once when I was eight, though, they both took off on the bus to Thaxted saying, mysteriously, they were going to meet "a man at a fair." All went well until teatime, when we became a little worried. Where were they? Preparing a meal was no problem for us. Incredibly, Bashie had been making Mum's morning coffee since he was four years old, including pulling up a chair to reach the grinder (it had been screwed to the wall at a grown-up's height) and bringing the pan to the boil three times, as she had taught him. He never spilled the boiling water or milk.

After tea and still no sign of the Roberts, Georgina said we should go over to Lillian's and she would look after us until they came home. Lillian and Len lived two miles away in a cottage, where we often went to watch television, since without electricity we didn't have one of our own. She was a French immigrant with a strong accent who had married Len, the carpenter. She was small and always wore a pinafore with a tea towel tied round her head. Both were very generous and were naturally the first people we would think of in an emergency.

As we set out it was with a spirit of adventure that had a very real edge to it. When we got to Len and Lillian's cottage she took us in and gave us tea while we excitedly explained what had happened. She then got up and left. I heard her and Len in earnest discussion in the room next door. She returned to tell us it was not possible to fit us all in for the night and we would have to go back. I never understood why she did this, apart perhaps from the fact that she had not had any children of her own and was alarmed to have so many stay overnight at her house. We felt rejected and very alone, but at least we had each other. It was now getting quite dark and the falling dew had a threatening chill to it. We knew we were going home to a cold and empty house. But most of all, we feared the woods.

The road home at dusk was not the same as in daytime. With a line of mist shrouding their trunks, the trees' upper boughs loomed menacingly when darkness fell. As we tiptoed along the track in a lonely Red Indian file the branches creaked and rustled like huddled witches. A startled blackbird suddenly shrieked in alarm and went chattering away down a hedgerow. We all heard a timber crack deep in the woods but no one would dare to ask why, as our nerves ratcheted tighter. We ploughed on, heads down.

Night had fallen completely when we finally reached home and by the light of a single candle we pushed our bunks into the same room and, chattering nervously, talked ourselves to sleep, one by one.

The Roberts returned the next morning with no explanation. The terror had evaporated with daylight and we all felt a lot more grown up, but an unspoken bond of trust was broken, especially with MacBryde. It never happened again, and anyway we could now look after ourselves. Couldn't we?

Mum always told me I could run fast because I had a larger than normal big toe and had inherited the swiftness of our Sioux ancestors. I knew she had been born in Canada, so being a Red Indian was plausible. I had discovered this gem of family history when I was rooting about in a deep cupboard in our bedroom. At the very back I thought I had run across the crusty carcass of a dead rabbit, but bringing it out into the light it appeared to be a pair of old slippers. They had small colored beads sewn into the blackened leather and were stiffened with age. Intrigued, I rushed off to show them to Mum.

"Yes, those are real Sioux moccasins. They once belonged to your Red Indian brothers. And you know when I call you home for tea? That's a real Red Indian war cry!"

It must be true. She had always called us with this strange "Woo-oo hoo-hoo," which only she could do. God, I'd been carrying round twin six-shooter cap guns in matching holsters since Christmas. I had been fighting on the wrong side. Then and there I dropped the cowboy swagger and took up a Red Indian hunting-trail lope. More important, I fancied I became fleet of foot. Never again would I start a race without first pulling on those moccasins and the mantle of the Sioux nation in my imagination. Sometimes, as I ran behind Mum to catch the bus, amid the banging shopping bags and helpless laughter, I noticed the power in her legs. She was very proud of her ability to run fast. After all she was a Red Indian too. Later, when I eased past her as we raced back from the woods, she crumpled up in tears and refused to run on.

Once, when the four of us were splashing by the edge of the millpond, flicking with sticks at the minnows darting through the weed, Rosie silently tumbled in. She was a toddler and could hardly walk, let alone swim. Georgina tried to grab her but couldn't reach. She turned to me:

"Go and get Mummy ... quickly!"

"Now," I thought, "my speed will save my sister."

I hurdled the two stiles between the barns, hared through the yard and, racing into the kitchen, screamed:

"Mummy, Mummy! Rosie's in the millstream."

Mum had been singing as she washed some dishes, hair neatly tied back in a ponytail, her back foot carelessly half out of a battered old ballet slipper. The plate she was washing hit the tiled floor and shattered as she leaped past me. I didn't recognize her face as I looked up and saw it flash by. It had been replaced by an urgent steely mask and the look in her eyes frightened me. I quickly dodged out after her, certain I could arrive before her to show her the problem. Some hope. All I saw was the back of her ankles, her bare feet flitting over the mud and her wild blonde hair, loose now, flying out behind her as she sped through the barnyard. As I turned the corner round the mill, I hoped I was at least in time to see Mum dive into the freezing waters.

But Mum had not dived in. For some inexplicable reason Rosie had remained calm and floated serenely out into the middle of the millstream on her back, a beatific smile on her face while Georgina looked on, helpless and terrified. As Mum arrived, the mill wheel had slowly started to turn and the black, still race had started to move. We all watched frozen in horror as Mum sank slowly to her knees at the water's edge with arms outstretched. Luckily the deep and usually powerful current was in a benevolent mood that day and it gently tugged Rosie back to the bank. When she at last came into reach Mum snatched her from the waters, dripping green weed still clinging to the back of Rosie's heavy Irish tweed coat. Mum had always told us proudly that because of the oils the fabric was impervious to water. Now I believed her.

As we walked back to the warmth of the kitchen, I found two black ballet slippers sticking out of the mud.

* * *

Bashie and me by the millstream, 1952
Photo by Russel Smart

The millstream, for all its potential dangers, was nonetheless a great source of fun. It supported trout, roach and carp, with a microcosm of lesser fry all thriving in the weedy shallows. Flashes of metallic blue would streak down its lengths, incandescent in the shadows of the overgrowing elder, as kingfishers fed on the columns of gnats. Thrilled, we would watch as luminous white herons, having daintily tiptoed the shallows, would rise into the air and flap off into the distance. The stream throbbed with grimy life and the pondweed that overgrew from the depths could hamper progress in our tarry old punt. But worse, we were warned, like a green sinewy serpent it could pull you under when you went for a swim. We had also been warned about the mill, which, if it was started up as you fished, could suck you along in the race. If you didn't moor up quickly you could then become entangled in its frothing jaws as the start-up rumble sucked a huge throatful of stream through its snarling grill.

The punt was the center of our fishing activities. We would tug it out from the mud under its collapsing wooden shelter. With patience we sometimes got results. We would buy a two-foot length of gut line and a hook from the fish tackle shop in Dunmow. Stripping a feather for a float and with a ball of twine we spent hours trailing our fingers in the clear midstream water as we waited for a bite. Some days we were rewarded with quite a catch. With MacBryde's help, mostly instructing us in how to be patient, thirteen was our record.

The millstream was used by a fishing club for breeding trout and they rented it from the farmer who owned the mill. It baffled me why these anglers would spend a whole day in thigh-length green waders flicking at the shadows with their rods and lines. They would pack up at sunset and go away happy with nothing in their baskets to show for it. I was told they did it just for the sport. Bashie and me, on the other hand, could moor the punt and run home with a glittering trout that MacBryde would roll in oats and grill for tea after only half an hour on the stream. Amazed, I even once saw an angler toss a trout back into the stream after a protracted and strenuous tussle to reel it in.

I had been struggling to keep up with my lessons at school. I would lark about at the back of the forty-pupil classes and answer back to Mr. Thomas, the fifth-form teacher, replying to him with lowered brow and surly mono-syllables. He ran a losing battle trying to control us, let alone teach, and I languished in the lower orders. Out in the playground, though, I had always been the fastest runner in the class and the smart money was on me for the school's best athlete when Sports Day came. Victor Ludorum or some-thing, they called it.

Being the fastest playground runner carried great peer prestige and I ran furiously in break time to maintain it. Once you had got the nod from your mates as *the man*, the title was yours to dispose of as you wished.

Jackie Baker had the title in the girls' playground and I often stole secret glimpses of her as she flew ahead of the others. In fact I was so besot-ted that other boys began to notice my glances. They set it up well. I didn't realize how I was manhandled over to where a group of girls were bounc-ing rubber balls off the schoolhouse wall.

> Over the garden wall,
> I let me baby fall.
> Mother came out,
> Gave me a clout,
> I asked who she was bossing about.
> She gave me another to match other.
> Over the garden wall

This last line required the girls to cock their leg over the bouncing ball as it came off the tarmac. My throat had constricted so I could hardly breathe, certainly not speak.

"'Ere, what you want?"

Jackie turned from the wall to meet us and all her girlfriends fell in behind her. I had never been quite sure if she knew who I was, but now there could be no mistake. The girls had physical training—PT, as it was then known—next lesson and she stood there in her blue Aertex shirt, slashed across with a red ribbon. Black woolen gym knickers crowned two creamy stilts that were capped from the ground with black plimsolls. She tossed her blonde mane at me, but I could hardly look.

"Nothing. We reckon I can run faster than you," I said.

I toed the grit with a total lack of conviction. That was the hook. She had spotted my doubt.

"Don't talk daft. Do you want to do it now?"

"Yeeeeah," they all roared.

So the horde sped over to the end of the parallel white lines painted on the playground tarmac. Two sets of seconds took the runners to the top of the track and in my mind I slipped on my Sioux moccasins.

"Ready. Get set. Go!"

Within three strides I knew I could beat her. I caught sight of her out of the corner of my eye and she seemed so earnest and eager. As she flew along beside me, my urgency evaporated and a physical sweetness seeped through me as we ran. I let her slowly inch past me till her red ribbon breasted the tape ahead of me. She was delirious. She jumped and twirled, punching the air. I slunk away with a secret grin. I got some strange looks from my mates for a bit as they took the flak from the girls, but I never let on.

Saint Mary the Virgin would sound her Angelus bell and the peels would echo off the remnant of an old section of abbey wall left standing in the nearby buttercup meadow; an ecclesiastical dorsal fin on the meadow's back to steer the supplicants to prayer.

The Reverend Cecil Cuthbertson ran a High Church and the tolling that reached my ears from the old abbey flints meant I had another appointment with the incense casket. It was all mumbo jumbo to me, really. I went along with it because grown-ups seemed so urgent and insistent about it. When I heard the first peel, though, I *did* pray: "Oh no. Why me, God? Why me, at this time?" Can't He see I'm only halfway up the walnut tree and need every ounce of courage to join Bashie, recumbent as he sways in the top branches? I could lose serious face here. But then, wait. Perhaps He *has* heard me: "Oi, Bash. Come on. Time for church. You'll have to come down." How many times can that happen?

Racing up to Saint Mary the Virgin, we tumbled through the heavily studded church doors and catapulted across to the vestry, elbowing one another to be first. Reverend was running late and a little agitated.

"Quickly now, boys. Into your surplices. The first hymn's starting."

The procession was already halfway down the nave aisle and my friend Dave Pitcher was swinging my incense casket, so that meant I would be on the organ handle. We knew the routine. If you're late, you take the last job left. But as Bashie joined the end of the line, hands sweetly together in prayer, I darted across the front of the leading silver crucifix as it headed for the altar and sped over to the organ. Seizing the upper end of the pump handle, I started heaving in unison with Tim "Tyke" Rice. He was the small gypsy boy from the caravan allotment and couldn't reach the top of the stroke anyway. The creaking and wheezing from the old organ's lungs was seamless as I nudged him out. Sweet treble voices filled the rafters:

"The day thou gavest Lord is ended."

George would, through these years, make the occasional visit, and these were awaited with great excitement by us children and not a little longing by me. The trouble was, for me they always seemed to be *visits*. George never came back to claim us or be what my school friends had: a *proper* dad. Why wasn't he like these fathers? I wanted to see him trudge out in the morning and navigate a Ferguson tractor through the Essex sludge. I wanted to regale my classmates with my father's skill on a combine harvester or the number of bales of straw he could carry. To describe him to them as a "poet" would have been met with incredulity, and so I started my schooldays with a half-blank family background. When talking about Dad, I would try to ingratiate myself with a scanty knowledge of George's cars. I knew the subject was close to his heart, but I never had quite the right information. A colorful tweak in the telling was often necessary.

He once arrived in what was no more than a rattling rust bucket. We had spotted him turning into the drive and raced to meet him, skipping along beside the car as we guided it home by the door handles. It must have taken all of his famed driving skills to avoid us as we tripped into the dust trying to get a foot on the running board. When the boiling engine had finally clattered to a halt, he waved us back from inside the car. He then emerged, peeling off his oily string-backed driving gloves. He tugged his flat cap forward off his head and slapped it back on. "To the victor the spoils!" he said as he scooped us up in his arms.

"So, dear hearts, waddaya think?" he asked. "Fangio, that charioteer of the gods, let me have the beaut for a song. Had her up to a ton on the Mulsanne Straight at Le Mans!"

We all looked at the smoking wreck and pretended not to see the missing bumper, cracked windscreen and broken light lens. I knew I could never let him drop me off at school in it (in the extremely unlikely event that he should he ever make the offer).

"Bumper, windscreen and light all on order from Talbot ..."

And he would metamorphose these trifling shortcomings into merit badges received while testing on the race circuit. You just had to believe him. Later, in the playground, I couldn't make all this translate properly, and rival tales from the council estate boys of mythic Sunbeams, Armstrong-Siddeley Sapphires and Wolseleys got more attention. The dubious knowledge that a sports version of my dad's Talbot Lago-Record had come third in the 24 Hours of Le Mans did give me a feeling of status, albeit defiant, but my tale never quite stood up.

The visits became a little more frequent, probably because the Roberts were on hand and he had drinking buddies. One Friday night, before a group of thirsty guests left for the pub, they came into my bedroom to see George demonstrate how a father should exercise parental discipline. This started as a little joke between them and it pained me to see the Roberts among this posse. Why were they now handing over their role of lax disciplinarians to George, who had forfeited this role by never being present? For the life of me I couldn't think of anything that I had done wrong to account for this castigation. Had any of them thought this through?

Nonetheless, this kangaroo court had deemed that George was to put me over his knee and spank me. Well, I considered myself far too old for this caper and would have none of it. As I flailed about in a desperate attempt to escape I grabbed at his balding pate and pulled out a clump of his precious hair. He let go and I quickly scuttled off to a corner, seething with hurt pride but brandishing a fistful of his last remaining wisps. His chums hooted with glee and they ambled off to the pub, leaving me feeling violated by a man who was little more than a stranger but who I yearned for as a dad. Those thin strands of hair between my fingers gave me grim comfort.

The mill was the center of Tilty and was guarded by a flock of aggressive geese that stationed themselves on the cobbles outside its front entrance. You had to pass between them and the bridge wall to get to the road. We had so much fun watching London visitors cope with this farmyard nuisance. As you approached the geese the natural instinct was to sidle over to the bridge wall away from them. That was your first mistake. As they were pecking away at the cobbles, they would stop. They raised their heads, which then spun round in unison like the gun turrets on a squadron of armored cars. They would eye you angrily and a cautionary hissing would start. If you didn't back off immediately, that was your second mistake. The hiss would turn into a furious screeching gaggle and they rushed you, yellow beaks in front of ramrod necks with wings battering the air. It alarmed me for years until Georgina taught me the trick: insouciance.

Not that she called it that then. She explained that it was just their nature and they couldn't help it. It had been bred into them by the Romans to guard the walls of their cities. We looked it up in *Legends of Greece and Rome* and it was true. All you had to do was say "Boo" as they charged, and then walk serenely past. I eventually mastered it. She could do it with everything—dogs, heifers, bulls, pigs, boars and, later in life, bores too. It worked for her. For me, they always smell my fear. Particularly the bores.

Visitors would dart this way and that, only to pull back with nervous little laughs. Georgina would then lead them grandly through the agitated flock with her nose aloft, declaring, "Just ignore them, they don't mean it."

If Bashie and I ever did manage to give the geese the slip and reach the mill door, we entered another kingdom belonging to Fred the miller.

"Oi, Fred. Can we come in?"

A grunt would come from the upper floors as he stamped about, heaving hundredweight sacks into line. Everything, including the opaque and cobwebbed windows, was thick with flour dust. When Fred disappeared into the bowels of the mill to start it working, he went through huge wooden double doors on the ground floor. A distant splashing turned into the hollow thunder of cascading water on a gigantic drum and he would re-emerge, brushing his hands. In a large gap above the top of the doors we watched as a row of wooden cog teeth, blackened and polished with wear, slowly started to move. This was just a small segment of an enormous horizontal mill wheel that picked up speed until the teeth flickered, then fused into an enormous black mouth with a fixed and threatening grin.

"You can clear off now!"

Fred turned, put a hessian flour sack on his head and stomped off. We darted to a side door, descended the few steps to a dripping dungeon and watched the horizontal vanes of this massive drum rush up from floor to ceiling, streams of surplus water spilling down. I have no idea how we never fell in. We even tried to reach out and touch the vanes as they went slicing by. Fred was a mythic figure to us, made more mysterious when he donned the sack. It was, quite simply, a hessian flour sack with one corner pushed inside the other and worn within the confines of the mill to protect his grizzled locks and hunched back. He would hump the sacks of flour up to the top floor and line them up at the hatch door of the ridge-high overhanging cabin, ready for dispersal by horse and cart. He was a gruff Merlin who toiled all day up and down the dusty mill ladders in this pointed shroud. He would emerge at four-thirty to clump into our kitchen and put four hundred strokes into the massive cast-iron pump that our cold-water supply depended on.

"Can we come and help you feed the pigs, please Fred? O please!"

We rushed out to the sheds, leaving him standing by the stoneware sink as he finished his cuppa after the pumping. He was a stoical and taciturn figure, but he tolerated us, especially in the house and later in the sties after tea. He plodded after us with a weary sigh and fetched his pig-feed bucket. With a muffled tap on the sides with the mixing paddle, he loosened the furry dried crusts of swill from the rims. He then filled the bucket half full with a coarse mealy powder. Splashing water onto this mix, he expertly worked the bucket and paddle with his gnarled hands, whirling up a succulent creamy porridge. The movements mesmerized me, and for some reason my mouth watered as I salivated over the swirling pig-food gruel. I would take the bucket from him, slack-jawed and drooling.

"Do the little 'uns first."

I would stagger over to the sty gate that Bashie was hanging over, prodding the pigs with a long stick. Releasing the gate latch, Bashie would ride the gate open and I waded through an agitated sea of squealing piglets and poured the heavy mush into a galvanized-iron trough.

"When you've done the rest, don't forget the latch."

Fred the Miller, 1948
Photo by Michael Wickham

And off he'd go. Fred lived in an old terraced cottage two miles away in Duton Hill, with Daisy. To her he would retire, wearily crossing the fields with a slow and measured stride, picking up his long leather jerkin and flat cap from the mill as he went by.

While away at boarding school a few years later, we heard he had died. Daisy, although apparently perfectly healthy at first, went into a rapid decline and died soon afterward. Mum said it was from a broken heart.

"But Mum," I railed, "hearts don't just break."

"Well, yes, I'm afraid they do."

I wanted to go back and mend all those windows we had smashed at the mill.

Madge Girdlestone was our postie and you knew she was coming because you could hear her whistling. As she crossed the meadow down from the church she'd be "Coming round the mountains when she comes." Then, the clack of the gate latch into the farmyard. "Coooeee ... anybody at home?" she'd trill as she passed the kitchen window. Totally irrepressible. We loved her. Well, how could we not? She brought our comics!

She banged in through the door and swung her voluminous postbag round in front of her. The whole length of both her arms would dive to the bottom together and her hands came up filled with bundles of rolled papers.

"One for you, one for you" she chirruped as she tossed out our comics.

After a quick cuppa she'd swing the bag onto her back, ruffling my hair as she strode out:

"Next time I'll knock your block off and put a cabbage on!"

If Mum ever saw us reading *Classic Comics* (a cartoon version of the classic books), she would tell us to read the original instead, but I remember being lured into the original works by the startling graphics of *Dr. Jekyll and Mr. Hyde* and *Green Mansions*.

One day Madge's whistle wasn't heard. The next was silent too. And the next. No Madge for a week. How would we survive? Eventually a string of other posties replaced her to deliver our comics. MacBryde made some discrete inquiries and came back smirking. Apparently she had been caught stealing money from Royal Mail letters, something Mum had guessed all along when some expected checks didn't arrive.

"Can ye ken it?" MacBryde chortled. "Aye: *Regina versus Girdlestone.* Then, doubtless: 'Detained at Her Majesty's Pleasure!' Well, well. Who'd a guessed it? Madge in the slammer!"

At first we laughed too, not knowing quite what he meant. Then we were stunned. Happy old Madge in prison. It was impossible to imagine. Georgina said Madge would die if she couldn't be free and we were all very glum. Mum told us that all Madge had to do was to ask and she would have given her some money anyway. She didn't have to steal it. Slowly a sense of betrayal mingled with our sadness, as if she had stolen our comics as well as Mum's money.

The mystery and enchantment of the woods and surrounding countryside that colored our Tilty playground changed when night fell. Before the Roberts burst into our life and gave darkness a terror of a different sort, we would huddle together in the kitchen. The Tilly lamp hissed a gentle warning to the darkness and kept the shadows at bay with a cold green light. Mum tried to cheer us up with a song: "There's nobody here but us chickens. There's nobody here at all."

Georgina always dared to ask the feared question:

"Mummy, what would you do if a robber tried to come in the door?"

"Ask him to sit down and have a cup of tea."

Why on earth that would comfort me and steady my jangling nerves, I have no idea, but it did. When we had washed and slipped into bed we would call out for Mum to come and read us a story. At our insistence it was often a Grimm's fairy tale, perhaps *Rumplestiltskin*.

I think most children have a compartment that fills up with just so much play-fright and once it is full they are happy for the night as long as it stops there. This may have been true for my siblings but not for me. My compartment was a bottomless chasm and the ritual had to go on. Mum would turn the oil light off after the story, kiss me good night and vanish. Everyone else was instantly asleep and Bashie's somnolent breathing would signal that I was on my own. I would now turn onto my tummy and, putting one hand over the other, start pounding the back of my hands with my forehead. I hummed along to the bumping until exhaustion overcame me or my repertoire of songs dried up. Then I would stick my thumb in my mouth and suck apprehensively while the owls hooted in the woods and a branch scraped the windowpane in the wind. I desperately tried to identify and then confirm that each skitter and rustle from the floorboards beneath me was of this world. Nodding off early would be no solution. The whole thing would only have to be repeated later on when the broken routine would shake me awake. But then, oh God, the night-light would be out.

It happened once when I had dropped off after a hard day dispatching General Custer with Bashie in the barns. I woke up in the small hours. Not a sound could be heard anywhere. A wall of impenetrable black all round. The night-light had gone out.

"Mummy, Mummy. Can I come into your bed?" I wailed.

No answer.

"Muuuummeeee."

Not a sound anywhere.

"Can I come into your bed?"

Pitch black all around and a rising nausea of panic. I'd have to get to her bedroom somehow. No, nothing for it. It would have to be a *journey*. Come on now, through the bedroom door, down the landing and left down the long corridor to her bedroom. Feel your way along the walls. Her door should be here. But it isn't. I am totally confounded. Why am I in the bathroom? My head is spinning in confusion. I'll never get to Mummy's bed, and if I don't, how do I get back to *my* bed?

"Muuuuuummeeeee!"

Then I heard it. She was whispering to me from far across the fields.

"Come, darling. Come to me. I'm here."

My homing systems righted themselves. I was off down the long corridor without using my hands. Passing through the bedroom door I knew its layout and headed over to her bed. At last, at last, the journey's end. Oooooooo, the cozy hollow by her side as I slipped under the blankets. Now I would feel her soft sweet breath on my face and her soothing words. But what is this? No soft skin but the rancid smell of sweat. A muscular arm yanked itself out from under me. There was someone else in the bed. A horrible mountain of hairy flesh was rolled over on top of my beloved mummy and was hurting her. She seemed to be crying out in pain. It had all been too much. I bit my lower lip as the tears came rushing up. The fight next to me was over quite quickly, though, and Mummy seemed to win because after this short tussle the big man rolled off her and she leaned over and kissed me on the head.

"There, there. You've had a bad dream. Go to sleep now, darling."

Visitors from London would come in all shapes and sizes. There was little Bobby Hunt, who would keep Bashie and me spellbound for hours into the night with thrilling bedtime stories. After Mum had announced *l'heure apéritif* and the grown-ups had gathered in the sitting room, Bashie and me would drag Bobby out by an arm and he would have to postpone his first drink. He would refuse to go on unless we handed him a hat to tell his story under, so we gave him our black Stetson with the white tassels for the first story. Then, getting into the role, he would strap my twin cap guns to his side and, pacing round our bedroom carpet, weave us pageants of quick-draw gunfights from smoky saloons in the Wild West. He could do the same with a bath towel around his shoulders like a leopard-skin leotard and Tarzan would sweep us away to some treetop jungle hideaway. His stories were cliché-ridden heroic sagas with perfect detailing.

An hour after the start of the drinking and when Bashie and me were asleep, Bobby would plunge back into the sitting-room fray and routinely pick a fight with burly John Davenport, one-time theater critic for the *Observer*. John had been a pro wrestler and you could believe it from his squat stance. He became belligerent when warmed with drink and was easily goaded by Bobby. These evenings sometimes ended in a jest wrestling or boxing bout that would suddenly flare up angrily. We were often reawakened from our slumbers where dreams of barroom brawls in the Wild West fused with dinner plates and glasses smashing to the floor as Bobby was pinned to the dining table.

One of our favorites was Ricky Stride. He came spluttering down our drive in a two-seater Morgan sports car. This one had a V-shaped two-cylinder engine mounted in front of a silver tubular fuselage and only three wheels. He had goggles on his forehead and a beautiful girl in the cockpit next to him. He was built like Charles Atlas, whose pictures we saw in magazines, and he spoke to us children like friends and equals, not at all from an adult world. He roamed through the woods with us, teaching us how to build dens and climb trees. He said he could track anything, anywhere, and when I raised an eyebrow, he said he'd give us the count of a hundred before he came looking and he'd find us, wherever we chose to hide.

As Bashie and me were trotting urgently along a track in the woods looking for a hiding place, it struck me that you didn't have to hide beneath or behind something. The lateral thinking on this was, I thought, to merge with the background like a chameleon, which was why I knew Red Indians had feathers in their hair and could summon each other with birdcalls.

It was a bright sunny day and the shadows were deep under the lowest fir-tree boughs. All you would have to do was stand perfectly still under these branches and you were invisible. But it was also a hot day and I had no top on and only corduroy shorts. Bashie was the same.

Ricky and Robert Colquhoun, who for once had been persuaded to come out and have some fun, pretended not to see us as Bashie and me stood like statues in the shadows. Our pale skin could not have been more visible. When they were nearly level with us they both suddenly turned and rushed us, shouting and hallooing. Bashie went out laughing with his hands up. I scarpered and ran the wrong way as they chased me. The nettles were only knee-high at first and I could jump and splay my legs out to avoid the stings. As I ran the nettles got taller and taller. I could hear Ricky and Robert calling me from the edge of the patch to come back, but I was in a frenzied terror now from the nettle stings and would *not* be caught. I ran and ran until the nettles were way over my head then stopped in a catatonic trance, unable to move or speak. Ricky gingerly stalked through the patch to pick me up and carry me out. I was in torment as they ferried me home with every part of my body scolded with poison. Mum put me on her bed, covered me with calamine lotion and rubbed it in soothingly. A few hours later, when the stings had died down, I actually felt quite invigorated.

There were at least two professional photographers who were visitors at Tilty. One was Michael Wickham, of course, and the other a camp little fellow called John Deakin. Bashie and me loved his visits because he was the only adult male to come to Tilty who would challenge us both to a wrestling match. We would join forces and, as he squirmed with delight, wrestle him to the ground. I never understood why he seemed to be weeping with pleasure as we bounced in victory on his chest.

Mum always asked Michael Wickham to leave her bed by the time we brought in her coffee in the morning and she never let him into her heart. He was an old friend of Mum's from her days in Cassis, France, in 1938. He arrived just as her relationship with George had finally fractured.

He set up a darkroom at the other end of the long corridor from her bedroom and when I stepped through the door I moved into a twilight world of sour and pungent smells. Pin-sharp rays of sparkling light were focused from polished glass that moved up and down on cantilevered stalks. An eerie yellow light dimly revealed black Bakelite dishes in which blank sheets of paper shimmered in swaying liquids. These white squares would often slowly metamorphose before my astonished eyes to mirror my own face and then to be hung dripping from a string over the trays. The equipment in the darkroom overawed me as if potions and paraphernalia from a sorcerer's cave.

One visitor to Tilty who came and went on a regular basis was the poet W.S. Graham—Sydney, as we always knew him. At first he seemed like any other of George's carousers who were so often sweet and mild-mannered during daylight hours but, when dusk fell, could turn treacherously after a drink or two.

Sydney was long-legged and with dark curly hair. His ruddy complexion and sad bloodshot eyes gazed mournfully round his bulbous nose. When on fire with liquor, he banged the table with his massive fists and the roaring Greenock vowels spurting from a rubbery upper lip would skewer me to my chair and brook no argument.

W.S. Graham and George were protégés of the radical bookseller and publisher David Archer and both had their first works published under his Parton Press imprint. Archer, after the success of a shop in London, had opened another branch of the Parton Street Bookshop in Manchester, calling it the Manchester Contemporary Bookshop, only to close it down and reopen in Glasgow. There he had met Sydney, a young engineer from Greenock, and reactivated the Parton Press to publish Sydney's first work, *Cage without Grievance* in 1942. When his father's generosity, which had been funding his publishing, started to run out, Archer closed his Glasgow shop and, with the Roberts in tow, headed back to London. Sydney later followed and Archer introduced Sydney and the Roberts to George.

Sydney's friendship with George blossomed but was sorely strained later when, while taking lodgings with us, Sydney started a clandestine affair with Mum. From the evidence of letters they exchanged, the affair was a passionate one and carried on without our realizing.

When they were working, the two Roberts used a creaking wooden shed at the back of the garden as a studio. I think it had been purpose-built for this, probably by Michael Wickham, because one of its walls was a large window that had an outside shutter and could be raised or lowered from the outside. When I smell oil paint from a tube the wild mess of the interior comes tumbling back and my eyes smart with the memory.

There was usually an easel in one corner with a work-in-progress clamped to it. The palette was no more than a square of plywood mottled with smeared colors. Among a tangle of crossed brushes lay leaded tubes of paint, curled up like winded toy soldiers. Their fallen caps were beside them as gore of different colors oozed from their severed necks—a body count of discarded casualties from a frenzied battle out of which the work-in-progress rose triumphant.

Colquhoun spent most of his time in there while MacBryde tended to our needs. Sometimes he would emerge, beaten back from his work by the weight of his hangover. Then we would all sit round the kitchen table and compete to see who could draw a perfect circle. Though Colquhoun's circle was frilled, as if inked by the trembling stylus of a seismograph registering an aftershock, he always won.

MacBryde's mischief knew no bounds. He once put on a special tea and the treat was a plate of newly baked cakes. Among many old favorites was a particularly toothsome-looking meringue, nestling in a frilly white paper cake cup. Presenting the plate with this speciality foremost, he asked me to choose. Of course, how could I resist? As I bit into the glazed sugar carapace my teeth cracked on a lump of rock that MacBryde had cunningly baked into the center. The tea-time table of my siblings, in on the joke, fell about with laughter.

Although we were poor when we first went to Tilty, we were never really aware of it. I didn't notice the holes in my socks (when we wore any) or my torn trousers. The only way we couldn't keep up with the council house kids was with the latest crazes. They would all have pogo sticks, Hula-hoops, yoyos and Slinkies long before us. But we always got what we wanted from Mum on our birthdays and at Christmas. Now that I was a real Red Indian, I naturally wanted a real bow and arrow for my birthday present. To be proper it should have arrows with metal points and flights with real feathers. Mum saw the inherent dangers in this, but after much nagging and pleading she finally gave in.

My birthday present came in a long cardboard box, and as I opened it there the arrows lay, deadly in their machined straightness, with brightly glossed rings around the shafts and fledged with striped feathers. The arrowheads didn't have barbs but they were brass, pointed and very sharp. Strangely, the kit included a colorful canvas target. I hadn't thought of shooting a target, just dogs, cats, birds and perhaps the odd passing cowboy.

So, without even bothering with my birthday cake, I smeared war paint from my watercolor box onto my face, put my Red Indian headdress on and with Bashie close behind me we ran out into the garden to set up a range. It was a very breezy day and whatever I did and however I hung it, I could not make the floppy canvas target stand up. I had a brain wave. Surely Bashie could hold it up. He could crouch down behind the playpen bars and hold it over the side. I explained this carefully to him and he was reluctant at first but said:

"Yeah, all right. I'll do it. So long as I get a go after."

The first arrow skidded off the top playpen bar and buried itself deep in the hedgerow. That was my marker arrow. Now for the bull. As I was about to release the second arrow, a downstairs window behind me flew open and a voice bawled out:

"Stop that at once, child!"

A naked man stood at the open window and I failed to recognize him immediately because he wasn't wearing his flat cap. George leapt through the window and ran over to me and seized the bow.

"The arrow, dear heart, will penetrate the butt and then your brother. You are a very courageous Red Indian brave, but the world does not need another martyred Sebastian."

Now handing the bow back and completely naked, he folded his arms round us and led his two little painted savages back to the kitchen.

Actually, this close call could easily have been avoided if Colquhoun had been on my case earlier. With bows and arrows it's not the bows that give us Red Indians problems but the arrows. You need lots, because you are always losing them and the half dozen real ones soon vanished into the hedgerows. If you make your own they have to be the same, otherwise your quiverful doesn't look right. I put the problem to Colquhoun and he had it solved in an hour, and that included gathering the materials together.

At the end of the cowsheds was an unused garage. The walls were falling out and under the crumbling plaster were row upon row of two-foot wooden laths on which the plaster had been laid. He took six of these wooden laths and split them down their lengths. He sharpened one end and pulled a bottle cap with a hole in the middle onto it. He then cut a two-inch slit in the other end and pulled the cardboard from a packet of Woodbines through the slit for a flight. He had managed all this within half an hour.

"Huh. Yeah, but they'll never fly!"

Well, I'd never seen Colquhoun shoot a bow and arrow in my life before, but he knocked George's flat cap off the handle of a garden fork six times at thirty paces with the dozen.

* * *

The cherubs from the church choir were my trusted lieutenants in the ongoing gang warfare we waged against the council estate boys who were led by Sid Boyle. He was bigger, older and nastier than any of us and patrolled the streets of Duton Hill with his dog, Butch, laying down the law. Our gang was Dave Pitcher, Tim "Tyke" Rice, Gary Livingstone, Bashie and me. We used hit-and-run tactics to little effect while Sid Boyle set up clever ambushes.

When the bus returned in the afternoon from the school run, it whined down the hill in a low gear and slowly navigated the corner at the bottom. There it drew to a stop, ticking over with the engine cowls rattling. As I came down the bus steps my blood ran cold as I saw Boyle and his thugs perched on the concrete-and-pole fence over the stream. They had cycled back from school and were there ahead of the bus. When I reached the bottom step I quickly scarpered round the back of the bus and, as I did so, another gang came out from the ditch on the other side of the road. They had me trapped back and front as the bus pulled off down the road in a cloud of black smoke. Bashie and I would have to sort this out by ourselves, since the rest of my gang had got off the bus at the Duton Hill stop.

Sid Boyle swaggered out in front of his gang and snapped out an order for Butch to attack. The dog ran barking at me with upper lip curled back over yellowing teeth and stopped, snarling, in front of me. I froze on the spot.

"We gotcha now, you dirty little gypo," he smirked, spitting out a wad of chewing gum. He then slowly drew out his catapult and loaded it.

He only half-stretched the elastic for the shot and I misread its trajectory. I ducked instinctively straight into the oncoming stone and, although it didn't hurt, the wound bled heavily. Boyle and his gang melted away when they saw the amount of blood squirting from my forehead. As I wiped the blood from my eyes, Bashie led me up the hill to Dave Pitcher's council house and I bled all over his Mum's kitchen while she wound a big white bandage round my head. I left Pitcher's house for the walk home, feeling every bit the Red Indian warrior as the blood came seeping through the white mesh.

I soon had reason to feel even sorrier for myself. I was crossing the pastures where they made the bonfire on Guy Fawkes Night when Sid Boyle and his gang got me again. This time his gang spread-eagled me on the ground and with Butch springing in and out, snarling and growling, Boyle came over and dropped on top of me with his knees grinding into my biceps. From nowhere, Georgina and Rose appeared. They must have come home from school on a later bus. Georgina marched straight over to Boyle, pushing his henchmen out of the way. She drew out a long feather from behind her ear and stuck it in his hair. She then grabbed Rosie's hand and circled round us, skipping and singing: "Stuck a feather in his hat and called it macaroni."

Boyle became enraged as his gang started giggling. He made a lunge for Georgina, but she skipped out of his way and I didn't ask for a second chance. All four of us ran home hooting our Sioux war cry.

Reverend Cuthbertson was a kindly man who had only one authority—Virginia flake. He worshipped it and grew it everywhere. The vicarage garden shimmered with glass cloches. He had two old greenhouses leaning against the garden wall and in them hung an impenetrable jungle of desiccating tobacco leaves.

His daughter Cecily called from the only small patch of lawn left free of gardening frames:

"Oh Daddy, for heaven's sake. *Do* come out and join us. What *are* you doing in there?"

"'And blessed are the horny hands of toil,' dear," he quoted back as he emerged through the greenhouse door rubbing his hands and peppering his toe caps with crumbling leaves.

"Mmm ... good ... the crop's ready," he mumbled to himself, as he chewed on his waggling pipe stem.

He doted on Cecily, his only child, and there was nothing he cherished more. Nothing, that is, apart from this latest crop of *Nicotiana tabacum*, which was his best harvest yet. The last penny of his stipend was still not quite enough for Cecily's fees at the boarding school where she studied ballet, so who was he to argue if the Good Lord provided. He had to make the difference up somehow. We were there to make inquiries about this school and were in the garden taking tea with the reverend's wife and daughter.

Mum had started to move up in the London editorial and advertising world by now. After she had first presented her credentials at *House and Garden* she later went back there to ask for a job on the staff. They had taken her on, pleased with her first article. She was making good money. After a year of this comparative prosperity she was beginning to think of sending Bashie, Rosie and me off to boarding school. Bashie and I, she thought, were in need of some refinement. Rosie was still very young, but Mum was now further encouraged by Mrs. Cuthbertson and Cecily to think

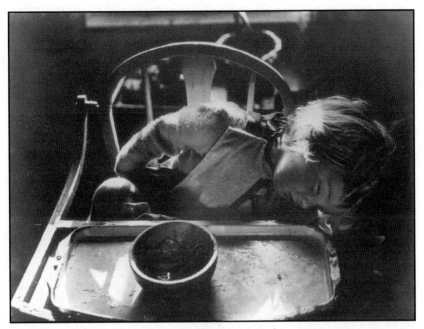

Rose, October, 1948
Photo by Michael Wickham

that under a mixed schooling of dance and academics she might thrive. The one drawback remained that, because of Mum's work commitments in London, Rose would have to board and she was only six and a half.

Georgina had been taking dance classes since before I could remember and was traveling to Dunmow for tuition, showing huge enthusiasm. She envied Rosie's luck. One day Georgina had gone round to see Cecily at the Vicarage, where she was working at the barre for her ballet classes, and Cecily had invited Georgina to join in. She whipped away from the barre fixed to her bedroom wall and, standing up straight and by her side, she threaded her arm through Georgina's:

"*Pas de chat, pas de chat.*" And they hopped across the room, shoulder to shoulder in chorus line.

"Change. Change. Change." And Cecily sprang into the air, scissoring her feet as Georgina tried to copy her.

"No, no, no. More *plié*, more *plié*." And she settled back into the first position. "Now the *entrechat* again. Aaand, yes."

After the lesson, Cecily took Georgina up to her bedroom to see her school uniform and she was hooked. Eighteen pairs of white ankle socks,

Georgina, January 1947
Photo by Michael Wickham

all carefully name-taped. Button-down straps on black, patent leather shoes. Brown cotton stockings. Full skirt with bibbed pinny. Djibbah underneath with a swagger jacket and topped off with a Sherlock Holmes cape. Everything had an elegant label: Rowes of Bond Street.

She stuck Herts and Essex for three years but could resist the world of dancing no longer. Also Rosie, who was turning into a passable dancer by then, had come back with too many colorful tales. So after persuading Mum, off she went to join Rose, turning her back on academia forever. It was probably the wrong call by Mum, to whom academic education was paramount. At this school the academics were minimal and ballet is one of the toughest careers.

1913

ELIZABETH (BETTY) SMART was the second of three daughters and one son born into a wealthy upper-middle-class family in Ottawa, Canada, in 1913. Mum adored her father, Russel Sutherland Smart, a benevolent and bespectacled little man with burnished cheeks and a pouter-pigeon chest. Despite his bookish and fusty background of law, regulations and records, he provided her and her siblings with a busy social life in a loving home that was frequented by diplomats, broadcasters, politicians and aspiring writers. He was a great reader and follower of the theater and perhaps sowed the seeds of a love of the English language in Mum.

Louise—or Louie, her mother—was the firm matriarch in this respectable household, insisting on decorum and a well-bred demeanor from her children, particularly her daughters. The secure family base led to a defiant and iconoclastic trait in them, none more so than in Mum. This defiance drove her to stubborn childhood insubordination, and early on she established a love/hate relationship with her mother. She would write later, recalling her earliest memories:

> I trudged upstairs, shooed by maid? nurse? mother?
> Unwanted.
> The baby slept.
> I trudged on up. Steps steep as Everest, revengeful, helpless, scouring the world for a small clutch to hold on to.
> Where did I go to? Rejected up in the dark, with difficult steps on two-year-old legs: an ineradicable memory of a journey with no arrival.
> Weren't there any warm cosy moments? I must have known there could be, for I screamed and screamed at the top of the stairs (some lower stairs) for my mother to leave her friends and gossip and cakes and tea and come.

But she never came. Or if she did for punishment, banishment into the huge deserted nursery, and the laborious folding and mating of those thick white woollen stockings and placing them two by two in virtuous rows, furiously concentrating, desperately muttering: "*Now* you are sorry? *Now* do you see how unjustly you abandoned me on that lonely landing?"[1]

Her mother's love was characterized by attention and then withdrawal. It produced a reciprocal love so strong in Mum that it was to remain particularly needy in her all her life, even though they had been separated for decades. Her mother was also hospitable, generous and warm, but her iron and indomitable will always got its way, and with Mum she would use emotional manipulation if she could sense any residual resistance when commands, tantrums and fury hadn't worked. Although not a social climber (she thought she was already at the top of the ladder, often declaring, "If the best was not for me, who then was it for?"), she was snobbish, telling her children she would have to "beat the Baldwin [black sheep family forbears] *out* of them" to instill some "decency and decorum *into* them." Because Louie had left school at grade eight, she was perhaps overly impressed by the trappings of learning.

Mum's dad, conversely, of whom there could be no better example of "new money," was always democratic about his use of it, listening sympathetically to any reasonable demand. This was a tendency all his children were to inherit and is a testament to just how generous he was, given how difficult it had been for him to acquire it.

With captivating nonchalance Mum would trace the ancestors on her father's side to a Benjamin Baldwin, one-time soldier in the Revolution and businessman whose grandfather had sailed to America from Hertfordshire in 1640. In the 1780s Baldwin had married a girl called Ruth Paddock in order to obtain ownership of Duchess County, then a part of New York State. Fanciful family lore had it that Ruth Paddock was a Sioux Indian chieftain's daughter and it always had an intriguing ring of truth until I learned that Ruth's parents were called Zachariah Paddock and Deborah Freeman, names which hardly have the ring of war paint and prairies. It was also suspect because Duchess County was a Huron enclave at the time and not Sioux, but we cared not.

Three generations after Benjamin Baldwin came Alanson Baldwin, who was a pencil maker and sawmill owner in Ticonderoga, New York. Alanson Baldwin was an entrepreneur and New World settler who had followed the expanding lumber industry in 1854 from America to Bytown, a year later to be renamed Ottawa (after the Outaouais Indians). In ten years he increased his ownership to two mills, two steamers and fourteen barges, employing 150 men and turning over 40 million feet of lumber per season.

During the Depression the business failed and Baldwin was left with cluttered yards of unsold wood. Ottawa was also hit by a huge fire and Baldwin had the ingenious idea of opening the St. Louis Dam and using the extra power generated by the torrent to work the pumps and extinguish the flames in the town. The local farming community in Carlton had been wiped out by the fire and he told them to go to the yards and help themselves to wood for rebuilding, telling them to pay him when they could. He was well out of business by the time the farmers were back on their feet. The debts remained unpaid.

In an attempt to emulate this, Mum would recall when, as a child, she once ran away from home in protest at a punishment and she too single-handedly saved the city in imitation of her grandfather:

> I kept on walking, brooding all the time on my persecution. I couldn't turn back to be treated cruelly. All the way up town, splashing unheedingly through the muddy puddles. At the great hotel, lying on the wet sand I found a match, still unstruck.
> A match, unstruck! Dangerous!
> It might catch fire and burn down the great hotel, perhaps the whole town! It was terribly dangerous! Perhaps God had wanted me to save the hotel, the town, from burning down, and so had sent me up here, to be a heroine. I, perhaps, was to save the town. This was my big chance!
> I struck the match and blew it out ... It was nothing. Yet I saved the whole town. I am a heroine ...[2]

When Alanson Baldwin first went to Canada from America he brought with him his ten-year-old daughter Kate. As Mum's grandmother she was best remembered for defiantly keeping the American flag in her underwear drawer. She had married James Alexander Parr, chief operator for the Montreal Telegraph Company, later to return to his hometown of Ottawa as an accountant. He was probably employed in this capacity by the Baldwin Mills and, thriving in this environment, produced nine children, seven of whom survived.

The splicing of the Parrs and the Baldwins at this point gives rise to another quaint claim in our family lore. When visiting England as a child of eleven, Mum and her family had gone to Poet's Corner in Westminster Abbey to see the grave of Thomas Parr. He was far from being a poet but had the distinction of living to the age of 152 (as verified in the *Guinness Book of Records*), surviving under the reign of ten kings and queens by conveniently changing his religion to suit the current monarch. I had often been told by Mum that Granny had primly talked of old Parr as passing away in the carriage after a feast given in honor of his longevity by King Charles I. The truth was, Mum delighted in telling us that he was in fact a loveable old rogue. He had married at eighty, been arrested for adultery at 105 and was forced to do penance by wearing a white shroud in front of Alderbury Church for "begetting a bastard." He was painted by Rubens, van Dyke and William Blake and died in 1635 from too rich a diet at the Royal Court where he had been paraded as a glorious old Methuselah.

Born in 1884, my Granny, Mum's Mum, was second to last of the seven Parr children. By the time she had met my grandfather, colorful though her background may have been, she was raised in a conventionally middle-class and fashionable part of Ottawa.

Mum's dad, though, had come to court Emma Louise Parr, her mother, in these leafy suburbs through a different route. Russel Sutherland Smart had been born a year later than Emma Louise, in 1885, to George Alexander Smart. His mother had died when he was six months old and George Alexander had abandoned his baby, absconding to America, to start a new family in Atlanta, Georgia.

Russel Sutherland was brought up by two maternal aunts in reduced circumstances, but it hadn't stopped him forging ahead in life. He worked his way through a practical-science degree at the University of Toronto by getting a job as a packing manager in his local Woolworth. Every day he would cycle to this basement packing floor from a tent pitched on the outskirts of the town. He got his B.A. from Queen's University through extramural studies and went on to join a patent and trademark agency. He quickly rose to Ottawa office manager in the agency and felt that, on this sound footing, he was able to ask and receive the hand of Emma Louise Parr in marriage in 1908. Not yet satisfied with his qualifications, he shrewdly mixed science and law by passing his bar exams in Quebec in 1911 and topped off his learning with a mechanical-engineering certificate from his old university in Toronto in 1913.

Canada at this time was expanding rapidly and demands for his services were at a premium, so with the help of a friend he set up a patent and trademark office, establishing himself within a short time as one of the most prominent patent lawyers in Ottawa.

Mum's neediness in wanting to be loved became a pattern of her behavior at school. After she had first attended the reassuringly named Ottawa Normal School, she was transferred to Elmwood School, in Rockcliffe Park, which reflected considerable social standing but was an imitation of an English prep school for girls. It flew the Union Jack over its neocolonial roofs in pompous declaration of fealty to the British Empire. When Mum was asked in literature classes to write an *Ode to a Nightingale* or complete studies in rooks or the lesser celandine, because her native Canada contained none, her defiant nature turned to resentfulness. As so often in her treatment of senseless snobbery, she turned to ridicule and became determined to sever Canada from the "Honouh of the mothah countrih."

She didn't develop much as a writer initially at Elmwood, preferring to gain popularity through clowning and conformity, "hiding all I knew and my mad delight in learning."[3] She and her sister Jane did, however, keep diaries (a habit she was to maintain all her life) and in one strangely isolated case she wrote a poem for an American children's magazine called *Junior Home*. "It was one of the best paid things I ever did," she said later, remembering the dollar fee.

Although Mum was often caught slacked-jawed when staring at the camera as a child, contemporary photographs attest that she turned into an attractive girl. It was strange that in 1924, at the age of eleven, this robust and healthy-looking girl was confined to bed for a year, due to the misdiagnosis of a "leaky" heart valve. Mum was an outdoor girl and I cannot imagine how her mother kept her in bed, save that she knew she would remain at the center of her mother's attention, getting all the love she craved. From her bed she also began to exercise control over her sister Jane, so often her childhood confidante and with whom she was ever to be embroiled in emotional turbulence. Much later, Mum wrote (in her diary of 1976) of this protracted convalescence: "All I asked was a bit of attention from a furious Mom. But there was nothing there to justify that long interesting year."

It was "interesting" because she had started to pen little stories while keeping up her diaries, and "nothing to justify that long ... year," because she never really felt she was ill. She also read and memorized voraciously, many books having been brought to the invalid's bedside. She systematically memorized the Latin names for all her favorite wild plants and trees, along with vast tracts of Shakespeare's sonnets and many favorite poems. This time in bed was the foundation on which her later obsession with literature was based.

Emerging into the social swirl of Ottawa, the butterfly that Mum had now become was "extremely pretty, pink and white and golden," according to Charles Ritchie, one of her boyfriends. She was less happy to learn that she had also been tabbed a "swot" by some of her acquaintances and hated being known as intellectual. At first she learned to be secretive, "having to camouflage books, read poetry secretly, pass ashtrays gracefully, be a Blonde," but this secret love of literature had metamorphosed with her beauty and she was often seen to carry *The Oxford Book of English Verse* under her arm wherever she went.

The Smart girls stepping out into society were corralled by their mother. Louie would drive herself into a panic awaiting the return of Helen from her parties. Three years older than Mum, she and her friends were often known to loiter on the way home and she would take the full brunt of Louie's repressed sexuality and Victorian prudery. Helen was often lashed about the legs by Louie, waiting with a switch of twigs as she scampered up the stairs when returning late. On one shocking occasion as Helen came home late yet again, Louie had the whole household, maids and all, lined up when she returned. As she attempted to dart by, Louie in a cold fury grabbed at her bodice and slapped her across the face. The bodice shredded to her waist and Mum witnessed in horror her sister's distraught attempts to cover herself. Helen, then aged twelve, burst into tears and sped to her bedroom.

Louie was to spend her whole life trying to exert control over her daughters. I think it must have been lucky for Mum that Helen, being the eldest, was the first to take their mother's zealous chaperonage. In 1931 Helen, now at McGill University in Montreal and perhaps fearing Louie's disapproval, eloped with an American college football player. The lovers were, however, brought back and placed firmly under the family wing as young Alan Swabey, the wayward football player, was taken on as a clerk in the family firm. Louie's fury abated.

At eighteen Mum had many admirers. They came to the balls and parties at the Governor General's residence at Rideau Hall, the Seigniory Club, the Country Club and, of course, the Smarts' Ottawa home, along with ministers, mandarins and politicians. Graham Spry, who later set up the Canadian Broadcasting Company, was one such and a constant companion. He was, in fact, deeply smitten, but perhaps because he was thirteen years older than she was (she called him Uncle Graham) and because Louie had selected him as an escort that could be trusted, his passion went unrequited. He said of a walk with her:

> She dressed in her sloppy shoes that would not stay on, she gave me a cane and then she would not go.... "You are coming for a walk," I insisted. We took the path along the stream that tumbles through Mackenzie King's property. The trees were arches, they formed an arcade, and the light seeped through.... Betty grew mad in the light. She ran, she leapt, she sang, she danced; she frightened me. "Horrible," she said when she came to the chasm where the stream drops forty feet over the rocks.[4]

Trouble was, although he had been enchanted, she had dismissed his reaction because he was too conservative. "What would you think of a man who walked through a valley in the moonlight and acted as if he were strolling down Sparks Street?" she had confided to Helen. She never mocked him but as a friend advised him:

> What is it you want out of life? Not just solitary meditation.... There is only a certain amount that you can think without stimulus. There are books of course, but even books should be read spontaneously and when sudden impulses come to you to read them. To read. On and on. If you have real work and play which means friends and exercise, which can mean any mountain, could you be happier? Retire to think for three months, for instance, near the sky and come back and fit your philosophy into everyday things. Oh, think a lot, which means anywhere—in church, in the bathtub, at the office.... It is sad to find out that you do not want to do the things you've always thought you wanted to do. I think you need friends. Doubtless I am wrong, but it is better to be wrong than restrained. I'm not using a peremptorily Oh, You Know tone, I was just thinking and it may be something different in a moment.[5]

Then he adds: "Be good. No. Be bad and repent."

If he was never to be her lover, he was her first literary patron, mentor and supporter:

> This panic, this blank ... sitting at my desk at Kingsmere in a catatonic agony. He told me to write, write, write. There is no other way to write. Fearing for me what I fear myself. How good. How good to feel he is

to the rescue ... he set the light of love of work alight and I was stimulated. Good. Even to write a tiny page about a bog is to feel fire such as I have not for ages. I *must will*. I *must*. I will.[6]

She tried to eschew the hectic social life that she found incompatible with her writing. When her father bought her two hundred acres of mountain in the Gatineau Hills for her nineteenth birthday, she constructed a cabin she called The Pulley, after the poem by George Herbert. She painted the doors and window frames yellow and in the isolation, rather than coming closer to God through restful meditation as her name for the cabin would imply, she began constructing her literary persona. *The Seed Growing Secretly* by Henry Vaughan was nailed to the log wall:

Then bless thy secret growth, nor catch
At noise, but thrive unseen and dumb;
Keep clean, bear fruit, earn life and watch,
Till the white winged Reapers come!

Although her literary ambitions could be nurtured by secret growth during occasional visits to her remote cabin, life was hurrying her on. In 1931, after graduation with first-class honors from Hatfield Hall, her secondary school, she asked if she could travel to England to study music. A suitably accomplished tutor was found, with extramural studies in history and English at the University of London. Mum, I think, may have wanted to take this visit more seriously, but her mother, who went with her, was expecting her daughter to be "finished" as a glittering debutante. Leading such a life in London soon began to pall after too many social engagements and Mum yearned for a more meaningful and urgent existence.

She returned to Canada for the summer of 1932 but in the autumn was back in London, with her mother, sister Jane and a chaperone, to continue her studies in music. Somewhere along the way, her motives for a musical career had evaporated and although she had been studying piano for thirteen years, and despite showing some talent for playing under this prestigious tutelage, she gave up. Or rather her tutor, Katherine Gooderson, of whom Mum was quite fond, suggested she seek tuition elsewhere. Gooderson had sensed that Mum's interest in playing had waned. Many years later I was astounded to hear she once had hopes of being a concert pianist. She loved classical music and I often heard her hum and sway to herself as a taped and battered old radio crackled out a favorite Mozart piece. But I never heard her play a single note.

Mum as debutante

This second visit to London with the chaperone was obviously designed to introduce Mum and her sister Jane to suitable young men, so they could marry well. The idea that they should study, the chaperone decided, was a cover and was totally at odds with any notions Mum had as to why they were there. However, the chaperone unexpectedly died (Mum and Jane always felt they had killed her with their "unkindnesses").

Mum at this time began to take her interest in literature more seriously. She flirted briefly with thoughts of reading English at Oxford University and went to a tutorial college to get her through the entrance exams. This interest fizzled out and she didn't take the exams. She had, anyhow, been lapping up classical reading on her own in a never-ending attempt to improve her literary learning.

Louie must have been pleased with the progress of her two youngest daughters. Mum could tell her that she had been to visit the author J.M. Barrie; had platonically dated the famous portrait painter Meredith Frampton (who was later knighted); had met the prime minister's son and future colonial secretary, Malcolm MacDonald; and had lunched at Downing

Street and spent the weekend at Chequers. Louie purred with bourgeois pleasure.

At this time Louie was approached by the formidable Mrs. Madge Watt (more commonly known as Mrs. Alfred Watt, after her husband), a Canadian founder, with John Nugent Harris, of the Women's Institute in England, who suggested she take Mum on as her secretary and traveling companion to Stockholm and Germany. Louie thought this was a suitable occupation for her daughter, although unpaid, and stumped up the fare. She even had Russel make a donation to the Associated Country Women of the World to demonstrate the family's approval of Mrs. Watt's cause. It seems unusual that Mum would have happily taken on a trip of this kind. As the personal secretary to an unimaginative but driven warrior of woman's rights such as Mrs. Watt, Mum must have known she was putting herself in the hands of an autocrat. She was often so troubled by her own indolence and lethargy that she would suddenly galvanize an urgent and demanding work ethic, which might account for her enlistment in the trip.

Her mother and background constantly stressed that a life of genteel pastimes in preparation for marrying well were all that a young woman should aspire to, and it started to frustrate her. She began to feel the need to be occupied: "With something ... anything, to make me feel more worthy. It was only an excuse to put off for a little while longer the settling of my future. It is my long winded excuse for never having done anything. An alibi, in fact."[7] A trip with Mrs. Watt was also a good excuse to escape the social rounds in London that she found increasingly tiresome.

Her personality was beginning to change. She often castigated herself for any feelings if they were not spontaneously generous and good, inspecting her motives carefully and constantly for anything bogus or counterfeit. Before leaving for her trip she was still continuing her music lessons while making preparations, and she records in her diary a touching incident that reflects the generosity of her nature but that still left her troubled:

> I joined my taxi again and hastened to Katherine Gooderson's to lunch. My taxi fare was immense of course—but I felt that way. The driver, after I had paid him, said, "If you don't mind me asking, Miss, who was the author of that book *Melody and Harmony*?"
> I looked puzzled.
> "That book you were carrying into the house—*Melody and Harmony*, I think was its name."
> "Oh—Stewart Maclaren. Are you a musician?"

He looked pleased and shy and said he was. He played the clarinet and the piano. "A man has to have some relaxation you know," he said. He was fair and quite young, in his thirties—and thin and sparsely haired. He was the oily kind of man and had a rather suffered kind of face. I said "that's a good book." He said "It looked it." He had never heard of Katherine Gooderson. I said "Good luck" to him and went inside. I had been so surprised and startled by him that I never thought to ask him if he would like to borrow it—as well as my music for the summer—no one is using it—why not let it be enjoyed?—just what I should have done. Oh why do I always have to think so late? I looked out K.G.'s [Katherine Gooderson] little square sunny back garden, and then I thought—perhaps he's not gone yet. I rushed to the front door but it was too late. O—what a fool! What a lost opportunity![8]

During the trip she recorded in her diaries this continuing inner debate for spontaneity but now the self-censure started to transfer itself from her feelings to her creativity:

I looked at the queer lake and thought it is like something. What is it like? Oh! It's like a wet olive. That's good I said. It will go well in my diary. It's like a wet olive. It will be impressive. Then thought: I am copying Virginia Woolf. I am being influenced and "making phrases." I am cheating. I am not being myself—but taking her construction putting on a light meaning and saying O how original I am—and how apt. Then—isn't all this truth-speaking and self-analysis, isn't it all her influence or someone's—not your own? All this pretending to get at the core. It's not true, really. But then I thought as I scrubbed my back with a lint cloth and French Fern soap (brown and oval) isn't it permissible to be stimulated honorably, to be made more alert and alive and noting of things by others? To be shown and *taught*. Cannot I be stimulated by Virginia Woolf and Katherine Mansfield (who is sometimes reflected in V.W.) and Mary Webb and Barrie and others? Yes, why not? To be my own original nature self—to be the thing that is the strongest urge at my depths—that is to lay all that down and laugh at it and walk on a mountain alone—really alone in a wild place. And not want to meet a soul. And that is really true and it is the urge and the flame and it needs no fanning. Things seem false if they are conscious. Conscious fun—nothing—revolting. Spontaneous they must be—bursting and self-forgetful.[9]

(I do love her little comic self-pampering aside in the middle of her tortured auto-dialectic: "lint cloth and French Fern soap" ... and then, oh, even more degenerate, "brown and oval.")

Although this trip was not a great success Mum was able to keep her reading and diary going in this way, with a continually maturing style. Her abundant joy in the German ski resort of Mount Hausberg with a companion she calls Herr Wrizt, brings an exuberant delight to everything: scenery, people, animals and her emotions. In one passage, while on the road they drop into a bar and at first she cannot make herself understood. Frustratingly she pleads for the bathroom (while in fact wanting the lavatory), which an old woman attendant obdurately refuses to understand: "But then she thought I wanted a bath—she *wouldn't* understand—I said *you* know—*you* know. But she just looked amused. I hadn't the courage to demonstrate literally—how could I anyway?"[10]

(It occurred to me that later in her life she would have had no compunction in crossing her knees, putting her hands between her legs and squatting in urgency, to demonstrate. At this stage, she was still too much the demure young woman.) But she soon warms to her cause and speaks of having had cider wine with a couple from Hamburg:

> … and I was going "crok, crok"; we had jokes and things. He was nice. It was reviving. Oh for *definite* people to talk to! And to be wallowing in mind—I mean to have to use your wits to answer—to be exultant in the fray—K.M. [Katherine Mansfield] says 'the high luxury of not having to explain.' You can leave all the unnecessary things out—and take for granted the unsaid. Oh joy! And no matter how tired or washed out apathetic you are, you forget it and your cheeks glow and you are enthusiastic and alive and *alert*. And it's fun. Well it was good after six weeks of the other, if only for five minutes in a pub in an incomprehensible language. They got up, shook hands with the two old people, said "Heil Hitler!" and left. [11]

All through this trip she remained oblivious to the increasing unrest in Germany in 1933.

This Herr Wrizt must have been tough. They covered thirty mountainous kilometers that day, and Mum at the end of the walk came under severe pressure to call for a rest. But not Mum:

> Oh! It was a long long walk—my feet hurt—I could not bear to speak. I knew the meaning of "footsore and weary" but I felt endurance and willed myself on. I could go on and on forever—by will to endure—(women's)—but it was awful. As long as H.W. didn't ask me if I was tired or try to talk or teach me I could go on. I said I wouldn't speak till

we got to Ober-Mörlen. He understood. He is seventy years old. I could hardly believe it.

Herr Wrizt accompanied me to the door of the *Englischerhof* [small hotel]. He was joyous at the door. I thanked him. ("Oh! No!" he said, shocked and chiding. "You must not say 'Heil Hitler' to a 'Hund' [dog]!")[12]

During this trip, apart from the light relief of walks with Herr Wrizt, it was Mrs. Watt's overbearing personality and the unremitting boredom of the meetings that weighed heavily. Mum was happily charging through D.H. Lawrence's *Lady Chatterley's Lover—"great.* And pure. And, strangely, it was infinitely comforting."

Then Mrs. Watt: "It must be pretty disgusting if England won't allow it. They're really awfully lenient about literature. I think it's perfectly disgusting to want to read a book my country won't allow."

Mum was relieved to get back to Canada for the rest of the summer in the family country home at Kingsmere and then, for autumn and Christmas, in Ottawa, where she resumed a round of parties and socializing. It meant Louie could stage-manage Mum and Jane's social life and in January 1934 she and Jane were presented to Their Excellencies the Governor General and his wife, the Countess of Bessborough, at Government House. Mum came out as a debutante here and D'Arcy McGee, her escort for the day, accused her of being unfair to him, to look as beautiful as she did.[13] In Mum's eyes this immediately wrote him off as a serious lover, consigning him to the role of "admirer," where he languished with quite a few others.

Although she enjoyed this role-playing, as earlier in London, this way of life was once again trying her patience and she felt torpor sneaking in. Despite it flattering her, she always felt there was something more important she should be doing: "So, now though I have just been writing I *WILL* on sheets of paper, it is not wholehearted, and at the bottom I know it is only an excuse to postpone my work, and sit dreaming idly, of sensuous, earthy, vain things, that sap vitality, and are nothing, and leave nothing the next day, but more desire for the same, and a power of discontent without."[14]

And later in that year of 1934: "Oh it is awful. I have nothing to write about. There is nothing. I care for nothing, but the glorification of myself—and not even my whole self, as of yore—I am content to have my body extolled and eulogized in meaningless hackneyed words out of the mouths of 'smoothies' with 'lines' who speak for effect or result and care not about the recipient."[15]

She wrote a poem at this time that well summed up her feelings and had echoes of her later complaints about the "female muse" and "the great sexual necessities":

I'm going to be a poet, I said
But even as I said it I felt the round softness of my breasts
And my mind wandered and wavered
Back to the earthly things
And the swooning warmth of being loved.
Bright and hard and meticulously observant
My brain was to be
A mirror reflecting things cut in eternal rightness
But before I could chisel the first word of a concrete poem
My breast fell voluptuously into my hand
And I remembered I was a woman.[16]

Before Mum responded to an ever-increasing pull to go back to London, where intuitively she felt she could more ably shake off the shackles of her vain and shallow life in Ottawa and address her calling, she took a boat trip with her father to Sweden and Norway. It was a trip that bound her to him in a complicity that she deals with in her diaries in a mature and understanding acceptance and that for me begs many other questions about her father's relationship with Louie.

During the voyage she is latched onto by various suitors, whom she handles in a sympathetic but irresolute way, being flattered by the attention but slightly irritated by it all. Her father, on the other hand, who had just had his fiftieth birthday, indulged in a fling that from Mum's accounts in her diaries had a well-oiled ring to it. Implicit in Mum's record of the encounter is the certain knowledge that the goings-on were a secret between them and would never go any further. Her account is touching and funny:

"We ['Mr. Harris' and she] walked round the deck and saw Daddy with a beautiful Scandinavian in his toils. He was leering at her. She was giggling. He had only left us for a minute. They looked old pals already. We went in and met her. I went to bed … I undressed. In the bathroom I met the Finn washing her stockings. I washed mine and my underwear. She was friendly, smiling and affable—a generous woman with the proper attitude of woman to woman—friends not enemies or rivals."

She then adds:

D'Arcy had sent me some flowers—gladioli and cornflowers.
"I didn't say anything," Daddy said.
"I didn't say anything and I didn't imagine anything," I said.
"I think you're mean to even think such things."
"So do I," said he, "I said nothing." We both laughed.[17]

They both they felt they understood each other perfectly.

The sentence she uses in her description is interesting: "They looked old pals already." Slightly ambiguous, I feel. Was it "already" because they hadn't been long on the voyage or because they had known each other before the voyage? And it seems a very intimate thing to be washing and drying one's stockings in the cabin of a man one has only just met. For all Mum's woman-of-the-world understanding of this affair she could still write, "Then I got into bed. But I couldn't sleep. I tossed and turned. I felt sort of sick. Why should I mind? When I myself? I thought you were on the side of the angels [her father had said he was 'on the side of the angels' to her when she was a young girl] ... I thought why should I mind? It seemed as if I didn't sleep at all until the bright day."[18]

So she did somehow mind but perhaps didn't blame him. Also, he had brought his daughter along on this voyage and had trusted her with his secret. But there must have been great danger in putting all this in a diary. She knew others were prone to sneaking a look and Mum had added at the start of her earlier diaries: "Journal of 1933—This belongs to Betty Smart. A purely Practical Practice Book Recording Days Whether They are Worth it or Not. Of no Spying Interest!"

This trip must have been a great delight to Mum, who was spending cherished and close time with her dad, but one does wonder at the circumstances. Was she taken along as a cover for his affair with Lydia Mattson (she is named in *Necessary Secrets*, page 73)? The way Mum records it, she seems unaware of anything more than a brief fling on her father's part.

She enjoyed her time with her father on this voyage, but she forever seems to be restless and unsatisfied, as if in perpetual search for something that stubbornly refuses to appear. She continually tries to escape one life to resume another elsewhere, continually feeling all the answers may lie on the other side of the Atlantic.

On her return to Canada after the voyage this unrest sends her off again to London in the autumn of 1935 to continue her extramural studies at London University, where her courses now include English, Latin, French, Roman history and logic.

Through a friend called Bill Aitken, a nephew of Lord Beaverbrook, she met and had a close liaison with Lord John Pentland, son of Lord Aberdeen, who had been a Governor General of Canada. She had spent some time with him in the Swiss ski resort of Grindelwald, after they had met in Scotland. It is hard to imagine a more unsuitable suitor. A fastidious, mother-obsessed neurotic, he attempted to dominate Mum, who, even though she knew this, tried to shoehorn him into an image she might be able to love:

"His own personal dignity must have been his staff, he cherished it at such enormous price. I remember him always gathered together, his back to his fireplace, standing on his own ground, lights indirect, everything in meticulous good taste, no false notes but false notes for a purpose intended. I would rush into this room, flushed, eager, remembering things that never actually happened, but might have, between us, and he would confront me with this marble enigma of himself."[19]

As Mum unfolds her feelings for him in her diaries it is hard to imagine they were little more than trophy partners to one another, and he was hardly the free spirit who she could share her love of abandonment in the wildness of nature: "The urgency grew. His ununderstandable, unapproachable, dominant personality began to obsess me day and night. He imposed a strictness, a discipline on everything with which he came into contact. I was limited, schooled, our meetings cut to once a week, or as a treat perhaps an occasional accidental or unprivate being together. This discipline piqued me. These tastes made me desire more."[20]

Her mother, who had made a flying visit from Canada, lifted her spirits but surprisingly didn't fall prey to his correctness and title, rather steering her away from him with scorn, as Mum tells in an account of the affair:

> She was balm, riches, luxury, strength. I felt remade—because of her expensive talcum powder, and perfumes, her pretty underwear, hats, stockings galore … I began to revive.
> "John doesn't like me in black," I said.
> "Tush," she said. "What do I care what John likes?"
> "He thinks that common."
> "Pooh! My taste is as good as his. That I should live to see a daughter of mine kow-tow to a silly man! Have a little pride!"[21]

But Mum was dreaming of someone quite different: "Today Mummy flowed and she loved me, and so she loosened my atmosphere and I was happy. And every minute he is in my thoughts. But oh! To be met in a leap!"[22]

She couldn't persuade herself that Lord Pentland was the one with whom she could leap hand in hand into the future, and she knew that if there was even the slightest doubt about this then it couldn't happen. Even as she tried to take his hand for this leap she was frustrated, for in their attempt to consummate their relationship he proved impotent. She felt lucky to have escaped the overpowering rigidity of his world, and on the boat back to Canada she recalls in her journals:

"Mid-Atlantic. The further I get from England the happier I am I have left it and the more I resent John and the cringing shape into which he was making me. I stand up and blush for my humble acceptance of importances and his too reasonable, joyless unnatural view of life. It's that he *might* so easily have made me happy and *didn't*."

In her journal of March 1936 she wrote: "I must marry a poet. It's the only thing. Why don't I know any?"

In October of that year, while on the world trip and still thinking of John, she scolds herself and says in her journal: "Never egg a man on to be physical. If he wants to leave, say goodbye. This has always been a principle, yet why have I abandoned it at times? Anyway it defeats its own end. From now on I must be *mental* until I find myself a proper mate. However may that be soon!"

Then later, that October:

On awakening: this terrible problem of matrimony! I don't want to get married any more. I dreamt I was married to John. First of all we were all at church singing hymns. Peggy and Lady Pentland behind. John was very sweet and helpful. But then I had to make an enormous bed for Lady Pentland and she didn't like the way I was making it. It had piles and piles of extra blankets and things for padding. I was trying terribly hard, but I couldn't please her. John was somewhere in the background, sympathetic but unable to do more. How can I marry and sign away my life? Then there are always the velvet eyes of the world [her phrase for a handsome man]. I couldn't consider anyone else. Men, careers, one excludes all others forever. Where is an occupation that embraces all things? And where is a *man?*

At the age of twenty-three she had started to rationalize an ideal that was to set her on a quest. She didn't know *who* she was looking for but she was beginning to realize *what* he would have to be, and she was already feeling that she might be able to write as an occupation in her life.

The round-world trip proposed must have been approached with misgivings. Mum had come back from her European trip out of sorts with Mrs. Watt. To volunteer, so soon after, as a dogsbody without pay for a world tour with her seems a little rash. Undaunted, and largely because she hadn't settled her future and was doing nothing at the time (yet again she reprimanded herself for enjoying too much this slothful life), she agreed to go. The trip was to take six months. Starting in Ottawa and traveling westward through Canada, they would touch the United States before heading out across the Pacific to Hawaii, Fiji, Samoa, New Zealand, Australia, Ceylon, Egypt and Palestine.

She and Mrs. Watt were under the auspices of the Associated Country Women of the World, as with their previous trip together, and this time Mum describes her duties as doing "every conceivable job from ironing blouses and carrying luggage; to intervening on her behalf, writing her letters and soothing people she had ruffled. I didn't get paid for this and it was called 'valuable experience.' I charmed people she antagonized against her own interests; I gave her affection when she made it difficult for anybody else to."

She also had to carry the chamber pots and at many of the meetings it was her job to sell the ACWW books, magazines and pins. Much to the delight of the assembled meetings she would play piano too, after she had made an address on, perhaps, Canadian art or the natural world. There was, however, much to delight her, and all the while she was finding out more and more who she was: "I looked at Mrs. Watt in the midst of her country woman gathering, making a speech, and I realized that you have to be slightly blind to *thoroughly* believe in *any* cause."[23]

When she arrived at Sri Lanka [then known as Ceylon], she was enthralled by the vitality of the Sinhalese but flew into a rage at their treatment by chauvinistic colonials.

A nice Englishman who brought some Sinhalese to tea at his club was forthwith ostracized and resigned and joined a Sinhalese club. The attitude is so stupid, ignorant, narrow and intolerable that it makes me boil. If I were a Sinhalese I should be leading a red revolt. "The Governor tells me communism is rife all over the island," said Mrs. Watt. The Sinhalese are cultured, charming, witty, subtle, kind, sensitive and proud. Those arrogant blockheaded ignoramuses! Lionel Alty, the Australian, made me hate him forever by saying, "Now, you've never stayed with these people before, Betty, so if you should need anyone I am at the Galle Face and Mrs. Moore Jackson is at the GOH. You'd better take those names down." If he'd been near enough I would have slapped his face.[24]

The bigoted attitudes of the arrogant colonials and Mrs. Watt's censure annoyed Mum, but she still experienced many moments of tranquility. She had always been in love with the natural environment of her homeland in Canada, and although she never conscribed to a religion she seem to come as close to any religious experience when communing with nature:

I have just been swimming in the soft, warm, caressing Indian Ocean. The sun has just gone down. The young moon came out, gradually getting brighter and brighter, and there was a great shining star nearer and nearer. Beyond the sand bar the sky over Galle was pink and orange. The little fishing boats and the palm trees on the two little islands were silhouettes. Some of the sky was mauve. Leslie [unknown acquaintance] was with me. He has a short D.H.L. [D.H. Lawrence] beard and he wore trunks. He completed the picture, dark against the tropical dusk. We each had surfboards. I never swam in water so warm. I jumped back into the joyful pagan worship of the holy things of earth. It's such a beautiful abandonment. What else can most of us know but that blissful, permeating, all-embracing warmth. I don't know whether or not it is sex. I don't think so because it is complete. It's not a straining after, or desire for, it's a realization, itself, of being alive, or every little bit being alive, here and *now*. It's saying this moment is enough; this is perfect and I am alive in every particle to its perfection.[25]

I don't suppose she would have admitted it, especially as she had only just opined of Mrs. Watt "you have to be slightly blind to *thoroughly* believe in *any* cause," but *her* cause was passion and she was right.

The tour rolled on to Palestine, where Mum was much taken with the attitude of an Israeli girls' agricultural college—a communal ideal with no authoritarian platitudes or hypocrisy. She felt their ideals were straight from the heart. She even felt exhilarated enough with their life in Palestine to put in a request that she be allowed to return from London and spend two more months living with the girls at the college, although this did not happen.

Despite all the vicissitudes of the tour, as she returned to London she was able to comment, "I can suddenly see the result of my six month experiment and the things I have learnt on my travels. I am new made. And I am pleased. O, if it can only continue!"[26]

Back in London she took up again with Lord Pentland, but all was not right. One evening they went out to dinner, and on their return to her flat she read him her diaries. He commented graciously that he thought they were good. He got up to go and on his way out intimated that he wouldn't be seeing her again. She was astounded and had no idea why. She couldn't understand why they couldn't see each other just as good friends, but she quickly came to realize that perhaps it was best that the affair ended:

"Yet even now I have sobered down, with sleep and warmth and realize that perhaps it would be a good thing not to see him. I can become adjusted to anything. O but only remember the walks through the wet woods! What they might have been! The misery of the thought of what they might have been! O the wild dreams! Was it really the end, then, when I sailed, sick and exhausted, for Canada last year? What have I done? Is the fault mine or his? He said that he had learnt that he couldn't teach me anything, nor he learn anything."[27]

Although she was very fond of him, he only ever appears as a limiting influence on her, and apart from her investment of boundless enthusiasm in him the affair seems to remain barren of any real joy for either of them. She muses, not without a little prescience, before their final meeting: "John disturbed me for at least eight hours after I talked to him. What *is* that magical tragical power anyway? I am drawn to him, compelled to be miserable, chastened, subdued, humbled, curtailed, bound. Why? Is it some divine idea to discipline and tutor my easily inflated esteem? Would fate dare to interfere?"[28]

Fittingly, he walks away from *her* at the end. Although she had always admired him for his courage in trying to shake off his straitjacket of social mores and inhibitions, how could she not see that sex with him would never be the wild natural passion she wanted? She was "free of my tyrant John. He is pleasant enough to think about. I am free."[29]

She wanted to find someone more 'related to her species'. She also recognized that she should "seek a mate, not a way of life. I must satisfy nature before I invite God." Not surprisingly she got over him very quickly and had soon thrown herself back into London life, resuming her classes at King's College, University of London.

Louie was now building up a dazzling future for her beautiful daughter as the reports from London reached Ottawa. Mum had become aware on her voyage that Edward VIII had abdicated. Friends of hers had heard it through heavy static on the radio as they steamed into Sydney harbor on December 12. On her return to London she was once again caught up in the social whirl as London prepared for the Coronation. She still wrote her journal and from it started an account of her world tour that she called "Details of a Detour," as if in apology for the fact that this was not subject matter worthy of her talent. With mixed reviews from friends and people whose opinion she respected, including Lord Pentland himself, she had already written an account of her liaison with Pentland that she had called "My Lover John." She was tentatively beginning her life of literature, and although she was vulnerable to criticism of her work she had the strength and discipline to continue, despite being in the hubbub of a continually distracting social life.

Mum was fully aware at this stage that she hadn't found her voice or any worthy subject matter but nonetheless she was "hurtled on by her lucky genes," as she later put it. It would need greater cataclysms in her life to prepare her for what she wanted to say as a writer, and for the time being all she could do was bear in mind a favorite line of Henry Vaughan: "... bless thy secret growth, nor catch / At noise, but thrive unseen and dumb."

The "noise" around her at this time could not have been more deafening. In the buildup to the Coronation of George VI there was much partying to be had. She was living in a flat in Lowndes Street, in expensive and fashionable Belgravia, paid for by her father. She had plenty of admirers calling on her and was shopping at Harrods, charging clothes to her mother's account at Peter Jones, the Sloane Square department store, and keeping abreast of her reading with a library membership and subscriptions to many literary magazines.

She took occasional music lessons with the celebrated but volatile pianist Clifford Curzon and, renewing a friendship with the celebrated Pearson family, she was often at their flat practicing the piano. She recalls a meeting at the time:

"I went in. Mike [Pearson] was sitting by the fire, untidy, with long hair over his brow. He said, 'Hullo, Betty,' but didn't get up (I am bound to say his attitude improved during the evening and he almost began to get on his toes)."[30] Here she is comically berating the lack of manners from the man who was later to become the Prime Minister of Canada.

Louie was pleased to get reports in Ottawa (sometimes from Russel Senior, who traveled to England periodically on business) that her daughter was attending "at homes" with the peerage and garden parties at Sir Paul and Lady Patricia Latham's, and Buckingham Palace through the Coronation Hospitality Committee. But this life continued to make Mum restless and unless she could pen a few more lines to her ongoing "book"—

little more than a write-up of her world tour with Mrs. Watt—she felt frustrated.

She was feeling she ought to make more of her friendships with women and she picked up with Diana (Didy) Battye, who was to later marry, divorce and then return to live with Michael Asquith, the grandson of the Liberal prime minister and son of Lady Cynthia Asquith. Mum had first met her at Government House in Ottawa when she was a debutante and was immediately struck by her as being "right, true and unvain." She had bonded with Mum in a bizarre escapade soon after they met. She and Mum had been on a camping trip near Quebec when they went to see a traveling circus. Mum was appalled at the plight of a bedraggled dancing bear and in a wild and irresponsible gesture so typical of her, she decided they must buy it to save it from further punishment. They bought it back to Government House in her little Morris and hid it in some outhouses. There was, of course, an ensuing scandal. One wonders what became of the bear.

Didy was a writer herself, and a model, and Mum arranged to meet her at her Lowndes Street flat. Didy was two hours late, but Mum describes her as "looking absolutely beautiful. Fragile, sincere, breakable, innocent, incredible. I adore her. She is doing some work in the films, also posing for photographs (at ten shillings a sitting) and a bit of mannequin work. She can cry in the movies when they want her to."[31]

This last fact would have been immensely impressive to Mum, to whom acting was a discipline she would never master. She made this embarrassingly apparent when she joined a theater group for acting lessons under the avant-garde directorship of Michel Saint-Denis, who had founded the London Theatre School. These lessons were observed with a lugubrious eye by Sir Peter Ustinov, who, as a fellow student, noted in his autobiography that the class was a "veritable battalion of girls, all dressed on the first day of term in black bathing costumes—all, that is, except one, a Canadian girl called Betty—I will refrain from identifying her further—whose black costume had not yet arrived, and who crouched among us in salmon-pink bloomers and bra, looking like a Rubens nymph who had wandered into a sinister witches' coven by mistake ... she trotted round [in imitation of] an elk from her native plains, entangling her antlers with imaginary thickets and being hunted by erotic braves."

She had remained secretive and quiet to the other students while at the school and would have been mortified to know that the theater school games she was made to play would later hold her up to ridicule by such a discerning and comic commentator. (This autobiography of Ustinov's was published nine years before she died and I don't know if she read it or was aware she had been caricatured in this way. I'm certain she would have been delighted.)

Prior to this abortive foray into theater, Mum had been staying with Didy at Billingbear Lodge, Berkshire, and had been to meet Didy's mother and stepfather. Later she had gone down to Goodfellows in Oxfordshire to stay with Sir Stafford and Lady Cripps, who had been friends of the family in Ottawa. Through the Cripps, of whom she was very fond, she met other political figures and came as near as she ever did to making a political comment about the state of the world. Affairs of state were inexorably heading for catastrophe and Sir Stafford, who was later in the War Cabinet as Lord Privy Seal, and Lady Cripps would switch on the radio to listen to Mussolini broadcasting. Mum comments:

"'The Germans were defeated' means nothing unless you translate it into the effect it had on each individual German, unless you see the trivialities it produced or ended.... They are most unselfish, the Cripps. I almost feel a traitor to their great cause. I feel they think I am a deceiving, gay, capitalist, pleasure loving, pretending to be more serious than I am. Yet, of course, I know they don't think that."[32]

After the Coronation and with a dismay that her life was presenting her with no challenges, she returned to Kingsmere for the summer. She had now made this transatlantic trip twenty or so times, with each trip promising recuperation or a new fulfillment that refused to materialize. These mood swings usually depended on the direction she was traveling.

A small event occurred after she had returned to London this time that gave her a new focus and would ultimately redirect her life. In August, as she was idly browsing through the shelves in Better Books in Charing Cross Road, she came across a book of poems by a poet she had been reading called George Barker. Thrilled by the beautiful "rightness" of the language, she became intoxicated with the verse and from the enthusiastic blurb on the dust cover by T.S. Eliot. She realized he was exactly the right quarry for her quest and determined to run this man to earth. In fact, more—she decided she would marry him. The blurb was correspondingly vague, because it made no mention of the fact that he was already married.

She had been fraternizing with upper-class friends on the London social circuit using her Canadian connections as a springboard into society. Becoming more and more disenchanted with this way of life, she began to seek out people of a different focus and temperament. During this search

GEORGE BARKER

Russell Clarke

George Barker, from the frontispiece of one of his books, with the title that Mum amended to read "Portrait of Contributor," in a photo that Mum stuck in the front of our family photo album

Photo by Russell Clarke

she ran across a man called Jean Varda at a party. He was a Turkish artist who had been raised in Athens and was older than Mum. He was an imposing, arrogant Lothario who pushed her against a wall and smoldered in her ear, "Take care! Take care! I am oriental. I will not be played with!"[33]

At Varda's invitation, she hatched a plan to join a commune in his villa in the south of France. He had invited a group of six middle-class English intellectuals to turn their backs on the rumbling drums of war and join him in artistic pursuits on the Côte d'Azur. So, early in 1938, and against the backdrop of Hitler's annexation of Austria and with the Spanish Civil War raging 150 miles from their intended destination, Mum and a group of artists and photographers set off to Cassis on the French Mediterranean coast. They intended to live and work together in a derelict multiroomed château that Varda was renting from his contacts with an English peer.

She thought of Varda as disturbing and, although living with his girlfriend, Simonette, he presented a wild and alluring interest. She records that after a party in Paris on the way down to the villa, "Varda changing shapes and colors and moved in and out like a tune on the radio which fades and grows sometimes disturbingly loud. The fading and the increasings seemed for no reason, and the images were endless."[34]

Predatory and voracious, he could not have presented a more antipathetic personality than Lord John Pentland. She describes him as "like an element. He was a wild and manly gale. He smelt of wet brown earth and grass. But he had satyr's eyes. I knew no conventions would restrain him. Virginity to him was a fruit to be eaten, to be taken in his chaotic stride."[35]

When they arrived at Cassis it wasn't long before Simonette broke off her relationship with Varda and he turned his attentions to Mum. As she tried to escape his advances she came across an aspect of sexual passion she had never before encountered and one she was certainly going to meet again. He became abusive and physically violent. But she was never cowed by physical bullying and, as she did later in life, dealt like with like. She fought back with a ferocity that surprised but didn't stop him. He gave Mum the room next to his, assuring her there was a lock on the adjoining door should she need privacy. She was soon to find that the key turned in the lock from Varda's room, and having told her that "on the thirteenth you will be mine," true to his word he slipped into her bedroom from his side. After a wrestling match across the dirty floor, he took her virginity by force. She, with commendable cool, comments, "Varda, the first day alone, attacked me in my room. I bit and fought like a wild animal, and we scuffed

around on the dusty floor. The nightmares that night! The cold shudder-
ing fears! Face fear. I faced fear. Ah well. Flowers must fruit."[36]

Mum carefully recorded the details in her journal and, with it, her literary voice started to change. The encounter, although robust, was never
brutal and she treated it as a rite of passage from which she metamorphosed
into a writer. Her love of the metaphysical poets had never colored her
writings before, but she now started to employ their metaphors with a new
authority. In Paris she had met the radical thinkers Wolfgang and Alice
Paalen, who were both to have differing influences on her. An unmistakable echo from both Wolfgang Paalen and Varda's interest in surrealism
influenced her diary entries:

> There was a question mark in the sky only it was backwards.
> There was a pine tree but the rest was blue. This is all. This is the
> key.
> The yellow eyes are glaring at me without a melting. "*D'ou viens-tu,
> Bergère?*" [Where do you come from, Shepherd?].
> From the beginning of the heart O! like the pulse of the sea, uncon-
> trollable, for a vision upwards through the thorns.
> Should I have expected these tearings of the flesh by the way? For
> the *toiling* I had set my teeth against. Rip! Rip! The disobedient flesh
> and on top at last a soiled remnant gasping its goodbye. For me, these
> visions are a consummation worth the world beside. All I would give
> away and accept fiend's puny jeers. Then that unspeakable largeness
> wipes away those cloistral pickings of the nose, less than my sporting
> with the eight-day long Atlantic.
> You see, even now, through tears just defeated, comes the balm, aer-
> ial souls of pine.
> This is enough, and the upward mingling of the sun.
> O you cricket, whom I agonised in vain to recreate on those too calm
> fields (fearful with the impotent vision in the rain but treacherously
> soothing to the unwilling liar). O you cricket! *Now* and among the
> flowering rocks!'

The summer in Cassis was the most defining period of her life up
until then and from it she armed herself with what she was later to term
"a furious weapon." Her pen now subscribed to a new language and she
emerged from her cathartic experiences with Jean Varda as a writer with
an unmistakable voice. So happy was she in her newfound life that she was
oblivious to the outside world and was able to write to her old mentor
Graham Spry:

"I am so happy. It is so sunny. I think I shall never come back.... I feel shut off by time & distance & cash from the whole wide world. Days slip by. But I've written several poems, ten new pages of John.... Life is cheap & pleasant here & I can work at last unhampered."

She told the same story to her mother and father but adds coyly at the end of a letter to them, "My bed is a folding camp which is very warm and chaste and smells of fresh hay." This hardly kept them informed of how her life had changed and was to become a pattern of understatement and veiled communication born of many sore clashes with Louie's iron will.

Leaving Cassis in August 1938, and with the Nationalists having just taken Barcelona across the border, Mum returned via Paris to Ottawa and Kingsmere. She had fully intended to return to Paris in the autumn, but because of the threatening hostilities her father refused to fund her travels. Kept from her newfound lover, Varda, and the paradise she had left, she raged against the bellicose war-mongering and fervent patriotism in Canada in a new poem. The lines were to echo her mounting passion with the works of George Barker:

"What do you think of the war scare
Bill, my good man?"
    (I like to get the opinion of the people when I can)
"Looks pretty bad. But I guess I'd do the same again."
Says Bill offhand (His imagination shutting like a trap
    All true news banned)
"Honour above life" says the complacent wife
 · 3000 miles from death
"I say it now and shall continue to say it till my last breath."
And the gaunt dreamers in their disturbed garrets
Disaster-provoking eyes
Seeing really, as they have seen so often in mind
Bombs hurling from the skies?
They rise trembling, they foretold him here
The nerve-straining wait done
They are relieved their role of prophet is over
And doom at last begun.

With the disturbing but thrilling romance of the previous summer fast fading and her father hinting that she might start earning a living, Mum worked briefly for the *Ottawa Journal* as a trainee feature writer. Louie, thinking it no fit way for a daughter to proceed, pulled her the other way, encouraging her social life.

Varda, who was in New York for a one-man show, announced that he was coming up on the train to Ottawa to see her. In honor of his presence, Louie threw a dinner party where she determined to meet him. For the occasion, Mum dressed in white as a June bride. The meeting was not a success. Louie was later to remark (in a letter to Mum of 1943): "The more I see of the 'arty' life the more that I think they give small return for the confusion they create."

Louie had always been suspicious of the "creative instinct." Varda soon left.

Mum, who could no longer stand home constraints, departed for Helen's flat in New York for the summer. Louie realized all her daughters had left and voiced disapproval down the telephone to Helen. She had got it into her head that Mum intended to marry Varda. She became overwrought and threatened suicide (her son Russel was talking about enlisting in the army to go and fight in Europe too). Mum commented

> I wrote at last to Mummy and mailed it in the night box. She had phoned and was hysterical. If I were going to marry Yanko [her nickname for Varda] she might just as well commit suicide. I would have killed her etc. Also Jane had brought up again the subject of marrying D'Arcy [Jane's boyfriend], and she had a cold, and the war was getting her down. I am glad I was out. But way below I am afraid she may catch me and drill her fierce bitter will into my escaping life, and I am troubled by her and for her. Yanko says she is a flagellist, a passionate woman who never got her share of fun in bed.[37]

It's not surprising that Mum developed a shrouded wording in letters to her mother. But Louie needn't have worried about Mum's relationship with Varda. Although she was very fond of him and he had helped in her voyage of self-discovery, Mum never considered him to be the one she was searching for. He was far too much of an egotist and sexual predator to be tied down by a single affair. Her primary and deepening love was with the English language, and so it was to remain all her life. Varda was a painter, and although he had introduced her to ideas of surrealism and new ways of perceiving the world, he didn't know how to really touch her being.

On September 3, 1939, the Second World War began and it started an agitation in her that remained with her the rest of her life. Her innate pacifism and naturalism was disgusted at the clamor for hostility: "The ghoulish aboriginal rites over the air of Hitler's 'Peace or Destruction' speech. The clapping and foot stamping like a tom tom's beat, gathering hysteria."[38]

She was finding it impossible to get any serious work done: "I am not honest enough. I am too fond of the veiling metaphor. I cringe. I acquiesce; I am a coward to hurt people's feelings. I haven't the dignity to speak out, to dare to be myself even if it offends. But I don't want to offend. But I can't call *anyone* fool. I must find a solution."[39]

And she did. She had received an invitation from Wolfgang and Alice Paalen. At the outbreak of war they had relocated from Europe and had invited her to visit them in their new home in San Angel, a suburb of Mexico City. This was exactly the break from the hectic and dreary office routine in New York she needed. In order to take up the Paalens' offer she paid for a steerage ticket on a ship carrying refugees from Europe. The *S.S. Siboney* was to take her from New York via Cuba to Vera Cruz, where she was to disembark and from there she hoped to take a night train to San Angel.

During the voyage she experienced euphoria from the release of her humdrum life in the city and the ever-present contact with her controlling mother. It made her enthuse in general with a joy for all mankind and in particular with those who shared the lower decks as they crashed through the high seas:

> I am alone. I am alive. At last, at last I can think. I can pray. I am filled with that spirit. Or, if you will, god, that individual who loves and dwells with me—eking each power to gather its evasive gold.... Here I was taking the vomiting body of humanity to my bosom, living their greed over the last tuttifrutti cake; their fear, their imaginary ills, lulled in the very rough arms of father neptune himself.
>
> I said smiling when I had to lie on the canvas cot, and they vomited on all sides so that it splashed right onto my face, and the stench was everywhere.[40]

That she could find love for the desperate and dispossessed humanity that crawled around her in the gloom of the lower decks was a reflection of how trapped she had felt and what a marvelous release this trip had become: "O I am in the thick of it. I love, love, love this my humanity, my people, themselves."[41]

It was an outpouring of empathy for all those that, like her, were escaping to a better world, and although for her it was a rich girl's adventure, for her fellow passengers she saw clearly that the voyage was a frantic rush for survival. She had love to spare and was ready to extend this love to all around her.

She may have thought she had escaped the controlling arm of her family's influence, but it wasn't to stay that way. A first-class ticket arrived via a steward who ventured down to the lower decks to fetch her back. When later writing about the trip she was to make her mother responsible for the upgrade, but it is more likely that her father, repenting his first refusal of funds, had sent the ticket anonymously. She only knew she had to put herself in the real world with its attendant discomforts in order to experience life more keenly: "Can I sustain my great adventure in this familiar comfortable isolation? Cherished and guarded, my work is double—to break through the misty clouds that lull and ease, and to translate when I get there."[42]

Her writing continued to reflect her wild love of the natural world and to stay in touch with her emotions:

"These grey days all sky and sea, are wild with innuendo and submerged life. The green, blues, whites, half greys, large embryonic clouds floating, the unformed bigness of potentiality. The whitecaps' foam, the gulls' flight—the strong warm wet air—like the spring message wind it goes through everything, through every pore, the brain, the sex, the mouth, the hair; it ravishes, exhilarates, possesses, cannot weary—O to leap into the sea—to *be* sea—to be sky—to be air. I will be there. I will by willing *be*."[43]

On first moving in with the Paalens, Mum was impressed with the environment of diligent writing and painting and set about her own work. The Paalens and the writer André Breton (later editor of the magazine *La Révolution surréaliste*) were organizing an exhibition of surrealism in Mexico City. Mum wanted to explore the strong ties of mother love and started work on her "Mother Book." Ever searching for a new form of expression, neither poetry nor prose, she wanted the book "to be about love. But love is so large and formless. (But so full of new worlds) ... but what form? Infinite pains for a poem. But I need new form even for a poem. I have used up my ones. Tricks begin to slouch about. Each word must rip virgin ground. No past effort must ease the new birth. Rather than that, the haphazard note, the unborn child, the bottled embryo."[44]

She particularly admired Anaïs Nin for her "feeling of naked, terribly condensed and understated truth—her feeling of every moment bursting to capacity with awareness of itself."[45]

While at San Angel she was whisked around by the Paalens to meet Diego Rivera, the Mexican painter famous for his murals in public buildings depicting the life and history of the Mexican people; the Peruvian surrealist poet César Moro; and Breton and other local artists. She took immediately to Alice, who was translating her poetry into English but would continually defer to Wolfgang's overbearing presence. She had once been a mistress of Pablo Picasso and now in her association with Wolfgang had taken the subservient role. She had a fragile and needy personality that Wolfgang sensed and worked to his advantage. At first for Mum this new life was stimulating and fascinating, but Wolfgang's attitude soon started to grate. After she refused to join his sexual *ménage* as another acolyte, she became infatuated with Alice, who she liked as a beautiful and sympathetic woman but in whom she recognized a troubled past:

"But Alice carries her beautiful hanging gardens with her wherever she goes, and smiles, and watches when the light changes, and leaps for joy when a housefly, even, makes a joke. Her fingers caress life's pulse. Life flies by him and he grumbles because he feels the draught."[46]

On the pretext of Alice's needing the sea air for health reasons, they decided to go (or rather Wolfgang allowed them leave) to the Acapulco shore together, leaving Wolfgang to his work and a girl named Eva Schulz— a Swiss friend of the Paalens' who had earlier joined them both in a ménage à trois—to look after him. On the Acapulco beaches Mum, Alice and a coterie of Alice's friends enjoyed a week of sunshine and sea together. While there, through her close sexual relationship with Alice and while still working on "The Mother Book," she was at last able to address how her mother's emotional manipulation exerted its grip on her. Until she had dealt with these demons, she felt she wasn't free her to write:

"I want to work at some definite work so that I can measure my accomplishment. But since mother forgave me, and I could feel some tenderness again, I am no longer possessed by her and my dissipated forces embrace wind. Fiercely free the concentration till and willy-nilly pearl is born. *Think.*"[47]

She was able to pass an emotional milestone in her relationship with her mother and move on. She abandoned her "Mother Book", because, as she later recalls, "Alice presented me with the pity.... Hearing, trembling with, her [Louie's] cries, her frantic unfair efforts to sabotage me, but going unflinchingly on.... So I forgave my mother for causing the passionate love I had for her, for casting me out of Paradise."[48]

The birth pains for her new "book" got stronger as she finalized the form it would take, especially after reading Anaïs Nin's *House of Incest*, in which she was particularly taken with the method of recording her experiences in dream-like sequence with little narrative or character assessment. Unlike Nin, though, her form was to employ a very strong metaphorical interpretation. Nin presented to her "the feeling of naked, terribly condensed and understated truth ... her feeling of every moment being bursting to capacity with *awareness* of itself."[49]

All she now needed was an experience to base the novel on.

"Alice's tearful articulate love" toward Mum in Acapulco had turned into affectionate companionship after the first erotic union. This had begun under Wolfgang's nose at Los Cedros y Begonias and later flowered as a full lesbian relationship. By the time they had returned to Wolfgang and Eva, the physical side of their affair had abated. Although Mum had helped to prepare Wolfgang's first International Surrealist Exhibition in Mexico City, she missed the launch.

Within a week of her return to San Angel with Alice, she had departed to join Varda, who had invited her to Hollywood. He too had left New York and was now working on paintings he hoped to open as an exhibition in Los Angeles. While living in Hollywood with Varda, her relationship with him started to cool, and when he left her to attend the exhibition, although missing him and feeling lonely, she had already told him they must part.

Ever since that hot August day in Better Books in Charing Cross Road when she stumbled on George Barker's poetry, his work had continued to fascinate her. While corresponding with the writer Lawrence Durrell about submissions to his poetry magazine *Booster*, she mentioned, among other poets' work, how much she liked George Barker's. Durrell gave Mum Barker's address and so, using her clothing allowance from her mother to fund it, she wrote to him under the pretext of buying the manuscript of a poem, "O Who Will Speak from a Womb or a Cloud?"

Thereafter George Barker loomed large in her imagination as Varda faded. Even without knowing much about him she started to fantasize about him, although for the time being it was no more than his written word that excited her: "growing into a long and dangerous image and is woven among the undertones."[50]

Mum replaced the thoughts of mother love and its effects on her with an absorption in Barker's poetry. "It is the complete juicy *sound* that runs bubbles over, that intoxicates till I can hardly follow (and the recurring lines in "Daedalus" 'the moist palm of my hand like handled fear like fear cramping my hand. OO the a— a— a!')."[51]

Later, when she received his latest poems, she said: "and I say O how ashamed I am to have thought *mine* were poetry, for he alone says *exactly* what I wanted to say, and even the very word sounds I was wanting to utter and the same elastic bounding back. That is my maddening injury. His are all true. Mine limp and labor. But when I opened the book my excitement made me too impotent to read. My head ached with too much greed. My eyes were glazed with wanting too much at once."[52]

Until she had read these poems (which were probably from Barker's *Lament and Triumph*), Mum's interest in Barker had remained no more than that of a devoted fan, but now her feelings intensified into something more like an obsession and she fixed all her "determined will" onto him. She decided then, without having met him or even seen a photograph, that he was to be the one with whom she would "leap bellowing with jungfreud into the arms of the infinite."[53]

The entrancement with George Barker's poetry and her newfound freedom after joining the Paalens in Mexico induced an intoxication with life. She determined not to let one minute escape without living it to the full. In her diaries she wrote: "But this afternoon *oil* brought back the placid flush to my cheeks and I ran upstairs to change happily suffused and clasped Paalen and bit his arm on the way—it lubricates—right then I could have taken the whole world in my bed—and the fresh flowering the only act of living. *Life*—the name then is a caress, a warm bath, a flower garden vainly breathing after the sun's insistence. I want to *act*! I want to be *used*!"

Varda didn't fulfill her ambition for life. She needed a voracious tour de force:

> He *must* devour me. Minute by minute pouncing on it ravenously. Not for my sake—because he loves me so much he wants me to be happy— For his own sake—*Only* because he is compelled.... The things to be written are water drops only to be collected, or just to lie savoring is enough life. IS ENOUGH. ("Distil in some inviolate casket the yellow sun.") I am so happy, so lovingly open to the world. The timidest breath of a joke can shake me with laughter like a hurricane, and I roll with it in the wildest glee on the inexhaustible flowery grass."[54]

As she marshaled these exuberant thoughts and feelings throughout this period of artistic liberation, it's as if she had been orchestrating a literary crescendo that she hoped would culminate in the book she had been preparing to write all her life.

While in Mexico, on December 22, 1939, Mum wrote a letter to George Barker. She had been told by his publisher, Faber and Faber, that he was lecturing on English poetry at the Imperial Tohoku University at Sendai, north of Tokyo. She asked him if he had any more manuscripts that she might purchase. Five days later, she recorded in her diary on her birthday, December 27 (her "Perennial Day of Tears"), and thinking of his "Daedalus" poem: "I think of George Barker leaping to his death (as it would be so easy to do here on the edge of this precipitate cliff) and falling falling—only to wake up at the bottom, not dead, bruised and battered, but not dead."

As this image occurred to her, he was—of all the places in the world he could have been—a few miles away as he steamed by on the *Fushimi Maru* for the Los Angeles port of San Pedro. He was on his way to Japan and the boat was to dock in San Pedro for some sightseeing before the last leg of the voyage to Tokyo.

At the beginning of March 1940 Mum wrote in her diary,

> My world begins to be all dancing. The gathering of the energy in goblets for the concentrated moment of its release. But this my book I carry everywhere, and its blank unwritten pages and shabby cover—its menial use for dancing notes, addresses, and accounts deglamourize it. I must not forget IT is my heavenly key—my work—my purpose. Dancing only my prayer (those sacred rites of Greece—man and earth in a love kiss) … if George Barker should appear now I would eat him up with eagerness. I can feel the flushed glow of minds functioning in the divine understanding and communication.

Unbeknownst to her, George Barker was beginning to find the duties of his lectureship at the Imperial Tohoku University not to his liking. Fearing that if he were to return to England he would be conscripted into the army and back to a life that had shaped his unsympathetic father, he decided to attempt entry into America. No sooner had he signed his contract of employment with the university authorities than he was penning Mum a letter in anxious appeal for help to leave the country. At this stage he knew little about her, only that she appeared to be an apparently rich American patron.

On arrival in Japan he had received her letter and request for more manuscripts, so he wrote back, "I am going absolutely nuts here and unless I can succeed in getting back across the Pacific in a matter of months at the most, it's flowers and curtains for the Chrysostom birds inside me."[55]

He offered her the unpublished manuscript of his journals if she could arrange to rescue him by sending two tickets and two quota numbers (necessary for anything more than a brief stay in the US). The fact that he needed two tickets came as a shock. Mum hadn't realized that he might in fact be married.

He waited for two weeks and then, in his diary, beseeched: "O charity, loosen the hands of E. Smart!" and wrote a letter to her including the manuscript of a sonnet and repeating his plea. Three days later and still not happy with the urgency of this, he sent a telegram "O begging rescue."

She replied by cable forthwith: "Come to the California shore," and with commendable but unfounded confidence promised to send $300 and all possible help. Undaunted and with zeal she set about raising the money. She wrote begging letters to all poetry lovers she could think of and anyone else who might possibly help. She even worked as a maid for a short period, but was sacked for touching her employer for a loan as an advance on her wages.

In her journal she reinforces her determination: "All day and all night I wrangle ways to rescue Barker from Japan. One by one my begging letters are refused or worse ignored. The promise I made him (and WILL keep) begins to be a center of radiating apprehension sending shivers from the bottom of my spine."[56]

Meanwhile, having returned to Hollywood after his show, tension between Mum and Varda rose as Mum felt she was being used as a his personal valet, running errands and doing domestic chores: "Even is it better to live in filth than empty resignation of hours preparing for a *something* that never arrives."

Her time was fully occupied dealing with the weight of begging letters she had sent out (now over a hundred) and she didn't have time to clear up after Varda. She asked her father for $300, but he turned her down. He later relented, sending a letter of support for the visas that the American consulate required, but no money. This, of course, meant her parents had found out about her obsession with George Barker. Louie immediately castigated her "passionate desire on your part to assist a British poet stranded in Japan [that] seems to far outweigh your interest in a very vital human problem in your own family." She felt that, as George Barker was married and had chosen to work in Japan, Mum had no right to interfere in his life.

In the end it was Christopher Isherwood, the English poet and author then working as a scriptwriter in Hollywood, who eventually came up with $200, asking only that when George Barker arrived Isherwood be allowed to meet the two of them. But the money did not arrive and it was a measure of Isherwood's generosity that when Mum rushed over to see him in person, showing him the telegrams and letters from George Barker, he simply wrote another check.

As her relationship with Varda deteriorated, he thought a new environment in which they could work might improve the atmosphere between them. He decided they should move out of Hollywood to Anderson's Creek on Big Sur. Varda had heard that they could live in wooden shacks left behind three years earlier by a departing workforce of convicts building the Carmel–San Simeon highway. This news had reached him from a commune of indigent European artists who had sought these huts as a refuge from the war, where they could work untroubled by the authorities and in comparative peace. The shacks were perched atop cliffs at whose feet the Pacific Ocean crashed in turbulent surf. Here, among this motley gang of snake charmers, oddballs, musicians, philosophers and painters, Mum began work, striving for a new form of writing for the book. She cajoled herself:

"Prose, please, prose for a while, straighten out the rushing water excuses—say, This is my whole duty. Don't take refuge in the automatic poem-formula. It increases the falseness—know that the only important thing is to extract the essence, the miracle—God."[57]

Then, with the form decided, she started work on a book that was vaguely about the love of a young poet. She started the book writing out passages that would later become sections of the second part of her new novel. She sensed the first part of the book hadn't happened yet.

George Barker, meanwhile, was in frantic correspondence with as many people as he thought might help him, including John Fitch, an American friend he had met on the boat from England and with whom he had stayed in New York. He cabled his brother Kit in England to send his marriage and birth certificates. Two months later, on May 16, Mum cabled him: "Better. Indisputable American documents posted today." And four days later the fares and money arrived, coinciding with pledges of support from John Fitch and the documents from his brother. He replied to his brother that he had just been "given the continent of America by an American who admired his poems" and sent Mum a copy of his new book of poems in appreciation.

He had sprung his escape from Japan after being there for only four months and three weeks. The Japanese university authorities were disappointed but tactful, given the perilous nature of international affairs. His predecessor, Professor Ralph Hodgson, had been incumbent for fifteen long and successful years. While on a last sightseeing trip to Tokyo from the university, George Barker had met a friend of Mum's from the Canadian Legation and after an idle inquiry was shown a photograph of her. In his excitement he wrote to tell Mum that he had seen a picture of "a blonde glory who was either Elizabeth S. or sunrise over the Rockies."

In reply on June 28 she asked: "All the people whose addresses I've given you are looking forward to meeting you. What do you look like? I never saw a portrait or anything, and only know what I deduct."[58] (When writing in her new novel she never identifies her lover by his appearance, remarking in response to later queries that "of course he is faceless; the *he* is a love object.") This letter from Mum was intended as a welcome to greet him on his arrival in North America, but it missed the boat, as the *Fushimi Maru* weighed anchor in Vancouver and steamed out for Los Angeles. She added self-deprecatingly:

"You are too generous because I've done nothing really, & I feel grateful to you for coming to America." She ends the letter saying, "I can't think of a welcome worthy Columbus. But it's yours if you can think of it."[59]

It is interesting that he never got this letter. He and his wife, Jessica, had disembarked when the boat docked in Vancouver from Japan, and had gone to stay with a contact of Mum's for three days. The letter had been addressed to "George Barker, incoming passenger aboard the *SS Empress of Russia*" and, having missed the boat, was returned to sender. In it Mum had suggested one of two options: either they come straight to Monterey, where she would meet them in a car that she said worked only "fitfully," and travel on to the colony at Anderson's Creek, or, alternatively, he might spend some time in Hollywood meeting people for two weeks. In the letter were details of contacts, telephone numbers and other arrangements she had made.

From Vancouver, Barker and Jessica traveled by boat to San Francisco and then took a bus direct to Monterey, surprising Mum in coming straight to her and ignoring the other arrangements she had so carefully laid down. This was because he never knew of these arrangements and cabled ahead that he would arrive at the bus station in Monterey at 10:30 Sunday morning, July 7, 1940. The bus underwent further delays and by the time it arrived in Monterey it was five hours late and so set up the charged and evocative meeting that Mum describes in the opening lines of her book:

"I am standing on a corner in Monterey, waiting for the bus to come in, and all the muscles of my will are holding my terror to face the moment I most desire. Apprehension and the summer afternoon keep drying my lips, prepared at ten minute intervals all through the five hour wait."[60]

Mum was in a frenzy of anticipation. All her expectations, her wild exuberance of spirit, the culmination of years of dreaming and obsession had come to this point. She had convinced herself that whatever else might happen to her, to this moment in her life she would always be true. This was to be her man and the moment upon which she had pinned her future.

Jessica was first to come down the steps of the bus, looking trusting and innocent: "It is her eyes that come forward out of the vulgar disembarkers to reassure me that the bus has not disgorged disaster: her madonna eyes, soft as the newly born, trusting as the untempted. And, for a moment, at that gaze, I am happy to forego my future, and postpone indefinitely the miracle hanging fire. Her eyes shower me with their innocence and surprise."[61]

Mum was already feeling guilty, knowing the intentions of her own heart, but on seeing Jessica, and despite the turmoil of emotions, the uppermost emotion was relief. They had arrived at last. With a voracious eagerness, she had set in motion an inevitable course of events. The "sunrise over the Rockies" dazzled and swept up all before it as the poet sees her "standing in a sideways stance of anticipation … with your hair like an apotheosis when I alighted from the door: and I stepped down into your lap, just as truly as I stepped down from my mother, and I have loved you completely and perfectly from that moment."[62]

When she first saw Barker he wasn't what she expected at all and certainly didn't fit her romantic image of a poet. Mum was to remark later that he was "all wrong." He had none of the "roar of authority" that he was later to acquire but sat at the café table fingering the tickets and blurting out small talk to Jessica. It didn't seem to alter Mum's intentions. They piled into her battered old car and headed off to the cabins at Anderson's Creek.

At first, there was no explosion of passion. The first few days were spent settling into the cabins, with Mum overcompensating for her unbearable excitement with urgent domesticity. Jessica made a home for George while he wrote his poetry. Mum, only too willing to please any way she could, volunteered to be his secretary and started to type his manuscripts.

Mum, California, 1940

All seemed well. Varda, who had been living with Mum all through this initial period, took another cabin and faded from the scene. For Mum, "the Beginning lurks uncomfortably on the outskirts of the circle, like an unpopular person whom ignoring can keep away."[63]

As she waited for sexual chemistry to do its work, as she knew it would, she was wracked with guilt about what she was doing.

Through the hot, high July of a California summer she and George, on heaven knows what pretext, left Jessica and roamed the local countryside together in her car. They would often go into Monterey, shopping for gramophone needles and 78-rpm records. Slowly the love affair began. At first they tried to keep it away from Jessica, although for her husband to head off into the hills with a beautiful, adoring fan and return flushed and excited at the end of the day must have aroused suspicion. But George resolutely maintained a denial and for the first few weeks at Anderson's Creek, Jessica was able to pretend to herself it wasn't happening.

George and Mum, however, both expressed harrowing consciences in their diaries that were testament to the guilt they felt for their deceit. Mum, in her diary and what was to become part of the book she was later to write said, "It [her face] was angular with the tears that should have blurred with liquid her unendurable torture. Her body was bent like a broken bow waiting for the wound which swung in perpetual suspension above her. But her eyes Oh my god pierced all the protecting veils that covered my imagination. Bleed me too in this terrible pool of birth."[64]

George was not without remorse either. An entry in his diary for July 20 ran: "I regard myself as that lowest and least principled of people and the simplest of p(o)ets: a dog."

Yet despite this guilt, they couldn't help themselves.

The dynamics of the situation proved too tense and in mid-August, in the nearest thing she could muster to an outburst, Jessica finally confronted George with her suspicions. All along he had denied any relationship and she had appeared temporarily mollified, not wanting to know the worst. In order to keep control of the situation, George told Mum one thing while telling Jessica another. At last she confronted George, weeping, accusing him of infidelity. She wailed that he had forced her to give up for adoption the child they had had earlier in the marriage.

For six more weeks they all lived together at Anderson's Creek with George shuttling between the two of them, placating them with the words they each wanted to hear. In late September, the three of them set off from Anderson's Creek in Mum's old banger. George told Mum the aim of the trip was to dump Jessica so they could run off to New York together. He told Jessica the trip was to look for somewhere for them to spend the winter. When they reached Hollywood, George and Jessica found a place to stay and Mum took a room with family friends a few blocks down the road, waiting. Here they remained, as frustration worked away at the two lovers, with George vacillating. On October 7, when George could take no more, he finally rushed over to scoop Mum up and they went to the San Bernardino hills above Los Angeles for a day together.

This day, although some time after they had first met, formed the zenith of their passion and was later referred to by George as his "nuptials" and by Mum in her book as her first sexual encounter with George: "Under the waterfall he surprised me bathing and gave me what I could no more refuse than the earth can refuse the rain."[65]

Afterward, in an exhilarated and carefree state on their way down, they decided to elope across America, going east for New York. Jessica, after all her selfless devotion and self-sacrifice to George and his career, was abandoned without a word, penniless and without a friend, thousands of miles from home.

The lovers planned an itinerary of literary stops along the route, the first perhaps at D.H. Lawrence's shrine in New Mexico. After three days on the road, where in fits of giggles they signed into motels under the invented names of Mr. and Mrs. Henrick Van Loon and others, they arrived at the first state border between California and Arizona. Here they were stopped by border guards, who handed them over to the FBI. The war in Europe had been going on for a year, and, although the United States was not yet involved in the hostilities, the authorities were neurotic about fifth columnists and spies. The FBI had reinvigorated the Mann Act at the borders to check identification. The Mann Act had been introduced in 1910 to stop prostitution by forbidding the transport of girls under the age of twenty-eight across the state line for "immoral" purposes, and had been revived as an expedient to arrest gangsters and their molls if no incriminating evidence were available. In the prevailing climate of unrest it was now proving useful once more. Fornication was allowed in any state, but you couldn't cross the state line for it.

George's papers were in order. As he had been traveling around the world, they had been carefully prepared at the outset, and Mum, in her haste to get him to America, had helped to ensure they were. Mum's papers were a different matter. The previous January, when flying from Mexico to California to join Varda, she had been waved through customs without her passport being stamped, as Canadians often were when entering the United States. This time she was detained for making an illegal entry into the United States.

After a brief interrogation, George was released. He scurried back to Jessica, with barely a comment. He explained his absence by saying he had been stopped and sent back from the border while motoring to New York on business, without mentioning Mum. She, meanwhile, was put through an interrogation by the FBI for three hours. As the feds fired questions at her, she said nothing but murmured verses to herself from the *Song of Solomon* to remind herself of the serenity of her love. In her book the passages of interrogation and reply become juxtaposed in an agonized and pitiful liturgical paean:

When did intercourse take place?
  (The king hath brought me to the banqueting house
    and his banner over me was love.)
Were you intending to commit fornication in Arizona?
  (He shall lie all night between my breasts.)

Behold thou art fair my beloved, behold thou art fair:
   thou hast doves eyes.
Get away from there! Cried the guard,
    as I wept by the crack of the door.
      (My beloved is mine.)
Better not try any funny business, cried the guard, you're only
making things tough for yourself.
    (Let him kiss me with the kisses of his mouth.)
Stay put! Cried the guard, and struck me.

After taking fourteen pages of notes with six carbon copies, the FBI agents locked her up for three days while they tried to get confirmation of her story. When they had asked her for corroboration of her story, she had given them the telephone number of family friends from her lodgings in Hollywood. After the FBI contacted them, her hosts in Hollywood immediately telephoned her father. He then called the Canadian ambassador in Washington and a visa was sent. She was released in the custody of these Hollywood friends.

She and George were now back at the beginning, but it didn't stop them from making another attempt to get away. Jessica was under the illusion that Mum had been stopped at the border while traveling alone, as George had said. So now, telling Jessica he was off to see a poetry editor in New York, on October 9 he and Mum set off by train, financing the trip with the last of Mum's allowance. George was without an income since he left the University in Japan, and the last of his salary had gone. By the end of October Mum wouldn't be able to get hold of her allowance anymore, since wartime restrictions in Canada (which had been at war since it was declared by Great Britain and her allies) prevented cash flow beyond its borders. A pang of conscience led Mum to ask her hosts in Hollywood to sell the banger after they had left and to give the proceeds to Jessica. This raised a mere thirty dollars, but it was all she had.

The lovers arrived in New York penniless and went straight to the apartment of Mum's sister Helen. They roomed there for a few days and then went to stay with Oscar Williams, who was the poetry editor George had spoken of to Jessica. He had picked two of George's poems for his new anthology. But this didn't serve their immediate need for cash, so Mum decided to go back to Ottawa by bus to pick up her allowance and more if she could.

The second Mum left New York for Ottawa, George was on the phone to Jessica in Hollywood. He explained carefully to her that although Mum appeared to love him he had no feelings for her whatsoever. Jessica, who had been going quietly out of her mind with worry in Hollywood, was so relieved to get word, any word, from him that she persuaded herself his absence was necessary and that out there, somewhere, she still had a husband. He told Mum he had informed Jessica that their marriage was over and Mum sent him the ticket to Ottawa. This was the beginning of a pattern of behavior that continued for some years and presented George with a conundrum he was never able to solve. Out of pity for Jessica he would leave Mum, and then return to Mum when he couldn't be away any longer. He became very adept at coming up with reasons for the latest departure from either woman, and both were only too ready to believe him.

Back at home, in a desperate attempt to raise money, Mum tried to sell her cabin she had called The Pulley in the Gatineau Hills along with its two hundred mountainous acres. Although her parents had little sympathy for her plight because they felt George was "letting his country down in her Hour-of-Need,"[66] she did manage to raise his fare to Ottawa, and so Mum wired him the money to come up from New York and join her.

On arrival George went to Coltrin Lodge, the Smarts' residence in the affluent Ottawa suburbs, and met Russel, Louie, Jane and Russel Jr. The meeting must have been less than edifying because the outcome was that Louie refused to have him in the house. Undaunted, Mum found him some cheap lodgings in Hull, Quebec, across from Ottawa on the less salubrious north side of the Ottawa River. From his new vantage point George could see the grimy match factories choking the damp air as they coughed out yellow sulfurous smoke. He felt his humiliation was complete.

Through the help of Jane, Mum's younger sister, who acted as go-between, they were able to enjoy fleeting trysts in grubby cafés. George was not enjoying his roll as pariah and became increasingly mortified by Jessica's plight. Writing a letter to him on November 7 she had cried, "If I had a home to go to and a father to fight for me it would be different, but as you know I had not a soul to turn to.... I may mortgage my soul at any moment to come to you." This was something George was keen to avoid.

As Jane and her husband, D'Arcy, came and went from George's seedy lodgings to set up these meetings with Mum, on a sudden impulse he joined D'Arcy on a trip to Montreal as he chased a journalistic assignment. As they crossed the St Lawrence River they were stopped by police who were on the lookout for escaped POWs and who found that George's papers were not in order. As an unexplained alien, George was thrown into prison overnight. From there he used his one telephone call to contact Mum, who rushed down in her car with his passport. After his release they spent a couple of days in a Montreal hotel.

(It always struck me as odd that until much later in her life, when it became imperative for her to negotiate miles of muddy track to her remote Suffolk cottage, I didn't know she could drive. She was always the most timid and terrified of passengers in a car and I was amazed to learn that she had done so much driving when younger. For perhaps thirty years she didn't get behind a steering wheel or mention to anyone that she could drive. After her second try, she passed the British driving test and crawled around the country lanes in a battered minivan. Later she was to become much more intrepid and, dressed like a lumberjack for the icy Suffolk winds, would roam far and wide on a doughty moped festooned with carrier bags full of bulbs and plants.)

George was very perturbed by this ordeal, although it was far less intimidating than it had been for Mum after her arrest and incarceration when they crossed the Arizona border. She remarked that he looked "all shook up," so she returned with him to the empty country house at Kingsmere. It was there that Mum had spent her summers as a child, she hoped they could lie low until he recovered his composure. But the trauma of his arrest, his worry over Jessica and the icy temperatures of an early winter on the eastern edge of the Laurentian Mountains brought George out in tonsillitis. This was a complaint that had plagued him from childhood, especially when he was at a low ebb.

They had to return to Ottawa to get treatment, and once again he had to lurk in lodgings in the choking air of Hull. From there George was able to excuse himself on the pretext that the air made his throat worse and seek treatment in New York. He also had to attend to work on *Selected Poems*, which Macmillan, his publisher, was bringing out.

Whether he was beginning to tire of passion or he was run down, the excuses he advanced to Mum for his departure were woolly. Largely they were a clumsy attempt to conceal his guilt and concern for Jessica, who had written to him from Los Angeles care of Mum's parents at Coltrin Lodge in Ottawa. Mum returned from Kingsmere, calling in on her own at Coltrin Lodge, to find this letter waiting and had given it to George fully aware of what it must contain. In fact, and not hard to believe, Jessica was denouncing Mum on every score. She reported to George in the letter that in Hollywood Mum had gone around posing as his wife,

"People gape if I am introduced to them as your wife, since you are Elizabeth's poet and genius from Japan and apparently I rose like Aphrodite but from the Pacific."[67] She said the Smarts were ruthless people and would use and then ruin both of them and begged for some money.

When he reached New York he cabled her ten dollars and told her everything was fine. She was overjoyed and forgave him everything:

"It's silly but directly I start writing to you I weep. It is distance and not having the right words and everything. But I have been trying to think only of you today, without my emotions sweeping in on everything, and I am dreadfully sorry that you had such a ghastly time and I believe in you and love you and all the nice things I thank you for a thousand times. But will you shelter me and keep me safe in future, Gran dear [his name was George Granville Barker]. I want to be covered and protected so that I can get resistance and some sort of capability back."[68]

He cabled her to come east by train and she set off sending a letter ahead: "I did not know that one wire could please me so much."

Unwisely, George arranged a quick meeting with Mum in New York before Jessica arrived and, having found a room, awaited Mum's arrival on the night train from Ottawa. Unfortunately he became confused, such was his consternation and worry, and he failed to make the appointment. When, on her arrival, there was no one there to meet her, Mum spent a few hours in an all-night greasy-spoon café bewailing her lot—a forlorn scene that was later to become the climax of her book. From a cable she later sent to George to remind him of his remission, the book's title, *By Grand Central Station I Sat Down and Wept*, was born.

After this horrible night she went back to where she knew he might be staying and on the next night, November 24, conceived the child with which, in her book, she was heavily pregnant while waiting to meet her lover at the station.

Three days later, as he kissed Mum goodbye on her way back to Ottawa, he promised to meet her for Christmas. As he did so, he was worrying about Jessica's arrival by train from Los Angeles and how he would settle her into the bed Mum had just left.

George now resumed his familiar juggling act with the two women, shuttling back and forth from New York to Canada, and it left him confused and miserable. He spoke to Mum of his undying love and then returned to Jessica and promised he would look after her forever.

In New York he was working on new verses and renewing his acquaintance with John Fitch, whom he had first met on the boat crossing the Atlantic on the way to Japan. While in Canada with Mum they would talk of running off to Nova Scotia. "Let's be randy in the Bay of Fundy," she laughed,[69] but they had their worries with these plans. Together, as strangers in this area in wartime Canada, it meant they would be taken as spies and George's problems mounted.

Through Christmas and into the New Year he prevaricated, making himself ill. On New Year's Day, when on a short visit to see Mum in Montreal, he contracted another bout of tonsillitis and was admitted to the Royal Victoria Hospital. He spent the whole visit in hospital. He was able to return in mid-January for another visit, but this time was confined to bed with a cold, and when back in New York expressed his frustrated love in a letter:

"Oh when I think of you I cough poppies and sneeze diamonds and sweet amber: have I endowed you with all those diadems of intellectual brilliance and kisses and fingernail polish and sexual ecstasy which adorn you whom I never cease thinking of? No, it wasn't from me that you received them, it was our connubial regalia bestowed by episcopal circumstance in honor of our nuptials. How could circumstances ever be praised more than by our act of union? And in return it makes us mythical, so that the slightest of your gestures remains in my mind better than the Elgins or the Russian dance."[70]

He exacerbated the frustration in each of his relationships either with letters of undying and carnal adulation or promises of faithfulness and eternal devotion, never coming up with a serious commitment either way. Now back in New York with his throat still inflamed, he was due at Harvard to give a reading for the Morris Grey lectures, an engagement that Mum had booked through Frank Scott, a Canadian poet now living in Harvard. Since this was Mum's contact and it was her turn to be visited, she contrived to have Frank Scott pose as her uncle, inviting him to send her the funds to leave Canada so she and George could steal a visit to Harvard together.

After croaking through the lecture, George, ever eager to impress Frank Scott and covering his low ebb with bombast, outrageously declared Britain had a duty to capitulate to Germany in order to supply her poets with new themes for wonderful elegies. Ignoring the women, both men drank their way through the night. The next day, with his throat scalding, his head banging and with the romance of this meeting completely destroyed, Mum and George went their separate ways. George went back to Jessica in New York and Mum to Canada, with a promise from George that he would come up to Montreal on February 9.

On February 7 George entered a private clinic in New York, where, with the funds from the reading, he had an expensive tonsillectomy. So involved had he been with these concerns that he had failed to make contact with Mum concerning their rendezvous on the ninth, and when he hadn't arrived she telephoned his flat in New York. It was the day he was due for discharge from the clinic but hadn't yet arrived home. Mum's telephone call was taken by Jessica, and the two women had a crisp exchange, with Mum letting Jessica know that George had arranged to meet her in Montreal that day. Jessica, in disgust, packed her bags and went upstate to White Plains to stay with John Fitch and his girlfriend, the only friends she had in the United States. She left a note: "You really are a louse. It's staggering what your 'great love' has done to you."[71]

George, on coming home to an empty apartment and finding no one to nurse him, attempted to re-establish his relationship with Mum and in a needy emotional letter declared:

> This is to tell you more than I can ever tell you O far more than colors love one another in poems or rooms love one another in houses or the masculine of Italy loves the Mediterranean or than anything and if you do not love me I shall go straight back to England and I mean if you do not love me more than all the world. Now I know quite clearly and quite overpoweringly that it is no one else of the five hundred million that I belong but to you and if you will not have me I am finished for the species homunculus, for all truly. I want absolutely nothing from anything but you from it all and you only and you are totally and you alone and when I think of our maternal urns hanging in my hand or at my lip then I feel the bitter diamond at the corner of my eye because you are far away.[72]

Appealing though this may have been, Mum felt the time had come to leave home and save her parents the embarrassment of witnessing her pregnancy and the shame they would feel it brought on them. Because of the currency restrictions, if she wanted to go on receiving her allowance she couldn't leave the country and so she wrote back to George in New York:

> I'm not running away from you because god knows that would be an impossibility since you are what makes my blood continue to flow, but I am not the right shape to stay in Ottawa any longer so I'll have to leave & soon. So next week by Wednesday anyway, I'm going to go to Victoria, B.C., & look for cottage in the north of Vancouver Island & plant my potatoes & all my withering & sprouting roots.... There will certainly be difficulties about keeping the remainder of my life secret but

if I go into wild & inaccessible enough country & cover my tail with enough lies & alibis & appear back home every so often to reassure them, perhaps there will be a solution. But I am absolutely determined that they shall never know or have a chance of any one telling them. I owe them that at least … and now I won't even be able to give you a birthday present or make a wish before you open your eyes on Feb. 26.…
In case you don't get here before I leave you can write me c/o Head Branch of the Royal Bank of Canada, Victoria, B.C. I'll leave about Wednesday, March 5.… I do love you more than anything else in the world or the world. That's not the trouble or rather perhaps that is the trouble. E[73]

On reading this George was spurred into catching the night train to Ottawa, arriving just in time to join her on the journey west, and they set off to find a place for Mum to have their child in secret. Mum had chosen Vancouver Island because it was the furthermost point from her home in Ottawa that was still in Canada. It also wasn't completely remote from medical help when the baby arrived.

They traveled across Canada by train and before the final decision concerning finding the child a birthplace, they dallied in a seedy hotel in Vancouver called The Almer. Mum worked on her novel, bringing it up to date now she had some action to fill the first part. George was also now at hand to read her entries, often annotating them in a dialogue that she was to make use of in the form the book was later to take. She must have felt him to be a very influential and authoritative voice at the time, and some of her friends even advised her to leave the writing to him, since he was the acclaimed poet; she could never be as great as he was. Although these comments were always to hurt and anger, they didn't deter Mum. She had written, and would continue to write, poetry all her life but only ever thought of herself as a writer, not a poet. Her new and evolving form of expression she didn't view as poetry anyway and took heart and stimulation from his criticism. She had always thrilled to the sound of his poetry, and for George to be the first person to tell her she could write closed her ears to the Jeremiahs who told her to leave it to others supposedly better equipped.

George had eloped with his pregnant love in a fever of fidelity, apparently happy to support her in her hour of need. But somewhere along the way this commitment evaporated and now, holed up in a grubby hotel with the threat of isolation on a lonely island beckoning, he sought secretly to escape. They had been ten days cooped up in the hotel when George secretly cabled his friend John Fitch, now on leave from the US Army Air Corps.

He and his girlfriend had Jessica staying with them in their house in Valhalla, White Plains, New York. George asked Fitch to bring Jessica with him but not to mention Mum to her. The first Mum knew of these plans was when Fitch suddenly arrived at the hotel in Vancouver. He was alone, and the three of them spent a few days at The Almer while George was able to put the finishing touches to his *Selected Poems*.

After asking her permission to dedicate the volume to her, George— on the pretext of popping out to post the typescript—left Mum in their room in the hotel. He jumped into John Fitch's red Buick and with John raced down to Big Sur and on across the US to New York for an impetuous joyride, leaving Mum bewildered and alone. As they left, Fitch had the decency to inquire about Mum's condition and how she felt about their trip. George flippantly replied that she had known this was going to happen all along.

Hoping that he might yet re-appear, Mum worked the ordeal of waiting into a diary entry: "It is not possible that he will not return. I sit here on one elbow hourly expecting his tight peremptory tap on the door. Each time the inefficient jangle of the elevator gets into motion, I start up. Will this monster stop at my floor and disgorge my miracle?"

Some later passages from the diary are turned into her book: "The wallpaper drips gloom, and the walls press in like dread. This dark hotel room is the center of the whirlpool where no one can any longer resist."[74]

She also wrote George a letter from the hotel a day after he had left:

Friday Morning. This is impossible. I simply cannot live without you. You must come back & get me. There's nothing, nothing at all in the world but this. You can't destroy me like this. You can't. If you must go to England I'll go too—I find I can get a permit if I volunteer to stay for the duration to get a job.

As for the baby if I don't stop crying & beating my head I'll have a miscarriage. Why did you ever think it would be possible? I could no more write a book now than a fish on the death brink could. I can do nothing, for you have rendered me nothing. If suicide is the only way out for you then I will die too only let me die with you.

George I am going crazy. My brain rattles around like a dried pea. I can't get to sleep & if I do I dream of corpses hidden in ice. I didn't think you would really leave me like that how could you? I could have gone with you at least. Come back & get me. O come back. I simply cannot endure this. I don't know what will happen—did you really say you loved me & do this? Don't you SEE there's nothing else you're giving me worse than you gave Jessica because the reason is less good & the results will be worse.

O God really I am dying I am truly dying.

He didn't return, and after another day of waiting she looked at a map of the area and opted for Irvine's Landing, Pender Harbour. This was a promontory on a peninsula stretching out from the mainland and she chose this rather than Vancouver Island, across the Strait of Georgia, where she had first envisioned she might go. It was sixty miles north of Vancouver and the six-hour ferry called only twice a week. Here she rented a disused schoolhouse opposite the harbor.

Across a rocky coastline she could watch the sun setting over Texada Island, eight miles away, and she could just make out Vancouver Island, visible as a thin blue line on the horizon to the southwest. She unpacked her records and books and awaited the arrival of her baby.

Although Mum had always been a child of nature she wasn't particularly practical. Later she would be able to fix things round the house with tape and string, but changing an electrical plug would defeat her. Horticulture was yet to appeal to her and she hadn't yet learned to cook, but despite the cosseted nature of her upbringing she put her dungarees on and did what she could.

When she had been eight years old, Mackenzie King, the Canadian prime minister, had moved into a house with extensive lands next to the family at Kingsmere. He felled the pines and had the land cleared to erect a folly. To Mum this was worse than murder and she had flown into a rage, running through his property, knocking down walls and leaving cryptic notes everywhere. Her mother had similarly underbrushed a nearby wood when they first moved onto their property, and Mum had become inconsolable with grief and fury for two days, not eating or moving in her tantrum. Now she was faced with a lonely survival at the edge of the world, keeping a vigil for childbirth. Daunting though this seemed, she was in her element. As a "survival pack" she had brought trunks full of evening dresses, party frocks, and parcels of precious books. She carefully arranged her treasured copies of Rilke, Auden and Wordsworth along the schoolroom shelves. When stocking up on provisions from the local shop, not knowing conventional shopping quantities, she had ordered ten pounds of tea.

One thing she was able to do was make her cabin look loved, and she painted the front door a bright yellow to remind her of her The Pulley in the mountains at home and next to Blake's words "The cut worm forgives the plough" she had Henry Vaughan's poem "Be clean. Bear Fruit. And wait." Over the windows and walls she stuck Madonnas, Christ heads and other favorite pictures. The prying locals were ignored and the curious Mounted Police, investigating new arrivals, left her in peace, labeling her a religious fanatic.

It worried her that in an emergency she would have to be ferried to the mission hospital and, this being her first pregnancy, she was convinced she would die in childbirth and so, dispassionately, she wrote out a will, in case. To her parents back in Ottawa she said she was happily out in the wilderness working on a novel and, although her sisters knew, her mother and father remained oblivious to her true state.

As her condition became more apparent, she began to arouse local curiosity, especially since she tried to explain her condition by calling herself Mrs. Barker. Her letters, though, coming through the post office had been forwarded to Miss Elizabeth Smart. That was also the name on her registration card. This nosiness from the locals might have driven her into further isolation, but her situation was a direct result of her own choice and her determined will. Inwardly she exulted in it. Nothing had happened from luck or chance. If George had been living there with her, it would have been the goal and the heaven she had been working toward for ten years. She was as close to the wild natural world as it was possible to be without becoming a hermit, she had a baby inside her—by "he for whom I waited so long, who has stalked so unbearably through my nightly dreams"—and she was about to start the last few pages of the novel she had wanted to write all her life.

She made friends with a Viennese woman called Maximiliane von Upani Southwell and her family in the village. She was twenty years older than Mum and despite surviving on the welfare she received for her fisherman husband's infirmities, she was cultured, elegant and well read. When she first entered the schoolhouse she turned over a book on the table, noticed it was by Rilke and said, "I see we shall be friends." Mum remained in touch with her for the rest of her life, and she dedicated *By Grand Central Station I Sat Down and Wept* to her, giving her the first copy, which Mum wrote out by hand.

George was two days into his motoring spree with John Fitch before he made contact with Mum again. He wrote trying to justify his departure, saying he could not simply ignore the fact that he had a wife and he was going to New York to sort it out. He promised to return once things were settled. He and John Fitch had first met on the Japan-bound *Fushimi Maru* on its first leg to New York. They had both had partners with them, but their friendship was to deepen and they were indulging in a homosexual relationship as they sped across America. On April 5 he wrote to Mum:

"Either I must receive a divorce or never forgive her [Jessica]: and she must acknowledge the process of the personal inevitable: but I shall not desert her; least of all when all the cards are stacked against her, and the wolf screaming at the window. But never will I let you, whose umbilical I also hang upon, live at a remove from me."

Yet he had put the best part of 1100 miles between them in the two days since he had vanished from The Almer. With John Fitch he had revisited the waterfalls in San Bernardino, to where he and Mum had first eloped as they deserted Jessica eight months earlier. He was moved to wire: "I send you this from a coast indescribably haunted by you. Prepare a corner for me and read Solomon." Overjoyed to hear from him at last, she replied care of John Fitch's apartment in New York, writing on the back of a letter from his publisher and being careful to annotate instructions on the envelope to return to sender should he not be there and therefore not receive it:

> Your first wire & your letter entirely resurrected me from the grave on that very day Sebastian [the baby was to be called Sebastian if a boy and Georgina if a girl] began kicking uproariously & hilariously. Come quickly for all I do is sit with folded hands waiting.... I was delirious with being too happy when I got your wire & letter. O it was the final final reaction & not just for passing through California? Anyway I am become an idolater & everything is for you daily & hourly. So come very very quickly This place is extraordinarily beautiful & peaceful & we can drink tea anytime we like. I do pray that Jessica is all right. Please do let me know as soon as you can & hurry for S. is impatient.

This letter had been written to him as he was finally arriving in New York, having covered 3700 miles in twelve days, sleeping in the car.

On the road from Vancouver, Fitch had phoned his girlfriend to let her know when to expect their arrival. George took the opportunity to invite Jessica to accompany them back to Vancouver. When the two men now threatened to reappear she fled. She had adopted a healthy skepticism concerning George's motives and was, as so often since he had left her, completely penniless. She realized she could no longer rely on George for support and had managed get herself a job as a live-in girl Friday in a country and swimming club in Rye, not far from White Plains, whose beach stretched down to Long Island Sound.

When George and Fitch arrived in New York, they went to his Riverdale apartment, at the northern tip of Manhattan, in the Bronx, instead of heading to Fitch's White Plains flat. There George sent telegrams to Mum on April 15, promising to return, and on the 28th, saying he was marooned in Manhattan with only three dollars and couldn't raise the money to make the return. He was, and had been, living entirely off John Fitch on their journey. Fitch, who must have found the apartment up at Riverdale not central enough, decided that together they should move to a new apartment in Greenwich Village, to where Mum addressed her desperate plea:

> *George!* This is April 27th and today there was no letter & the sun didn't come out & the Art of Egypt & Othello & the entire Faber library were powerless. Nor could Nature give me a slap of revival even though I found dogwoods bigger than my baby's head & my whole room smelled of Lilac & Appleblossom & the wind lifted my skirt ...
>
> ... 24 days have gone by & by now what can I think but that you have betrayed & forgotten me in all & every way, for I have had one letter only from the Monterey coast where a perhaps too violent reaction precipitated you back to me. Are you mine then? Are you really mine? And when O when are you coming?

Before she could post it she got a letter from him, so when replying she sent three letters: this one; one outlining ways to get some money together for the travel fare, which contained the line "But I expect you don't want to travel four days by train third Class, as once when I sat down by Grand Central Station & wept, choose comfort instead of love," which George later suggested she use as the title to her book, claiming it as his invention; and a third:

> Now it's April 29th & at last your Letter has come & I want to do nothing but sit down & cry for ever until you arrive. Will you ever arrive? O I am so sad & so in love. Beg, Borrow or Steal. But if you say you can't I'll say you don't want to ...
>
> ... But anyway you aren't here. You are betraying me in N.Y. at every opportunity & though I love you madly desperately solely & forever I am dissolved dissolved dissolved with my tears overflowing all Pender Harbour. E.[75]

She also cabled him several times, pleading for him to come, but he laconically replied that he was mooching around New York trying to ignore the "tarts with key rings under their eyelids and boys with hour glass waists" and to think only of Elizabeth Smart, 'my saffron, my brindle, my Brom-dinagian-breasted; my uraeus urethraed, my sweet (christ, I'm out of breath)." He wrote these words even as he was trying to set up a date with Jessica in an attempt to win back her affections. He suggested they meet uptown at Columbia University to see a new musical play by Benjamin Britten and W.H. Auden.

John Fitch was recalled to the Air Corps in Florida and it became nec-essary for George to leave the apartment that he and Fitch had been living in. Suddenly George had to find rent and subsistence, and so before he departed he touched Fitch for a loan. Fitch reminded George how gener-ous he had been in the past, refused, and so enraged George that he com-plained angrily to Mum:

"He said that he had been compelled to sell the ford to buy the Buick. I said of course. He said I have sixty dollars with which to enter the Air Corpse. Here you have forty of them. And as I know this untrue (he had, only two or three days previously, announced the windfalling of 220 bucks). I took the forty and parted.... And now I know how Aristotle felt about that ungracious and ungrateful agrarian Alexander. Requiescat in astra Johannes Fitch."[76]

After Fitch had left, George managed to struggle through May with the rent (the forty dollars from Fitch helped), but June was beyond him, so he turned his attentions back to British Columbia. In May he had dealt with the imminent publication of his *Selected Poems* and watched his rep-utation emerging on both sides of the Atlantic. Manhattan, however, was proving an expensive place to live, so before every last cent had gone he bought an airline ticket to Vancouver. He also felt he had won back Jessica's loyalty.

Mum had been alone a long time by now and although her sympathy for him was all but gone, she wrote, still true to her feelings for him, in her diary:

"I am lonely. I want the one I want. He is the one I picked out from the world. It was cold deliberation. But the passion was not cold. No it kin-dled me. I begat. This time last year it hung in strips. Now there may be sadness and sorrow and delay but no more precariousness. It is pinned down. It has confessed. This is the *one*. This is the one. And you try to ful-fill a precious proposition of fate by being his. It is O a rare conjunction as a spark that settled into clarity."

On May 22, while on a stopover in Winnipeg, George realized he was completely without funds and so took his air ticket and cashed in the second leg for a train ticket, thereby giving himself a little extra loose change. He also cabled Mum of his indigence, saying the eighteen cents he had left wouldn't pay for the $2.50 he would owe for the hotel. He would be either evicted or arrested, but he would get to her one way or the other. Attempting to tug at her heartstrings with this display of bravado, she resisted its appeal and steeled herself for his charm offensive. Her diary entry for May 24:

> No I will not allow him to wreck my life or turn bitter and broken because, after all, he was only certain of loving me for perhaps three days or weeks. I will not say it was any less because now his incredible capacity for what is surely unnecessary deceit to both of us knocks everything from under me, entirely dissolves me so periodically ... but I don't invalidate even the moments when I was most deceived. For they remain as good and I do as completely love; nor can I cease loving nor will there ever be another who was all the things I wanted so completely and the only one destined.... The worst thing is the deceit. Even she [Jessica] who sees the offence itself so large (but then, to save herself from total wreck she was able to make *me* the monster) minds the deceit most. "My dearest love—you reign empress in my heart—you totally reign my mind."

> Dearest Elizabeth I am all Elizabeth my head my heart my hand.[77]

Both these quotes from a letter of his.

George finally arrived on May 28, four days after this entry, and they spent the longest time alone together since they met. This for Mum must have been deeply satisfying, but he, arriving in hat, tie and thick jacket in flaming June, must have felt incongruous and uncomfortable. He was always the consummate urbanite and it was hard to imagine a more rural setting. It took him only a month before he began to feel restless.

On June 28 he left for Vancouver to stay in The Almer to think things over, and he could now write to Mum, demonstrating a strong new resolve: "For six weeks, we must again be parted for a purpose. I am going to New York to get a divorce. For fifty hours I have watched my life struggling on the pin of my thinking and from this transfixion which is indeed a minor martyrdom I have received the determination to Alexander these Gordians."[78]

On the way to New York on the train he wrote better to underline his determination to get a divorce and return before the baby was born: "I love you, Elizabeth my golden bough and this is to implore you to believe what

I have written." It suggested perhaps that he understood she was beginning to acquire a skepticism about his promises.

But he never returned. And he never "Alexandered his Gordians" with Jessica. When he reached New York he had to wait a few nights in a cheap hotel for the return of his prospective New York publisher, Oscar Williams, and on July 11 he managed to scrounge floor space with Williams. He also took up with Jessica again, telling Mum he'd seen her once but wasn't able to broach the subject of divorce with her because she looked so depressed. As the month wore on he took to seeing more of Jessica, who now had a little money from her job.

He escaped the sweltering humidity of Manhattan in July to sun himself on the beach at Rye, where Jessica would join him for her lunch break. He had managed to talk to Jessica about the divorce proceedings, he said, which were successfully ongoing, ending the letter, "I am dying for you, canada, dying for you."[79]

Since their last leave-taking at Irvine's Landing, George's relationship with Mum went into a tailspin as his one with Jessica flourished. Now communicating only through the carefully censored letters he sent her, nonetheless she felt she could predict what he was up to. She realized that his professed ongoing divorce discussion was more truthfully a reconciliation, and from a very unreliable quarter Mum heard that Jessica was pregnant. She accused George of being responsible for conceiving a second Sebastian and, livid, he forgot his professed longing and spat back:

"You crazy witch. Where did you ever conceive the idea of Jessica and a child? This is the first I've heard of it and I'm sure that Jessica is unaware."[80] He identified the source of this false rumor, who turned out to be a mutual acquaintance, and went round and hit him in the face. Feeling pleased with himself, and that honor had been satisfied, he wrote to Mum begging for more money.

Fully immersed in finishing her book, Mum ignored his pleas. The book was written largely back to front. She completed it on August 14 and wrote to Louie to tell her, letting her know the job was now to find a publisher. She also sent a typescript copy to George.

He had been aware of how the writing was going because he had been overseeing it at Pender Harbour, but on reading it now he was amazed and wrote her a critique:

The passion of intellect and by this I mean the sensuality over words & images and the whole ballet of semantics is tremendous and marvelous in Grand Central. Indeed I do not know of anyone now writing in the English language with a more florid fountain of simple sensuality than you, my dear Lizzie.... Now I will get my nose down to your St. Catherine wheel of a book and tell you what I think should be done with and about it. First it is the book that you have been waiting for these twenty nine? Thirty-two? Thirty six? years. This I recognize because of the natural authority with which the most dangerous of its statements are made: such statements can only be made when the irrefutable ratification of true Sibylline instinct is at work: this Sibylline instinct is everywhere in the thing. I recall for instance the superb phrase This is the hour I once rose up and, beautifully equipped with scorn, commanded the sun to rise. This is the speech of the human addressing himself to his creator and, my darling, I kiss your hand in oblation.

The critique was lengthy and very generous, helpfully outlining a few quibbles he had which Mum was to carefully implement later.

Knowing the birth was imminent, she took the opportunity to move in with Maxie next door, resigning herself to the fact that George wouldn't be present for the birth. He had written to her on August 8 saying he couldn't see how he could arrive in time "without holding a gun to a Guggenheim head. Read Goethe, watch over me, pray for my poems, and die every day of love for all things including myself and my son who draws life from your right and your left breast."[81]

As so often in George's life, all sources of money had dried up and he was further harassed by the draught board demanding an interview with him on August 12. Mercifully for him, this was later deferred. In his frustration he lashed out at everyone, including his hosts, the Williamses, and they evicted him, so he moved in with a young poet he had just met. On arrival at the Brooklyn flat of the young writer, he collapsed and was admitted to hospital with suspected pneumonia. While recovering he determined to make a last attempt to get to Pender Harbour for the birth. On his discharge he managed to rustle up a few dollars through loans and handouts but failed to raise enough cash for the trip. His desperate letter to Irvine's Landing demanding "IS MY SON HERE?"[82] fell on deaf ears, as by now Mum had felt the first labor pains and had left on a rowboat for the mainland to prepare for the birth.

On August 28 at ten past four in the afternoon, my sister Georgina Elizabeth was born. On September 13 George set out from Brooklyn in an attempt to see his second child (Clare, his first, by Jessica, had been given up for adoption). He already had an application for immigration to Canada

pending but as yet had not heard if it had been successful. He got no farther than the US–Canada border at the northernmost tip of New York State
when an official demanded a current reentry permit. When one wasn't
forthcoming, the official put George on the line to the director of immigration. The director asked for references and, for reasons best known to himself, George unwisely gave him the Coltrin Lodge number. It was lucky
Louie wasn't in, but Helen told the director that George wasn't welcome
in their house. The director then checked the files and found that George
had been refused entry to Canada on the grounds of "moral turpitude,"
which if it hadn't been so inconvenient and frustrating at the time would
have brought a smile to his lips. Louie, through Russel Sr., had brought
her influences to bear in the Department of Employment and Immigration.
Although this "moral turpitude" was an official charge for entry refusal, it
was never to be seen on official government records.

A week later, having beaten a retreat to New York, George received a
letter from the director of immigration telling him that his application for
immigration had been turned down by the minister. They also explained
that they had "a great deal of information on Elizabeth Smart and her ille-
gitimate child."[83] The baby was only three weeks old and yet they had felt
the birth important enough to have it recorded on file already. Surprisingly,
Louie hadn't learnt of Georgina's birth despite this.

Mum left the hospital and returned to Irvine's Landing. She found that
Maxie was an enormous help with the baby and she quickly settled back
into the schoolhouse. The need for a trip back east was becoming overpowering, and when she heard that her father was ill she needed no further excuse. Her first priority, however, had to be George. During this
postnatal period he had been regularly in touch and was keen to run over
her novel with her. He sent her his new *First Cycle of Love Poems*, professed
undying love for her, reiterating that he was talking to Jessica about divorce
and wanted to marry Mum:

"Of course I have spoken. This has devastated her devotion. You know
that she is a Roman Catholic and I say this as I would say it of Thomas
Moore [*sic*] or Edmund Campion: it violated her fundamentals to con-
template divorce. I pray for the tongues of angels to persuade. And in the
end in the long end I shall. But you must understand that it is like intro-
ducing an iconoclasm in her."[84]

Having been squatting in sordid conditions with alcoholics and
bums in the Bowery in Manhattan, he had now in fact moved in with Jessica in a rural cottage upstate. Not surprisingly he was less than candid

Mum and Georgina, 1949

concerning his whereabouts, but Mum could stand waiting for him no longer, so she left Georgina in Maxie's care and on December 9 set off for New York.

(Mum would spend the rest of her life trying to explain this abandonment to Georgina, but the urgency to find George was stronger than her love for her child: "Then three months of anguish & despair and running through the bushes. & then off in a boat, leaving Georgina a tiny figure in Maxie's arms.")[85]

Worried about her father's illness, she should have made Ottawa her first call, but nonetheless she went straight to New York, where yet again George failed to meet her at Grand Central Station. Leaving her bags with a friend in Manhattan, she sought George out and arrived to stay with him and Jessica in their cottage in Nyack. This is the first time that all three of them had been together since leaving Big Sur with its ensuing treachery. Her pocket diary for the year ends: "This was a very sad year for ES—it was spent mostly in having Georgina—& the very great joy it was turned to the worst unimaginable sorrow. 'I came too late in time etc.' It is really too terrible to record."[86]

On December 24 she went back to Ottawa to see her stricken father and wrote in her diary: "This was a hellish time. George phoned often & said Will you marry me, but that didn't help."[87]

While in Ottawa and with the help of her father, Mum was able to obtain an American residence visa with a view to finding a job in Washington, where she knew a friend, Grisell Hastings' husband, Eddie, was in the British Navy. She left Coltrin Lodge without her parents' finding out they had a grandchild, and in Washington she managed to find a job as an office clerk with the British Army staff.

She was still smarting from her meeting with George and Jessica when, despite his rhetoric, George failed to broach the subject of divorce. There had been an occasion before she left Ottawa for Washington when Mum had phoned George at Nyack. She got Jessica on the line and after a frank exchange of words, Jessica let Mum know she and George were living in conjugal and domestic bliss. George, sensing he was losing his hold on her, was quick to cable Mum:

"I happen to be very much in love with you and no one else in existence and I am prepared to take all the consequences. But to subject Jessica to the anguish of having this said when you were actually there in the room would have been diabolical."[88]

Mum ignored his entreaties and threw herself into mastering her new job, and from tea girl she quickly rose through the ranks, moving within a few weeks from the Army staff to the British Embassy as a personal assistant to the minister of information. She was living in Eddie and Grisell Hastings' house and it was to that house that George paid a visit from New York. He found Mum a busy working girl who had little time for dallying with him, and at the station to catch the return train he was not even offered a parting kiss. He blustered later in a letter:

"What kills me about you is your self-consciousness for do you know—naturally you do know—that when we parted I was not permitted to kiss you not even merely kiss you because your 'boss' (love, thou art absolute sole boss of life and death) happened to be hiding in the bushes? I AM NOT

PREPARED TO PLAY 2ND BOSS TO ANYONE INCLUDING CHRIST AND SIR STAFFORD CRIPPS."[89]

Back at Irvine's Landing, Maxie's son John had come down with a nasty eye infection and Maxie had to ferry him to Vancouver for an operation. Unable to take Georgina with her, Maxie had put her in a foster home through the Children's Aid Society, and while Georgina was there Mum frantically tried to maneuver her round US immigration requirements to get her into the United States. For an American visa the consular general required that she should fulfill three requests. First was consent from the father, second was her declaration of marital status and third she was her provision of documentary evidence to show that she was the mother.

Georgina languished for two weeks in the foster home before the visa came through. Mum also had to keep the secret from her parents, not an easy thing to do if a five-month-old baby was to arrive off an airplane by herself. In order to forestall possible inquiries, Grisell Hastings and Mum conjured up a story in which Georgina was the child of a woman who had died in British Columbia and was stopping off on her way to join her father, who was stationed in England in the British War Services.

Maxie duly put Georgina on the plane, but when Grisell Hastings showed up, tight-lipped and sporting a rakish feathered hat, the waiting press soon learned that Grisell was Lord Lamington's daughter and was taking possession of a mysterious baby, known only as Georgina Elizabeth. The flashbulbs started to pop and next day the *Washington Times* headline ran:

LONDON-BOUND BABY PASSENGER IN PLANE PROVIDES MYSTERY AT AIRPORT HERE: INFANT ENDS ONE STAGE OF MYSTERY JOURNEY

An accompanying photo showed Georgina being handed over by the stewardess. The copy ran on:

> A five-month-old bundle of pink mystery flew in last night. And disappeared. When American Airlines' Trip 24 arrived at the airport at 7:45 p.m., an extra stewardess disembarked.
>
> "She left Vancouver early this morning," said the stewardess. "I had orders to prepare her formula in Chicago. She arrived there at 3 p.m.— a stewardess had cared for her on the United plane from Vancouver— and I held her in my arms all the rest of the way. She was an ideal passenger. The purr of the motors seemed to soothe her, and she slept most of the time. When she woke she would drink her formula. But I don't know her name."

The passenger list identified the child only as Georgina Elizabeth. Airline officials couldn't clarify the issue. Immediately, rumors spread. "Royalty! Nobility?" And some were emphatic that the baby's mother was a mysterious lady who stood in the background. In a Baltimore paper the headline ran,

EARL'S DAUGHTER MEETS MYSTERY BABY

Grisell refused to give the baby's last name or any other details of the onward flight, save she was London-bound.

Grisell whisked Georgina off to Helen's, who had a house across the state line in Baltimore. Mum had come down with measles and didn't want to infect Georgina and so, agonizingly, couldn't meet her. Unfortunately, Russel Sr. was visiting Helen at the time and listened carefully to the explanation of the identity of the baby as told to the press—and, just as carefully, bought none of it. He took one look at Georgina and then looked back at Helen and said, "Georgina Elizabeth is yours, isn't she?" and they told him who Georgina really was. When he got back to Ottawa he kept faith with his daughter's secret and it was two years before Louie found out.

It took George three more weeks before he got to Washington to see his daughter. She was now seven months old. When he left to return to New York he arranged that Mum and Georgina should come and visit him in a month's time.

When Jessica found out about Georgina's existence she sent a charitable and forgiving telegram of congratulation to Mum. Jessica had to swallow her pride to send the telegram, because only two days earlier she had written to Mum:

> Of course he [George] has been living with me all the time and happily and very passionately (this because from your letter it counts more than anything with you) and is finished with you and is just forgetting the last remnants of you etc. etc.... Also I was not to get in touch with you as you would lie to me. The arrangement now was that we should ask you down and he would tell you in front of me, so that I would be convinced for all time. I know he loves me Elizabeth and I believe now what I first believed. That he enjoys sleeping with you but does not really want to live with you. Obviously he could have been living with you all this time if he really wanted to and he says that all the lies are to prevent me from going from him and it must be true. After all I have

left him once already. But you pursue him Elizabeth and apparently you would rather ruin his life than let him continue being happy with me.... You certainly have made your mark on our lives my sweet.[90]

In selflessly congratulating Mum on Georgina's birth, Jessica must have found it particularly difficult. A week later she left George again, and when Mum brought Georgina up to New York to visit him two weeks later there was no chance of a final showdown with the three of them, luckily for George. Mum appeared at an apartment that George had arranged for her to stay at, resplendent in white summer frock with Georgina on her arm, to claim her man.

George, during this period of his life in Manhattan, had been enjoying a spell of increased industry. He was submitting regular poems and articles to literary magazines and writing critical reviews, and Macmillan had published his *Selected Poems* in New York. He was relieved to hear the draft board had turned him down when he attended their rescheduled meeting.

Remuneration and fees from all this new work still left him short, so when the French writer Anaïs Nin, whom he had first met in October of the previous year, suggested he come in on a project she was inaugurating, he didn't hesitate. The project was a circle of writers, among them Henry Miller, Robert Duncan (one of a group of poets associated with Black Mountain College, a liberal-arts college in Asheville, North Carolina, that became, in the 1950s, a center for anti-academic poetry heralding the Beat Generation) and other friends whose job it would be to turn out erotica to order for rich businessmen at a dollar a page.

Nin was increasingly concerned about George's welfare. Beguiled by his charm, she romantically pictured him as an obsessive genius drinking himself into the gutter, and in order to save him decided to become his patron. He never really took much of a liking to her, though, finding her pretentious. But he was quite capable of enhancing their relationship for cash, especially if the writers of this erotica were guaranteed anonymity for their contributions.

They set to work with relish, and their first offerings were much enjoyed by the clientele. In fact the clientele was a chain of agents, presumably all taking a cut. Nin passed the manuscripts to a pornography publisher, Gerson Legmann. He handed the material to one "Slapsie Maxie," who then dealt directly with the connoisseur, Roy Melisander of Ardmore, Oklahoma. Melisander was under the impression that Henry Miller had written every last lascivious word. The enthusiasm for their product was diminished only when, playing fast and loose with poetic licence, too much exuberant surrealism was introduced into the sexual athletics.

George had been introduced to a wealthy bohemian couple called Willard and Marie Maas. Willard was a poet, and Oscar Williams had included him in his anthology of poetry. Marie was more visual and had been to the New York School of Fine Art. She was now making avantgarde films. They were starting a new experimental film with George at the time when Mum and Georgina came up from Washington to stay in their apartment.

With George commissioned to prepare the voice-overs and script, Willard took on the direction and Marie was on camera. All three were to act as subject matter. On 16mm black-and-white stock they shot a slow-motion, distorted, almost forensic examination of their three naked bodies, paying fond attention to the orifices. The working title was to be *The Desire and Pursuit of the Hole*, with George's cultivated vowels parodying a Pathé Pictorial newsreel, as he facetiously recalled a familiar Californian background:

> Then Sappho, distraught with the frustration of her passion,
> Gathered up her skirts and, crying in a voice that will be heard forever,
> Threw herself off the cliff of her lover's disdain.
> From waterfalls under which brides practice their long-awaited nuptials,
> Vikings with battles in their hands emerge like murderers …

They called it *The Geography of the Body* in the end, fearing their mock reference to the writer/painter Baron Corvo's *The Desire and Pursuit of the Whole* might not be picked up by a wider audience. After cutting and editing, it surfaced a year later and enjoyed an underground reputation for contemporary experimentalism, but for lack of professional distribution it survived only in cult status.

George had been at his happiest when his wife and his girlfriend had daylight between them. He could control them and visit them, if he had the money, when the need arose. Through 1942 Mum had come to feel that George would never leave Jessica and that although she loved him, living with him was impossible (an explanation by her to account for his absence to us children many years later). He would come down from New York to see her and in order to spare the blushes of her Washington host and family friends, Grisell and Eddie Hastings, they stayed in sleazy hotels where so much of their past romance had taken place.

On the night of November 9, 1942, after a visit with Helen to see Georgina, they checked in to the most affordable room the Mount Royal Hotel, Baltimore, could offer and, attempting to re-ignite past passions, eagerly set about my conception. Despite the ardor of this night, Mum felt the relationship was cooling and had already begun to feel alienated from George.

It was, indeed, only a month later that he was conceiving more children with Jessica in New York, who could now see that threatening to leave him brought him to heel. On the strength of this, and to put an end to the prevarication between the two of them, Mum decided to leave America for England, hoping that George would follow. Her US work permit was due to expire and the trip was, after all, one she had made many times. Also it would force George either to follow—and declare his allegiance to her, and put the Atlantic between him and Jessica—or to stay with Jessica. She would also escape the anticipated hysterics from her mother on the day she found out about the existence of her grandchildren. These reasons belie the fact that she was prepared to take a trip with a perilous North Atlantic convoy, risking the lives of her child and her unborn baby, and live in a war zone that would imperil them all. She would also distance herself from her adored father, who had been ill in this risky attempt to get her lover to make a declaration of fidelity by following her.

She knew how dangerous this trip might be. In case she, Georgina and her luggage went down with the ship, she left a copy of the manuscript of her book with the Maases. She also knew that Maxie had a copy. She had handwritten the complete manuscript and given it to her as a present for looking after Georgina. (It now resides in the Library and Archives Canada.) She was beginning to feel there was urgency for departure, because her second pregnancy was beginning to show. Under wartime restrictions, pregnant women were not allowed to cross the Atlantic in a ship. She quickly made plans. The first thing she had to acquire was a job to go to in England, in order to get her exit permit. She managed yet again to prevail on her father's good offices and with help from her old flame Graham Spry, now working in London with the Ministry of Aircraft Production, they came up with a junior position in the British Information Services.

Her mother had to be told and without any knowledge of the real background to her daughter's move, she trilled in patriotic fervor:

"It's all very exciting! I understand your wanting to go & am quite in sympathy provided you can be of use in the country.... There is one thing that I know & that we as a family share & I wouldn't say it if you were not going into the danger zone. We have *guts* & we can stick it & if the worst happens I know you will not be afraid. The only fear I would have would be falling into enemy hands which would be much worse than death for any woman—especially a young & pretty one."[91]

Mum had no time to make a last trip to Ottawa to see her parents and left Washington with Georgina for New York on March 3. She had three weeks in the Maases' apartment on Brooklyn Heights awaiting a berth on board a ship that had to be taken up at a moment's notice. During this time she had many furious rows with George. She knew that Jessica was pregnant too. George would spend time with Mum and Georgina at the Maases and then slip quietly away to Jessica, who was living round the corner in Cranberry Street. He successfully managed to keep one woman from the other, while maintaining that he only loved the one he happened to be with at the time.

The Maases proved implacable friends to Mum. She termed them "the informers," as they kept track of George's movements for her, and she was to continue a correspondence with them for years afterward. Before she left, and perhaps realizing how final her movements might be, Mum elicited promises from George that they would meet in Kew Gardens on July 1. However much she may have worried over the steadfastness of his plans to meet her in England, they were kept secret from Jessica.

On March 25 the call came from the shipping line and Mum bundled Georgina into a warm overcoat and rushed down to the docks to board the *S.S. Tyndareus* for the three-week crossing. They waved goodbye to New York, with no sign of George waving back, and began their voyage to sea, where the starting convoy of forty-nine ships was joined by eighteen more from Halifax, Nova Scotia. A flotilla of thirteen gunboats hooked up in mid-ocean. The convoy was into its tenth trouble-free night when an attack started. The convoy was a comparatively large one, of eighty ships, and, since the commodore of the convoy, Admiral Sir C.G. Ramsay, was aboard the *Tyndareus*, Mum's ship was well protected.

The conditions for an attack on this tenth night were perfect, however, with the northern lights making night visibility exceptional. A marauding wolf pack of U-boats picked off and sank three ships. The next night, the gunboat escort was kept frantic, driving off thirteen more attacks, but in the end the escorts' protective perimeter was penetrated and *Tyndareus* was torpedoed and started to ship water.

Mum was sitting in her cabin reading, with Georgina asleep on her bunk. The other six women and two babies in her cabin were already asleep when she heard a muffled boom and felt the shudder of the metal walls. Seconds later an alarm bell jangled urgently down the corridor and a voice on the public-address system told them to muster up on the boat deck with their life jackets. She was halfway to the door before she stopped herself, remembering Georgina, and turned back. Her nineteen-month-old daughter picked up her head and was looking round bleary-eyed as Mum tugged two woolen sweaters over her head and pulled her overcoat on. She could lay her hands on only one life jacket and, hugging Georgina to her chest, she quickly threw it over both of them. They scrambled along the corridor with the others from her cabin and up to the deck. While she was waiting to board the lifeboats in barely controlled hysteria, a sudden wave of calm swept over her and the immediate panic evaporated. She felt "full of relief, a kind of wicked joy, that I should be offered such an effortless way out of my pain."[92]

The vague rendezvous with George in London in five months' time gave her little solace and she thrilled to the idea that an to end her despair was out of her hands.

The passengers were kept in the muster groups for an age. They felt that the longer they delayed from boarding the lifeboats and plummeting down from the shipside davits to the dark icy waters, the better their chances were. Oxyacetylene torches flared down the gangways as sailors raced up and down, some bearing metal cabin doors to patch the breach. The mustered passengers were frozen top to toe in the cold clear Atlantic night before the all-clear sounded. Three more sister ships weren't so lucky. They were picked off by U-boats before the convoy docked in Liverpool on Saturday, April 10.

Mum was six months' pregnant, and when she turned up for work at her new job on the next Monday morning her condition was evident. By Wednesday she was sacked. The service was not prepared to take the responsibility of having a woman in her condition in their offices. She was turned out for "procreational activities."

No longer required to reside in London for work, Mum phoned Didy Battye, whom she had last seen two years earlier and had first met in Government House in 1936 while she had been touring Canada with Lady Tweedsmuir. Didy—now Didy Asquith—was living in Gloucestershire, in the converted stables of Hinchwick Manor at Scarlet-sub-Edge. Here Didy was alone with her five-year-old daughter, Annabel, and a nanny called Mrs. Foster. Michael Asquith, her husband and the son of Lady Cynthia Asquith and grandson of the Liberal prime minister, was a conscientious objector and away on duty for the Friends' Ambulance Unit, run by Quakers in London.

"This is Betty Smart. Do you remember me? Could I pop by for tea?" she inquired and Didy immediately invited her to come and stay.

When Didy picked Mum up at the train in her MG TD two-seater sports car, Georgina sat on Mum's lap and they sped off into the Cotswold Hills towards Scarlet-sub-Edge. As they careered along the wooded hillsides in the open-top car, Didy and Mum excitedly shouted to each other as they tried to catch up on the years in between. Mum told her a poet called George Barker was the father of Georgina and her unborn child and that although he was now in America, tentative plans to meet him in Kew Gardens in ten weeks' time had been arranged.

On arrival, Mum was shown the converted rooms over the stables at Hinchwick Manor, where she would share the accommodation with Didy and Annabel. That weekend, her first in England with Georgina, must have felt like a haven of peace and quiet, as they had picnics on the manor lawn with the gentle Cotswold countryside bathed in the April sunshine. She managed to spend the next eight weeks recuperating under these glorious conditions before her peace was disturbed.

George arrived on June 15, having convinced the authorities at the British consulate in Washington that he would make himself available for war work in England if they repatriated him. He had been getting more and more agitated in New York, drinking heavily, and in frustration had thrust his fist through a glass windowpane in the Maases' apartment. He had given Jessica "the one decent thing he could do for her before leaving her [making her pregnant]."[93] So, his wife pregnant and penniless, he again abandoned her, this time with an ocean between them and with only vague promises of a return.

He dropped in to see his mother and father on arrival in London and three days later telegraphed Mum to say he was on his way to Moreton-in-Marsh station and could he be picked up?

George, too, immediately settled into the calm atmosphere at the manor and, stretching out on the sun-drenched lawns, fancied a stay to await the birth. For the time being, all five of them were able to squeeze into the converted stabling, but with Didy also pregnant with her second child he understood this arrangement would be temporary.

Mum had by then become used to wandering off into the hills on long walks with Didy and lazing on the lawns around the empty manor pool with the children. She had also spent many hours carefully smock-stitching dresses for Georgina and drawing up long lists, of which she was an inveterate compiler. These included a bibliography of the complete works of George Barker, "a poet and there is none better alive this day in England or anywhere else," details and dates of all movements and maternal and paternal relations (later gathered into little handmade books for each of her children, with photos and contributions from George; mine was termed Xtopher's Book), with an ancestral bloodline and pedigree.

Although George appreciated the rhythm of life at the manor, it wasn't long before he began to tire of the domestication. He rowed with Mum continually about Jessica's pregnancy, with Mum accusing him of faithlessness, to which, in his defense, he would grandly reply that men and women had different motors and polygamy was the nature of the beast for men.

The desire to throw himself back into his London haunts became overwhelming and, despite the terrifying air raids, he went back after only a brief stay at Scarlet-sub-Edge. The threat of these air raids, however, and his parental curiosity did bring him back on three two-day visits in June and July, but just before the expected birth he left, saying he would soon return. Two days after his departure, Mum went into labor and on July 23 she was admitted to Moreton-in-Marsh District Hospital, where I was born at 5:35 that afternoon.

With aplomb Mum duly noted every last detail, later entered formally in Xtopher's Book:

> Admitted 2:30. Slight Show this morning. Pains began just before midday. At 5:35 p.m. delivered herself with a little manual assistance. "Placenta membrane and perineum intact. Loss average." Dr. J.E. Jameson delivered him with assistance of Sister Armstrong, he weighed ten pounds and eight ounces when the dirt was washed off.... Placenta fifteen minutes after birth with a bearing down pain. No drugs, local anesthetic or ether. Sister Armstrong pummeled around for a "clot." There were thirteen babies in the hospital, one two? hours before CB. Cord came off eighth day. Milk flowed abundantly. Left hospital Thursday August 5th 1943.... Saint Christopher and Christopher Columbus guard this Christopher Barker: whether he carries Christ or looks for islands that aren't there: may his extra-big toe and his athlete's heel and his shoulders that stuck in the vagina come in handy. When Christopher was severed from the umbilical and laid in the basket, he said, in a loud pleasant voice, "Da" which is, "So be it."

Many more details were to follow.

Mum telegraphed the good news to George, to Maxie in Pender Harbour, and even to Alice Paalen in Mexico City. George, in replying to the telegram, added a postscript for me: "Forgive me."

It took me a long time.

With no further word, a week later Mum wrote from her hospital bed:

> Darling George: Where are you & what are you doing & are you very unhappy & harassed & if so why don't you write & tell me about it since who's supposed to be your helpmeet but me? And even if it's only something else then I want to understand & even in jail I thought of you & if they'd given me a pencil would have written you all I felt. If it's the bloodhounds or the beautiful pilot (John Fitch) or the gay paraders or the tigers of regret or whatever there must be a use for me since my love is not sporadic & periodic but like milk which if not sucked swells up till the breasts are footballs & has to be expressed by force.
>
> Christopher was circumcised today & has been dreaming about it ever since. Maybe he'll remember as you do. He's all dopey with ether. So far he's not the Acolyte type but I hope you'll like him. When I think he's my son I feel nice & cozy but when I think he's *your* son, I feel so pleased I cry.
>
> Please come & own him and me. Or if you can't come yet, then write us your instructions for the conduct of our hours, and lives. All love from Elizabeth with kisses from Georgina & Christopher.[94]

Mum was released from hospital on August 5 and George managed to get down to from his pressing engagements in London on August 9. On seeing me for the first time said: "Is this your latest production? You really are rather clever."

The next day, dressed in our best, we all set out from Scarlet-sub-Edge for London and, including her daughter, Annabel, Didy took a formal photo of the new family. George wore a battered trilby cocked raffishly on the back of his head, which he had combined with a trench coat, pipe and important-looking leather briefcase of work under his arm. Mum was in a tweed suit with peaked jockey cap and I was trussed up in a white knitted baby bag dangling from Mum's arm. Georgina was held in her other as she hitched up her knickers from below her smart double-breasted tweed coat. We were setting off into the blue with no home to go to and would not return for eight and a half months.

On arrival in London as a family of four we descended on George's mother—Big Mumma, as she was affectionately known—then living at Cornwall Gardens. We met most of the rest of George's family: Big Mumma and Bompa, or Pa; his grandma Taffe; his three sisters, Eileen, Olga and Monica; Eileen's children, John, Barry and Little Olga; and Monica's children Wendy, Pat and Mac. Ever mindful of George's charismatic way and with no sign of Jessica, Big Mumma gave Mum a big bear-hug greeting and welcomed her into the tribe, merely stating that it was a pity she and George had not met ten years earlier.

After a crowded few days in his parents' flat, George managed to find a small single room round the corner at Colherne Road. There he left us and flitted off into the night to stay at Monica's larger flat at Redcliffe Square. From there he made occasional sorties to Colherne Road to check on his family, but it was at Redcliffe Square that he did his writing and it was from Redcliffe Square that he made his forays to the Kensington pubs. It was while Mum was trapped in this tiny room with two small children that she learned of the existence of my half-brother and -sister, born to Jessica in New York on August 27. Under a death's head and crossed bones, Mum entered the following words into my Xtopher's Book:

"Addendum: when Christopher was five weeks old (August 27th 1943) he got a twin half-brother & half-sister by his stepmother Jessica (Jessica Winifred Barker, née Woodward) who were born in New York, USA: St. Clare's Hospital. Their names are Anthony Sebastian and Anastasia Clare. 'But thereof came in the end despondency and madness.'"

This was doubly galling for Mum, because George and Jessica had given the name Sebastian to the boy twin that once upon a time he and Mum had reserved for their first-born, who of course turned out to be Georgina.

So George now had twins in New York and a daughter and a five-week-old son in London. With his first child, the adopted Clare, he was now the father of five. Jessica wasn't aware of my existence at this point and George attempted at first to hide the fact from her. Jessica's sister, an old friend of George's from a time he had first met Jessica, soon informed her. Anxious to deny the facts, George said in a letter to Jessica that I wasn't his and surely she must know how promiscuous Mum was. Jessica didn't buy this, so he lashed out at her sister. Jessica replied:

"One day I must make out my testimony of the unforgivable and unforgettable things—it would surprise you considerably I think. You were always so sure you were getting away with things and that I was convinced by the most outrageous lies. Re: my vicious sister, I am not concerned with your behavior now and as she was not the father of Elizabeth's children, mention of her seems superfluous.... Will you never learn?"[95]

Since he was constantly arguing with Mum whenever he turned up at Colherne Road, he largely kept away, and Mum realized that the close confines of the flat were not helping their relationship. Casting about in desperation, she mentioned her problems to Julian Trevelyan, who was one of the original guests at Varda's villa in Cassis and with whom she was reacquainted. He had heard that a basement flat at Hammersmith Terrace on the Thames shore was available.

Our time there was not happy. The high tide lapped right up to the window of the living room and we shivered in the damp of the sunken room. On one such night a friend and fellow poet called David Gascoyne came round, and after we had been put to bed the three adults talked on into the night. As they talked, a sudden air-raid siren sounded and Mum rushed into our bedroom and grabbed us in either arm. She got as far as the stairs and there she cowered with us in her arms while David theatrically intoned Baudelaire's *Les Fleurs du mal* and a line of incendiary bombs smacked into every other house, setting the terrace ablaze. When the air raid had passed and the all-clear sounded, George reappeared from the cupboard under the stairs and he and Mum rushed around till they found David. He was in the sitting room, inspecting the corpse of a dead mouse in the fireplace.

George soon realized he couldn't continue to share this crowded and noisy accommodation with us and slipped off to stay with his sister at Radcliffe Square. Alone and becoming embittered, Mum wrote in a notebook:

Continuity lacking.
Fear invading.
I am doodling with my mind.
There is no urgency.
George has hardened his heart.
He is mad.
I am mad too with an inward curtain-like madness. A pall. There is no illumination.
I have children. But I have ceased to care about anything. I have no personal ambition or even the desire that people call me nice or pretty or witty. Nor do I have any use for sensation, nor do I crave cessation. It is a technical circling, encircling, cycle, of giving the body to be burned but having no charity.
When the raids come I am very much afraid, but merely afraid. Not saying, O let us die together in each other's arms. No for George nags through all, and my arms are not his comfort & his home.

True, he is harassed by joblessness & cashlessness, but if I were harassed & had external trouble it would be love I would crave to cool my forehead with.

What can I do? For without love I am truly dead. Will it awake in him & be renewed like the spring? Probably not now. (O but I don't believe this. If I did, why would I dare get up & walk down the possible streets—No I am merely bitter.) He sees now in everything I do, ulterior, & reprehensible motives: I wash my face, even, "for the wrong reasons." (Sic. cf. Jessica's: that noble creature who is so good herself that she can't believe in the bad motives of anyone else! Balls.)

Balls to you, Jessica, with your astute line of the abused. The reason you manage him so cleverly is because you don't love him. He's *your* husband, and *your* honor is at stake. You like the pose of the faithful wife. Besides you anticipate prizes. (Now you're being vulgar, Elizabeth. O, then, will the psychoanalyst judge? No, he will say: Tell me what you are afraid to tell me: Well, mother said I must never call anyone common.)

Well then, presume I am defeated. Am I defeated by English tricks, expediency or time? ("I came too late.") I have watched him lately trying to make all his lies true by posthumous actions—or to convince himself by man's puzzling situations to fit into a bubble.[96]

One thing she was very aware of as she lay in her damp room with two young children was that the luxury of a quiet place to write had been left in the cabin at Pender Harbour. She had been able to write only fragments of complaint in her notebooks since then. But one night, when she was able to get out to the Soho pubs on her own, she met up with a charismatic Ceylonese figure called Tambimuttu. He said he was editor of a magazine called *Poetry London* that was published by Editions Poetry London. He seemed largely penniless, bumming drinks and meals for himself, doing the Soho round with indigent poets and artists. But Mum learned that he had started his own publishing with very little and was able to drum up backers, including the publishing house of Nicholson & Watson, and was responsible for publishing early works by Henry Miller, Anaïs Nin and Vladimir Nabokov, among others. He now expressed an interest in her book and she quickly wrote to Marie Maas to send the manuscript over.

This was only a brief glimmer of hope for her, as she wasn't able to get any new writing done in her present circumstances and with her relationship with George at a very low ebb she expressed her frustration in an unsent letter:

To George
There are (for me) two things on which it was all founded: (a) I love you: & (b) you are a poet. Both of which are still true.

But as for (b): I & my children contribute nothing whatsoever towards your being a poet: you will be one whether we exist or don't exist, with us or without us. On the other hand if Jessica skins her knee you can be moved to elegies & write a series of lullabies if she has diarrhoea.

As regards (a) I am obviously not loved in return, nor needed, and I cannot bear to be by and watch the object of my love ignoring me, abusing me, insulting me, and every day forgetting the reason why we ever met. I don't feel that you have any respect for me, nor any consideration & if I continue to live in the radius of your hate and disregard, I shall lose my selfrespect, what's left of it.

We are obviously the supernumerary: You don't need us. Therefore for our own sake we must get out of it altogether & leave you with what is yours in all senses of the word, what moves you & what if anything you love: I mean Jessica & her two wrong reason twins. Perhaps she loves you enough to carry coals & wash floors & nappies & sweep & sit up alone night after night, or perhaps you love her enough to help her when she needs it & to want to be with her occasionally.... So now alas & farewell. You whose true wife I would rather have been than had all the other prizes besides.

I am very bitter & very angry & full of hate and revenge, but I knew too well the moment you closed the door that the love is not to be destroyed. It really is *IN DESPITE*. And though tonight I sat down to write you a reasonable list of reasons why I must leave you (or "we must part" if you insist on pedantry) I find my pencil still keeps wanting to write a love letter. This is because of (a) I love you, I guess. But if *only* loved you I would not for a moment have tolerated the abuse, the selfishness & callousness & betrayals for a moment.

Alone most of the time with the two of us crammed into a small room, Mum decided to escape the air raids and move out of the Thames-side flat into the country. George's sister Eileen suggested she come down to Modbury in Devon for a few weeks. She lived in an Elizabethan cottage with primitive amenities but made it available for Mum if she would look after her three children while she went on holiday.

Three weeks before she moved to Devon, though, Louie, back at Coltrin Lodge in Ottawa, had caught up with some of the story. Louie had gone down to stay with Helen in Baltimore, and when they were talking about war refugees Helen's young son Tommy had proudly announced that he could remember Aunt Betty's "little refugee" when they had come to stay. Louie instantly made the right assumption. "It isn't my hurt that matters," she wrote to Mum. "I am only hurt because you have hurt yourself and that beautiful child—she looks like a little flower escaped from some garden in Paradise—if only she hadn't escaped. I don't blame you darling & I certainly don't judge you. I just don't understand." But now the secret was out Mum let out a sigh of relief and felt she could make a further confession:

> Dearest Mummy,
>
> I don't know how to tell you what I want to tell you because I am afraid it will distress you perhaps more than anything: I mean that Georgina has a brother because I didn't want her to be lonely. He is fine and looks just like Daddy.... I have dreaded telling you about Christopher (after Christopher Columbus because he crossed the Atlantic prenatally looking for a new country) because I feel you may find this even harder to understand and perhaps you don't know how much I mind hurting you & know it is your distress that assails me when I have nightmares or get sick.[97]

Louie remained bewildered as to why Mum lived her life as she did and was sad that she felt she couldn't acknowledge us as grandchildren. Her Dad decided not to comment but did increase her allowance.

Mum spent two weeks in Modbury looking after four young children in conditions that made her life more of a misery than ever. The water was brought up by the kettleful from the coal scullery to a dank, cold kitchen that had no sink. She had nappies to change and a lot of soiled bedding that could be hung out in the yard to dry during the day but would have to be hauled in at night so the sheet's whiteness didn't contravene the air-raid blackout regulations. Besides Georgina and me, at two years and eight months of age, respectively, there was Eileen's youngest, Olga, who was half a year younger than Georgina, and her brother Barry, eight years old. Their eldest brother, John, thirteen, was at boarding school in Plymouth.

These were trying times for Mum, and it's interesting to note that in a contemporary homemade photo album that she had titled *Georgina Elizabeth and Christopher Barker's 2nd Book* (1944) she captioned a photo "Barry Jackson. This boy was beaten by ES with a dog leash in March, 1944 & he deserved it."

The fact that, excepting for one isolated occasion with me, she *never* resorted to beating or slapping any of her own children speaks of how frustrating these two weeks turned out to be. After the first fortnight, when Eileen came back, Mum took Georgina and me off to a nearby hotel in Bigbury-on-Sea for a week to recuperate. But Eileen went off again, and although Mum managed two more weeks at Modbury she had had enough. In an attempt to solve our homelessness she put Georgina and me in a nursery while she summoned George from London and together they went house hunting.

Georgina and I were taken to the Coombe Royal Residential Nursery in neighboring Kingsbridge, but the moment Mum left I flew into a tantrum that the nurses were unable to control. Mum told me later that they trussed me up in a baby's straitjacket, in which I remained seething for three weeks.

While we were at the nursery, George and Mum decided to go back to Didy's in Scarlet-sub-Edge. They became more reconciled with one another, pledging to start a new life together. Mum elicited a promise from George that they would have three more children. George later retracted his offer.

In the *Georgina Elizabeth and Christopher Barker's 2nd Book*, a photo depicts Mum sitting next to George on a Cotswold drystone wall. She has a wry sneer on her lips while George fumbles with a pebble, a nervous smile playing about his face. Blue fountain-pen ink captions the photo: "George & Elizabeth. At Scarlet-Sub-Edge, visiting Didy, & looking for a home, while the children were at the Nursery in Kingsbridge. On Easter Monday, April 10th 1944 xxxxx xxxxxxxxx [a line of emphatic deletions]. The night before this picture was taken George revoked his offer of five. (Mrs. Bach & Mrs. Donne bear me witness.)"

There is another photo in this series on the drystone wall, with Annabel, Didy's eldest child, being held by George (Didy had recently given birth to Stephen, or Kip, as he was to become known). Mum glares out from under a lowering brow and scowls at George from the corner of narrowed eyes. Although Mum had learnt to be sparing with unnecessary facts, especially with her mother, she always found it very difficult to hide her emotions and this is the aftermath of a blazing row, with Mum still smoldering.

Mum felt this was her best chance to try to make a life together with George, but even as they looked for somewhere to live he was recanting promises. She was also aware that he was in touch with Jessica, often sending her the little money he had and yet scrounging Mum's subsistence allowance from her father in order to provide cash for the pub. She knew he would be making plans to return to America to see the twins and if she

Me, 1948
Photo by Michael Wickham

let him go she might never see him again. She was beginning to doubt they could ever have a life together.

After the house hunting, when they arrived to pick up us children from the nursery, we had both been confined to our beds. I was still in my straitjacket. Both of us were severely underweight and running dangerously high temperatures. Georgina remained mute for three weeks after we left, traumatized by the experience. George, on seeing this, also fell sick and Mum took her ailing family back to Scarlet-sub-Edge to attempt to start a new life. She was never to forgive herself for leaving us like that.

Once more she had abandoned her children in an attempt to secure a life with their father. She resolved never to let it happen again.

Mum rented the ground floor of a house called College Farm Cottage in Condicote. In fact it had only one actual room. She had help from the landlady's teenage daughter, nicknamed Big Girl, to look after Georgina and me. Mrs. Foster, the landlady, was on hand to cook some meals, but there was no running water or bath and the room had only an oil stove for preparing food. Although there were many grounds for domestic discord and they argued continually, Mum tried to keep George happy. On the first night in our new home together, when they were involved in a particularly vigorous bout of passion, the bedsprings broke. George used the incident as an excuse to escape to London, where he was able to spin out the search for new springs for seven days before he saw fit to return.

Through May and June that year Mum was being increasingly marginalized in their relationship. In his letters to her from London she noticed his unrest and they now conspicuously lacked the glorious hyperbole and charm of earlier letters. Her own writing had descended to little more than a list of domestic chores done: "I realize that I am afraid to say the important things and therefore there seems little point in this book, except as an exercise in description of daily domestic tasks. Perhaps one thing will lead to another—or the truth will emerge from the omission."[98]

George's absences in London frustrated her, and what she termed her "woman's lot" had started to take its toll on her: "Can I be a writer whose tale is heard when the statistics are sifted? This morning I hit Christopher in the face with my fist because of George's letter, because of landlord's bills. It is unfair. I am crying out from guilt, despair, humiliation, love, being the one left out."[99]

He was writing to Jessica with new schemes either to repatriate her and the twins or to get them himself. For this he would need the twin's birth certificates, and while assuring her that his new book was dedicated to them he mentioned that he had not seen Elizabeth or even knew where she was. But Jessica, ever skeptical and knowing their own relationship was at an end, wrote back:

> Since that glorious day in Big Sur I have implored you to stop lying but you still go on and send me further from you with every lie. I hear from people we know in London that you are still seeing Elizabeth— I have never thought otherwise—and fighting most of the time … you

haven't the strength to break with her forever and if you attempt it she will track you down again and as you refuse to tell the truth there is no one that can help you, least of all me. I did everything possible to help you when you were here and suffered every possible hurt and indignity in consequence but you went to England and left me knowing that she would be there and what would happen … you both took the "gilt off the gingerbread" for me for ever and I am never, never going to enter it again.[100]

As George spun round and round frantically trying to make peace with his partners, he succeeded only in alienating them both. While Jessica had every reason to complain of his behavior, so too did Mum. She discovered he had dedicated his latest book to Jessica, and when she caviled it moved him not one jot. Her diary entry for May 14, 1944, read:

"In the evening we walked to Longborough & I had one and a half pints of cider and was nicely drunk. On the way home I dashed into the prickles because George made a tit for tat remark about dedicating his book to the twins (he 'didn't consult Jessica when he dedicated his book to me'). I lay among the prickles in the hedge & wanted to cease. When I got home George was having supper & reading. He got into bed & neither of us said anything except George who made a few caustic remarks. But when I got into bed we made love."

Then an entry for May 19, 1944, recorded how her world turned upside down and her quarrelling with George was forgotten:

A lovely sunny morning. Didy came early for the bicycle. I sat out with the children mending my blue striped dress. Giffy [Georgina's name for me and now adopted by Mum] had on his corduroy overalls & a sun bonnet & Georgina her starched seersucker dress. After lunch as I was hurrying to get the things ready to take on a picnic a woman on a bicycle stopped & said "Can you tell me where College Farm is?" & she had two telegrams one for Mrs. Barker & one for Elizabeth Smart & I said "They're both for me." One was from Mr. Harvey at the bank saying Daddy has died yesterday & and the other was from Bobby [Bobby McDougal, an old friend from Ottawa] saying how sorry she was. It was bewildering and too much of a shock to believe. I cried but then began agitatedly getting the picnic things together, & crying. And thought, all one can do after all is to cry. It doesn't seem enough. But I tried not to give myself time to realize it because I didn't want to collapse at the picnic or have to tell others. Nannie was there & we sat in the bluebell wood & I picked a bunch of orchids & Annabel let Georgina play with her big doll & pram. And of course the more things flowered the more sad it seemed & the nearer and more horrible death. I know that I am guilty because Daddy had so much on his mind & I did always so much want to make him proud of me & happy. And he was so optimistic. And now things really have fallen apart & how can the center hold. Harvey's wire said another from Mummy was being sent with a letter. I can feel the taste of death in my own mouth. But—there is never & nowhere a time for such a word. A form came for George from the American consul to emigrate to America to "join his wife and children." The evening by myself was horrible.

When he died, Mum's father was only a month short of his sixty-fifth birthday, and apart from his longstanding and largely untreated stomach ulcer condition he was in robust health. Too proud to make much of a fuss about his stomach pains when on a weekend stay at Kingsmere, he started vomiting blood. He was too far gone by the time he reached hospital to be successfully treated and died within three days. Today his condition is easily treated and but for this neglect of his health he would have had perhaps twenty more years of life.

His death came as a terrible shock to the whole family as well as to most of Ottawa, where his obituaries were fulsome in their praise. His benign authority had been taken for granted for so long by both Louie and Mum that they were overcome with deep self-recrimination. Louie felt she had never let him know how much she loved him and Mum felt she had let him down. He had always been obdurately optimistic for her, and for so long she had looked forward to the day he would be proud of her when she launched her book.

Mum secretly nursed her grief until the next day, telling George only as her brother arrived at the household for a stay. Russel Jr. had been stationed in England with the Canadian Artillery and when on leave would visit. Obviously he could see she was grieving over the death of their father, but he thought she was languishing from something more repressive and suggested she gave herself a break from her children and get a job with the BBC perhaps.

She was exasperated with George's wily ways and she wrote in her diary on June 10: "I am going to leave George. Didy says she's come to the conclusion I should too. She says we're incompatible. I say Jessica is ideally suited to him, not like me at all. Didy & I say we are, as they say of pilots, 'finished.' We quake at the sound of motors starting up. I am very sad & wonder if I will ever be strong enough."

On June 12 Mum went to London. She left a bewildered and miserable Georgina, who had sensed that her mother was leaving her again and clung on pitifully as Didy attempted to comfort her. As she was boarding the train, George was disembarking going the other way. He imparted to Didy the sad news that his friend from the wild days in America, John Fitch, had gone missing in action. He retreated to a room on his own. A day later he emerged with a new poem to his friend in his pocket and then, after visiting the doctor in Moreton-in-Marsh, caught the next train back to London.

In the *Georgina Elizabeth and Christopher Barker 2nd Book* (1944) Mum lists George's time spent with us in Condicote. In a column next to it she has listed, in accusatory detail, the time he spent in London. From the time we all came back from the nursery on April 25 George, despite his new declaration of intent to make a home with us, divided his time evenly between College Farm Cottage and London. He would probably have spent more time in London but had started to take Benzedrine, a stimulant he discovered he could get from the local doctor in Moreton-in-Marsh. He would take it in London to enhance his socializing but its aftereffects made him paranoid. On more than one occasion these bouts of paranoia, coupled with a new weapon visited daily upon London by the Nazis, sent him fleeing back to Condicote with tattered nerves.

The D-Day landings, heralding the beginning of the end of the war, started on June 6 as 156,000 assault troops crossed the channel to Normandy's beaches. Wave after wave of airplanes full of paratroopers, some towing frail wooden gliders, droned overhead all day long from the Moreton-in-Marsh airfields. The paratroopers were to be dropped in northern France, behind enemy lines, where many perished as they were blown out of the sky or crashed into deliberately flooded fields on landing. As this was happening, London underwent a new type of attack. Raids of "doodlebugs"—an early form of cruise missile called Vergeltungswaffe, or reprisal weapon—superseded the conventional bombings the capital had undergone in the Blitz of 1940. George, along with thousands of others, heard puttering engines announce the arrival, in ones and twos, of these flying bombs over the city. Even as they listened, the planes' engines would cut out as the fuel ran out and for a few seconds an eerie silence followed as the threat appeared to pass. In those few seconds the V-1s were plummeting down onto the London streets, to explode in random mayhem. In his post-Benzedrine paranoia George found these V-1s particularly unnerving and he reluctantly fled London to the sanctuary of the countryside, complaining that the flying bombs had been ruining his sleep.

Back in London, with his new poem and a bottle of Benzedrine pills in his pocket, he went straight to his mother's flat at Stanhope Gardens. There he and Mum, on a break from domesticity, met up and for three days he made Mum's life hell. Her diary reads: "LONDON Benzedrine—George's ashen stiff face. Flying bombs. Staying with family because of G. Didy's tight shoes. Ulrica & George & his pocketful of betrayals & repudiations escape me never. Next time if it comes, what will I be able to do but die?"

At the end of that week they returned to Condicote and the atmosphere between them did not improve. George replenished his stock of pills and ten days later left for London. He was back at Condicote the same evening, though, seeking refuge from a swarm of doodlebugs that had fallen on the city. His mood turned vicious. Mum wrote:

> July 6, 1944. Nothing will ever be right till *he* wants more children, not necessarily per se, but necessarily & because of the nature of love. I know I know I know he is only trying to keep the situation OPEN for Jessica so his misrepresentations (I mean lies) will work out. O Hell O Heaven O horror & he expects me to take this merely marking time & call it love & be willing. Of course I can't really write in this book because he reads it & takes offence throwing up continually the fact that I wrote "I am going to leave George." I know I am not a wise woman or I could wait wisely or say nothing & never want to see his letters or know to whom he writes or what he does in London or how he feels about J. But it is four years since we met & it is still as messy if not messier than ever. The trouble is, for me, that there is always hope. i.e. either J. is a wonderful woman in which case a triple situation might be possible, or she is not, and he might eventually realize it. As for me, I feel myself getting less & less wonderful & I shall certainly not be able to make any more noble concessions, or stand any more chicanery, or sit back while he stands on his head to get back to J's devotion. If only, even for this limited period, he were really given to me & loving me without always considering whether he'll be able to camouflage what he's doing.

Mum still saw Jessica as a rival and George was trying to keep Jessica's interest alive by demands and threats. As his desperation increased he would tell Jessica of the sacrifices he had made for her, threaten her with eternal separation and then profess undying love as if these things would change her mind and make her love him more:

I insist that this is the showdown. The war itself would be quite enough for me to contend with but to go on for the next year and more hanging on the responses you may experience to the gutter lies of any tom, bitch or harpy—I'm not b. well going to, my dear, I'm not going to. It's about time that you understood that the truth is not the private prerogative of the Woodward family. I'm sick and tired and if you want the children to grow up without me then say so and you can all three spend a long life without me. I've told you I love you till I and the censor have got sick of it. I've sold my soul and my typewriter to keep you at the rate of six or seven £ per week in the States. I've ruined my reputation as a writer &, until this morning, I had nothing in the world to hope for except reunion with you.[101]

These entreaties went unheeded, though, and on July 25 she replied: "*I will not return*—certainly until after the war. I have nothing to return to and the longer the Atlantic is between us, the happier I shall be. And that is definitely that. There is no need for us to discuss it again. Be happy and for God's sake stop telling such fantastic lies."[102]

Mum may have now thought the way was clear for her with George. When he was staying with her at Condicote, which during that high summer he did for nearly two months, their relationship was volatile. Her diary records George often sulking and hating her, once because she had written and got a reply from her old platonic admirer Meredith Frampton.

The arguing was occasionally interspersed with passionate reconciliation and in August, despite the instability of their relationship, Mum became pregnant again. This time George was less than exultant and said that Mum had "stolen" the baby from him. Though Jessica had terminated their relationship, George was worried about her reaction, and Mum wrote to Marie Maas in New York as if in helpless explanation: "I simply can't help wanting babies if George looks at me erotically. Perhaps it can be psychoanalyzed away, but only if the love could be too & then what'd I be—Peter Pan, Medusa or a really nice hermaphrodite?"

Louie, of course, was scandalized and wrote to say: "How can you ask for my blessing on so wrong a deed? I can't think of any line of reasoning by which you could think it fair and right to go on having children."

She went on to say that because of Mum's irresponsibility and lack of decency her father had died a brokenhearted man. Disappointed though she was and lashing out in this way to hurt Mum, which it surely did, her criticism never seemed to stop Mum from her determined course. And happily it didn't stop Louie from sending parcels of food and clothing.

Even Russel Jr. was moved to write that he thought Mum's unfounded optimism hard to fathom. He cautioned her that relying on her allowance (which Russel Sr. had increased to $200 a month when I was born and which was reduced to $100 after his death) could be foolhardy, because if the new senior partner in their father's law firm should die she would be without a penny.

Even with these counsels ringing in her ears, her list of New Year's resolutions for 1945 included: "No. 3, Keep the children prettily dressed always," "No. 6, Keep bowels open" and then firmly entered at No. 7 was "Have a baby." Next to it a tidy tick with "Sebastian 16th April 1945." But No. 12 read, "Make a final decision about George, if he won't [make a final decision] about me, and stick to it. The years roll on & the freezing wind."

George's father had served his country with distinction during the First World War. He hoped his sons might be able to do the same should they be called upon. Pa's intransigence on the subject had produced a reaction that had seen his eldest son [George] draft-dodging across the world to avoid this very call.

Nonetheless, George's conscience continually troubled him and had been only a little mollified after he took Michael Asquith's advice and applied to the Friends' Ambulance Unit. On applying, however, he discovered that the National Service Act required him to pass a certificate of health from the Medical Board. This he duly sought but, despite priding himself as an athlete in his younger days, he found the Medical Board could list him only as grade four—unfit for any form of war work but the lightest. Strangely, the board also listed him as five foot nine inches tall and with gray eyes. Even with his characteristic stoop he was, at that time, five foot eleven inches and with piercing blue eyes. Surely they were thinking of somebody else.

A year later, with D-Day over and the Allied armies pushing through France, every able-bodied man in Britain was doing what he could for the war effort. The contemporary photographs of birthday parties and christenings in Condicote show lines of smiling children interspersed with their mothers, nannies and nurses as they dutifully pose for the photo call on which Mum would have insisted for her album. Reluctantly standing in the back row with a guilty grin and conspicuous as the only man present, George was occasionally caught on camera too.

He was present in the back row of the party photo for Georgina's third birthday on August 28, but on the 29th he heard the news that the launchpads of the doodlebugs had been found in the Pas de Calais and destroyed. By September 9 he resumed his commuting to London, confident the menace had gone.

Realizing that if she wanted to see George at all she had to make trips to London, Mum continued to do so through the New Year and into January. Once, memorably, she phoned him in London to suggest a visit and he crushed her by telling her she was not wanted. The next day she set off for London anyway but turned back at the station, too dispirited to continue. When, five days later, he turned up at Condicote they had blazing row and Mum fled to Didy's at Scarlet. George went back to London the next day in a sulk. She thought she was now ready to purge herself of him in a vigorous spring clean and her entry for April 4 read:

> Vernal Squill [springtime lily known for its purgative qualities]. The pear tree is blossoming & George is lying. I must think about the soul to whom I am about to give birth. I shall awaken myself with signs of frivolity. Why should I be paralyzed with fear now that I am over thirty? George will read this book and censure my secret heart. No I must abolish fear & let the Corn Grow. The perennial vines weeping along the wall in spite of the spring remind me of the empty road where I persevere always & at last, always out of reach, out of hearing, when the Act is enacted. Yet I have listened as attentively as most & I have been ready to be helpful to history or love or epitome. I expect that perhaps I was over eager like the scorned or outcast woman. Be off cloying & clawing Devotion, for I will be after the fickle whore. Like George, O too too much like George.... George has led me to a long & tedious contemplation of this dead-end tragedy. But soon I shall be taking to labyrinthine ways—with my bambino on my knee.

As the birth of her next baby approached, George's unreliability drove her to distraction. Her obsession with him transfixed and disarmed her and the only way she could escape him was for him to finally leave her—a move he couldn't bring himself to make. Four days before the birth she wrote:

"But he doesn't come on the train he says he will, & my hope is blitzed again & I am suspicious & I am doubtful & I remember how an odd drink is more important to him than I am, even in need, and revert to my expectationless neutrality. George, George don't you see how foolish you are?

(If it's me you want, I mean.)" A list of clothes follows and then: "*I HATE the Vulgar Mob and SHUN them. Hate Hate God God I could SCREAM,*" followed by a heavily deleted sentence.

Confounding her diminishing expectations, George on April 16 alighted from the 6:57 p.m. from Paddington at Moreton-in-Marsh station with Sue Asquith, Didy's husband's sister, who, by earlier arrangement, he had met at Paddington and traveled with. Mum had been nervously awaiting the train, hoping it would arrive before the baby, and they quickly escorted Mum back to the cottage hospital. There, three hours later, she went into labor. My brother Sebastian was born at 11:30 that night and was George's sixth child. Of the six births he had managed to attend only two, and indeed for Sebastian's he made it just in time.

Two days later, on the morning of the 18th, while Mum was still in hospital, Didy brought her a parcel from the first post delivered to College Farm Cottage. It was from Editions Poetry London, and in it were the proofs of *By Grand Central Station I Sat Down and Wept*. With Sebastian asleep in the cot beside her, Mum spent the rest of the day excitedly correcting the slim volume.

Mum's record of Sebastian's birth lacked the exhilaration she usually felt at childbirth. In spite of the arrival of her book her mood crashed again. On April 26 her diary read:

> It is *unbearable* loving George. I always *knew* he won't come & yet I always expect him & sit in that inane fever of anticipation, no matter how I keep telling myself his coming is out of the question. What can I do? I really *can't* bear it. It gets worse, not better. He won't let me leave him, & yet he won't stay with me. He won't settle my difficulties & yet he won't let me try to settle them for myself. I love him desperately but he continually arouses my hopes that we are going to live a happy married life together, and I *always* believe that *this* time it will really happen & there is never anything but the same disappointments & frustrations. He *never* comes when he says he will. He always stays away two or three times as long as he says he will. He always vanishes & lets me sit waiting for him in my best clothes, relishing the hour to come—O God George don't you see that I can't bear this life of continual frustration and solitude? Suddenly one day I will crack, snap, break into bits and BE GONE.

Her mood didn't remain down for long, and remembering the exciting arrival of her book and the infectious atmosphere from the radio and newspapers of approaching Armistice Day, she and Didy went to London to be part of it. On the trip, Big Girl took care of Georgina and me, and with Sebastian in Mum's arms Didy and her husband, Michael, joined the group. We all went up to London in high spirits three weeks after Sebastian's birth to celebrate VE day in Trafalgar Square.

Except for Michael and Didy, we all went to stay with Big Mumma at 23a Stanhope Gardens. She accommodated us along with her own children and grandchildren as best she could, but the confined living, with Big Girl sobbing constantly from homesickness, set us children off into a grizzle. George distanced himself as much as he could and soon became irritable. After yet more quarrelling, Mum took us back to Condicote.

Her book was duly published in August, with only 2000 copies as the first edition. Due to a wartime shortage of paper, the text was compressed into fifty-eight pages. This was four pages more than the uncorrected proof copy, on which she insisted on 231 new paragraph breaks. She wanted the text to "breathe" more, and later editions bear this out, expanding the book (with the same text) to twice the number of pages. At the time of publication and with great excitement she anticipated good reviews. But apart from a short paragraph by "L.A." of *The Sunday Times*, who wrote on September 23 that "it was an exciting, original book, half-way between a novel and a prose poem," and an enthusiastic review from Paul Potts in the winter edition of *The Poetry Quarterly*, the notices were mixed. The book quickly disappeared. She was left very disappointed.

The last blow fell when word filtered through of Louie's reaction to the book. Louie told Jane she had burnt her copy and rushed down to the local general store, seized the entire stock of six and burnt them too. She also pulled strings with the government's External Affairs department and had it blacked. She initially complained that the book was "erotomania" and a poor imitation of something Henry Miller might have scribbled, but underlying these objections she was convinced the book was a slight on her as a mother. Mum was deeply depressed to get the following letter:

> Thank god your father does not know that you are reduced to living as a char in some man's basement. What he did know completely broke his heart; and even admitting it as you once did, you could then publish a book to be read widely in Ottawa writing down your father & me & practically holding us up to scorn or revealing the most sordid details of an erotic "love" episode, to complete our sorrow & humiliation. The conclusion of the whole thing is very logical & how you could

have expected it to have ended otherwise is not compatible with sane thinking. The only redeeming thing about the whole affair as far as I know it, is that you have shown the most marvelous fortitude & endurance & courage. If only these fine qualities had been put to better use earlier in life, how different the whole thing might have been. Sometime I would like to know from you if, taking all the sorrow & suffering & tragedy into account, you feel it has been worth while.[103]

By now we had said goodbye to Condicote and Mum had taken two damp rooms in a basement in Markham Square, off the King's Road. Didy had moved away from Scarlet-sub-Edge and without her company Mum had moved us to London to be nearer George. Mum's reply to Louie had been delayed while she got over the shock of her letter and she got round to it only after our move to Markham Square:

Dearest Mummy, Your letter about my book came just as we were moving, & everything has been in confusion since. At the moment I am sitting in a cold room as the gas strike is on & I can't even get a flame to make coffee. I'm sorry that you took the parts in my book about "my mother" personally. I was writing about one thing: the emotion felt by a woman in love. The only thing that can compete with falling in love is the relationship with one's mother. Naturally mothers are possessive at this moment. I will be, everyone is, it's the nature of things—it would be wrong not to be. Someday I may write a book about you—then you will have more than a few odd sentences & you will not be referred to as "my mother."

I am sorry, though, for the sorrow it has caused you. There is nothing in the book except things as they bear directly on the one emotion. It isn't supposed to be a novel, but they use that for lack of a better word.

Russel is here & I have been seeing quite a bit of him. He seems very well & longing to begin work. I think he sails early in December.

I'm trying to find a flat which is agony in London now. We managed to get two rooms with a gas ring. I have a cockney woman to look after the children. I'm going about a job tomorrow. It's really awful at the moment—what with the housing shortage, nannie shortage, gas-strike, people's nerves, queues, inconvenience for the children.

I had lunch with Bobby today. She's just got up from a week in bed. Georgina goes to Sandy's [a friend's daughter] school every Wednesday for the dancing class. She loves it. Sandy is very big & tall & like Paul & has pigtails. She's getting very grown-up.

I need a double pram & Bobby suggested you might buy Gertie's from her & she could bring it over for me when she comes as she is coming very soon. If this is possible it would be heavenly, as I can't hope to keep a good nannie without a decent pram. Gertie's is a twin one, which is what I need for the three of them, and it's a lovely one. It could be <u>all</u> my Christmas & birthday presents. I hope she still has it.

I hope that all your plans are going well & that you are happy.

I am in such a whirlpool at the moment & having to make so many superhuman efforts that you will understand if I don't write very often. I'll try to, for I think of you all the time & hope you are well.

Love to John, Love Betty XXX from G C & S Sebastian has six teeth, stands up by pulling himself up, creeps, plays pat-a-cake. I'm still nursing him.

This letter must have gone some way to building the bridge with Louie, because we were soon in Gertie's twin pram, Sebastian sitting in it facing me, outside the Royal Bank of Canada, at Trafalgar Square. The bank had been Mum's family one and was run by old family friends. Mum was never refused an overdraft. She had gone in yet again to arrange credit and Sebastian had his nose and his six new teeth into a raw cabbage (cabbage was, for a long time, his favorite nibble). A Mr. Magoo figure strolling into the bank felt so sorry for the poor urchin in the pram with nothing better to eat than a cabbage leaf that he gave me a big piece of white paper. Sebastian snatched it from me and it was about to follow the cabbage leaves when Mum came out of the bank and rescued the fiver.

Mum didn't, of course, tell Louie what chaos those two rooms in Markham Square were. Although Mum had moved there to be nearer George, he avoided its jumbled gloom as much as he could, but it was here that he dubbed Sebastian the Basher. He was precocious for his age and had learned to walk and run by the time he was nine months old. He adopted a habit of creeping up behind visitors sitting in our decrepit old armchair and hitting them on the head with a book. Once, he bashed George just after his bedtime bath. He raced out the door into the basement yard, but no one bothered to follow. George knew this trick of his by then and knew there was a flight of stone steps to stop the child getting to the road. Not this time, though. I watched in horror as, for the first time ever, he scrambled up the steps. I expected him to come clattering down after each one but he soon reached the top and I started screaming for Mum only when I saw his little naked body hurtling toward the steady line of hooting traffic on the King's Road. I remember my limbs were numb with fear. Although I suppose I could have caught him, I was rooted to the spot as in a dream. Then at last Mum came flying up the stairs and as she sprinted after him, calling his name, he went tumbling into the line of traffic, giggling hysterically. He was caught by a bus conductor who had seen him come scampering down the square through the early-evening smog. He jumped off the back platform of a Number 14 bus with his arms spread wide, as if catching a piglet in a farmyard, and handed a squirming Basher back to Mum.

As with so much of the dire accommodation we had undergone it wasn't long before the claustrophobia and expense of this grimy basement began to wear Mum down. George was as elusive as ever, spending most of his time at Stanhope Gardens, often sleeping in a tiny loft room they termed the Doll's House. But it couldn't have been *every* night, for when Mum told him she was pregnant for the fourth time he offered his undying support by accusing her of puncturing her diaphragm and telling her he now had the fare and the papers to go back to the United States.

He left for Canada and New York on May 31, intending to meet up with Mum's sister Jane for a few days in Montreal. He had taken leave of Mum by declaring that his intention while in the States was to drum up old contacts and perhaps land some form of academic post. This was the realization of all Mum's worst fears and she knew he'd gone back to fetch Jessica or perhaps persuade her to return to England with the twins. Worse, he might start a new life in the New England countryside.

He met with Jane in Montreal and dallied there three days, the news of which infuriated Mum when she heard it. He then traveled to New York, only to find that Jessica had fled without leaving a forwarding address. He appealed to the Maases for news of her, but they remained implacably loyal to Mum and, although Willard was doing some speculative recordings of George's new poems in New York, he faithfully reported on his movements to Mum while he was in town. As a sop to Mum and perhaps to excuse his behavior, George cabled her, claiming that Jessica was at last obtaining an annulment. At this point he hadn't even seen her.

Jessica finally relented, leaving the twins with her friends in St. Louis, Missouri, and returning to New York alone. When she and George did meet it was plain to both that the end had come. Far from obtaining an annulment, though, and because of her increasing commitment to Roman Catholicism, a divorce had become out of the question.

The continuing misery of cramped and expensive lodgings in London and the depressing news from over the Atlantic engendered a new resolve in Mum. She decided to move to Ireland and wrote to George in America, inviting him to join her if he could.

Having heard from Jane that Russel Sr.'s will had been probated and knowing that no new work had transpired in New York, George decided he'd be better off on the other side of the Atlantic. He wrote to Mum to let her know of his flight arrival time at Shannon and added, "See you for tea tomorrow, you adored $100 a weeker. It will *natch* surprise you to learn that I love you."

Trouble was, when he descended the steps to the Shannon tarmac on September 22 and we all rushed to greet him, he was to learn that the probate had provided her with £100 per *month*, barely enough to keep us children in potatoes. He was not pleased. Mum had found a temporary place to stay in County Wicklow, south of Dublin, while she awaited more permanent accommodation to become available in a larger house in County Galway.

Mum, George and the three of us children made Ballyrogan, Arklow, our home for the next two months. The family photo album contained five gray-black rectangles instead of photographs as a record of this time. The continual half-dark had proved too low a light level for Mum's box Brownie and after a series of captions to these blackouts—they read "Christopher, Georgina, Bashie, George, Sept.–Oct. 1946"—they were underlined by the sad phrase "It always rained."

This was more discomfort than George was prepared to bear, and after a series of nasty quarrels he left for London. He explained that he needed to obtain more methedrine, which, along with the stimulant Benzedrine, was part of a drug-taking habit that he had never really shaken off from the wartime doodlebug scares and earlier times in America. Some of these narcotics had been readily available over the pharmacy counter in America, but in postwar England they required a doctor's prescription.

He had enlisted the services of a "tame" doctor who practiced in Kensington, London, and who was much favored by other writers in need of pharmaceutical inspiration. Although George had been taking Benzedrine when he could get it, he had gone to see this doctor in September 1943, just after I was born, to sort out ailments that amounted to little more than psychosomatic, including occasional stomach complaints and throat infections. When the doctor asked him about the state of his mind, George replied typically that he continually heard peacocks screaming. The alarmed doctor noted him down as a religious maniac and immediately prescribed methedrine, as in those days it was sometimes used to counter psychiatric disorders.

George also needed to make inquiries about a bursary from the Society of Authors. Before he went, Mum made the mistake of trusting him

Rose, Bashie, me, Georgina, 1952

with her allowance check, asking him to deposit it in the Royal Bank of Canada at Trafalgar Square. It was not deposited, however, and the local store at Arklow refused Mum credit when her check for the groceries bounced. Her memories of Arklow had not been happy, and with George now in London Mum took the opportunity to attempt a real break with him:

27th September 1946

I do not think that I want to lie down in your crowded bed for bouts of therapeutic lovemaking. Loving you, I see no beauty in lopsided true love. It really is in sorrow & not in anger that I say: I do not want you any more because *I simply cannot bear it*. It isn't only the unfaithfulness. It's the loneliness, the weeks and months of being alone, really cut off from you, receiving perhaps a postcard saying I fuck you as you pause for breath in fucking somebody else. It would have been better if I had married before I met you, because then you could have given me a few months of fulfilling attentions which is all, apparently, that women need, & then I could have returned to the someone who, possibly, would have cared for me. For you do not want the responsibility even of love & by this responsibility I do not mean either money or guilt.

I realize that if you had cared about me the small necessary amount you would not have left me alone with so much pain, but would have contrived to find some other way of doing what you had to. This is the depths & the final & the end of my misery & degradation & if I say good-bye to you now I will be able to keep from being bitter because I am so grateful to you for your last few moments of frankness.

Dearest George, I will NOT give up the belief in true love or if you will romantic love—IT IS possible I KNOW. I never *wanted* anyone since you. IT IS possible to cometh to rest in someone—but you have not evidently had enough pleasure & power. Maybe I want the middle-aged things now. I've had my fuck, but I've lost my love. My womb won't tear me to pieces now, maybe, but my heart certainly will. Good-bye. Elizabeth[104]

He countered quickly that it certainly demonstrated her romantic love for him if she preferred a sexual orgy to his genuine love and she could have saved him the fare from America if this was how she felt. But yet again his mood moderated and he followed this tirade with a charm offensive, saying how deeply and painfully he loved her and it would take the grave to separate them.

In November we moved from the temporary accommodation in Bal-lyrogan to a bigger house in a village called Roundstone in County Galway. It had an imposing facade with a flight of steps running up to the front door that was set in a portico entrance. It was known locally as Hillcrest, but because of its steps we naturally called it the Step House. The main dirt road of the village ran down a hill past these front steps. The middle of this concourse served as a duct for a rivulet of domestic effluent that, twice daily, straggling lines of lowing bullocks contaminated further, discharging excrement as they were herded to and from the lower pastures. We played happily around this sewage, bouncing our rubber balls across the street from one dripping wall to another as the never-ending drizzle swept down behind us from the Connemara Hills.

Looking out across the Bertraghboy Bay on such days, the distant islands loomed through the mists as we played with the local school-children, mindful of catching the lice they carried in their hair. Mum had a special metal comb that she continually groomed us with, hoping to keep the dreaded infestation at bay. She glorified in growing our long locks and would have been mortified had we, like some of the other chil-dren, had to have our heads shaved and our skulls painted in gentian violet.

I made no friends that I remember when we first moved to Roundstone, because at first I was too young to go to school. Later, although not yet four and to give Mum a quieter house, I was allowed to attend a few lessons, which I loathed. I couldn't understand what was being said because the lessons were conducted in Gaelic, and although Georgina quickly picked up the language, I sat huddled at my enormous desk in bewildered silence through the long unintelligible day.

Living this way while carrying a baby nearing its term, Mum came to the point of despair. As the cold days shortened through November and December, Ireland was about to experience one of the worst winters since records began. Mum's patience and love for George dwindled close to extinction. In a series of dismayed complaints Mum wrote to George of her misery. She received his reply by return from London and it was in stinging counterpoint on the verso page of her own letter:

"Hillcrest," Roundstone, Co. Galway. Wed. Dec. 4th 1946

Mum: George: There's Nothing left to a relationship like ours (if there's not straightforward trust) [*Crossed out and above it Mum had written* "there's none"]. It is obvious that you meant to stay in London for a month or more or why would you have Farrelly [an American poet and friend of George's] write you there & send MSS to 23a? Also, why do you deny us to him?'

George, in reply on the reverse page: I don't discuss you with Farrelly.

Mum: You can have Jane & anybody else you want: I won't make a fuss. Why should I? I haven't got you myself so I'm glad she has.

George, in reply on the verso: You are now making a fuss.

Mum: If you are waiting in London to have a private word you are merely going to unnecessary inconvenience.

George: I'm waiting in London because I have to broadcast on Sunday. Listen in & verify.

Mum: Also you alienate me by the sleight-of-hand & double-dealing.

George: What sleight-of-hand? The one you're <u>assuming</u> is happening?

Mum: Of <u>course</u> your love toward me lacks something if you can write Jane (or any other USA interest) that your life now lies all there.

George: This is a trifle speculative. You don't know, first, that I have got any American interests, or, secondly, that I write them if I have, or, thirdly, what I write. This remark of yours is as hysterical as all your violent guesswork. The truth is that I rather wish I had got some USA commitments. My European ones are getting as ugly as anything with swollen head.

Mum: I give you your freedom without grudging if I can get your 100% Confidence in return—otherwise I say Please do let us make a final end.

George: When I receive my "freedom" it won't be necessary for us to exchange anything, least of all "confidence" (all my confidences, you observe. Where are yours?).

Mum: Relationships can't be romantic when there's another contemporary passion going on. What remains—& it does remain, is a rock of Gibraltar starkness that stands anything except the indignity & the degradation of petty deceit.

George: I find that I am a little old for "Romantic" attachments. I know you're not, but I'm prematurely cynical in these affairs—thanks to you. Anyhow, it's impossible to go on feeling romantic (that revolting word!) about a woman whose only successful affair is the one she conducts with herself.

Mum: Kit is not happy here. He is restless & bored & my ill-concealed despair isn't much help to him no matter how hard I try for him. I don't really ask you for anything now and I don't even get really angry, but I do feel I deserve, and I now should get, worthier treatment from you.

George: Worthier treatment than what? Than all the hysterical hallucinations you inflict on yourself?

Mum: Perhaps you act without examining your own motives, but when you could so easily find them out, & are quite capable of true honesty with yourself, you should give me that at least. E.

George: This last piece is just conceited condescension disguising itself as a lecture on moral perspicacity. I know far too much about your motives to respect these little disclosures of your colossal sense of intellectual superiority. So, I'm quite capable of honesty, am I? You are not. I haven't committed any of the misdeeds this letter ascribes to me but even if I had there would have been a certain amount of poetic justice in them. How you hate seeing the methods used upon you that you use upon other people. A few truly prodigious accomplished facts and a healthy shot of hysterics—you might come to see that you are unliveable with. I have received your letter containing the sentence "so put my money back in the Bank." Unfortunately I had already dispatched it, or I would have used it for pleasanter purposes. By God, you're a neat hand at real rudeness of literary style. G.[105]

The last paragraph in his letter referred to his failure to deposit her allowance check from Canada, and although he says he had already dispatched it back to her, it never arrived and the money simply disappeared.

As a result, penniless though we were, we were about to become even poorer. All the same, with the swirling snow starting to settle on the frozen tributary of sewage down the main street, Mum rubbed her freezing fingers and in dismal and pathetic longing she doggedly carried on manufacturing miniature copies of George's collected works. ·

As Christmas approached, suddenly and without warning, George reappeared in Roundstone. This time, as if holding a shield up before him, he had brought along his young cousin called Wendy. She was the pretty and devout daughter of his sister Monica, and as a twelve-year-old was keen to be present at the birth of a baby cousin and so had agreed to travel to Roundstone from London with him.

While there and with his brother Kit also in tow, the two crawled the local pubs, running up credit where they could get it. When that ran out, they moved to neighboring Galway to run up more. Mum wrote to her old friend Didy Asquith:

> I loathe George now & am absolutely cured of him forever—he has been revolting all this time that we were eating potatoes & the little people were knocking on the door with their bills. He and Kit spent (I discovered last night) £40 this last month in the pubs here—while refusing to pay a single bill—or even give cash for food—& then complaining like mad at the lack of it—it isn't as if they'd even been jolly or gay—just abject and selfish ... he spent all my monthly allowance in London & my Family Allowance & won't pay anything back but gets furious if I mention money or bills. Thank goodness at last the pubs refused also to give credit or cash checks—but now he's got a store in Galway to send stuff & cigarettes and will *never* pay them. And if there are four chops for eight people he eats two whole ones—Jessica sent a letter last week, too, saying she's been hounded by debt collections & George has spent about £150 on *nothing* not even any fun. He's been *poverty-stricken* the whole time. It's definitely cured me.

Mum and Wendy struggled to put a happy Christmas together that year of 1946. Mum insisted that in the absence of any money for presents everyone should make books of their own choice to put under the Christmas tree. Mum had a ham brought in from Galway on the weekly grocer's van to add a little festivity to our meager table. But this goodwill did not go far. Much to Wendy's embarrassment, George's temper flashed often, fuelled by vain attempts to extract Benzedrine deposits from his lighter-fluid residue, and he wreaked havoc in the huddled household. His mood improved only when he was able at last, surprisingly, to source a supply of methedrine from the local doctor that his trip to London had failed to secure. He, for one, was able to ignore the cold and darkening twilight whose icy grip slowly turned into freezing candlelit nights, unrelieved by the comforts of electricity or running water. Mum even had to chop up the furniture to have a fire in the open grate.

Mum wrote to Marie Maas in New York: "'I am very old now & care very little what he does. We all sit hungrily in the dark & think we are going mad, which I daresay we are. I am very tired, tireder than Ireland, more irritable than England & more derelict than the unrehabilitated continent. Please send some 'Chix' nappies ... it would make life BEAUTIFUL to have some—it would be better than Romance, Sex or even Conversation."

The baby was due in six weeks and would soon urgently need those nappies.

George was desperate to abscond from this forlorn existence, so with Kit and Wendy as his conspirators, they hatched a plan for his escape. In early February Kit and Wendy made their way back to London and when they arrived they sent George a telegram that appeared to be from E.J. King Bull, a commissioning editor in the drama department at the BBC. It urgently recalled him for a pre-rehearsal consultation and script conference on a radio play George had submitted to him for consideration. As if with incontrovertible evidence, he threw the telegram on the table in front of Mum and, without further ado, made off for London.

Two weeks later Mum went into labor with her fourth child and the baby arrived at 4:03 p.m. on February 18 in the upstairs bedroom of the Step House. Mum took an ironic delight that in this shrouded Irish winter there was still enough twilight to give birth without wasting a candle. Rose came into this world with half the villagers clamoring on the doorstep wanting to see the new baby. But not her father. For lack of a cradle, she was laid in an empty coal scuttle, a shortfall that was quickly remedied in the following days by a local carpenter, Paddy Shaughnessy, who made a crib for Rosie and a small rectangular table for the rest of us with little matching stools. We all helped paint our new table in white gloss and watched enthralled as Mum painted a large surreal eye on its top whose pupil was a large spoked cart-wheel. As she emblazoned each of our names in red around the sides she said:

"There, that's to keep an eye on you all and make sure you're always safe!"

The crib's two interior corner support posts had been crudely carved to look like two figures standing to attention. As Mum dotted the eyes of these figures with red paint she announced that they were Rosie's Mummy and Daddy. Those two wooden effigies were to remain a pathetic totem for many years—a symbol of an unfulfilled hope that one day George would come back to us and we would be a complete family. For the time being he was too busy to lay eyes on his new daughter and it was not until she was six and half months old that he finally managed it.

For the two months after George left, Mum just about managed to find the rent. Finally, with her allowance money gone, we were forced to move. Mum had to ask Bobby McDougal, her old school friend now living in London, for some money to survive. Bobby had been instrumental in delivering the twin pram to us in Markham Square from Canada and it had faithfully followed us from London. Mum put ten-week-old Rose in the pram with Bashie, and with Georgina and me hanging off the side panels we set off on the cold and windy two-mile walk down the coast road to our new home.

To get us there in an eager mood Mum made this new home seem very alluring with colorful stories of how the tide came right up to the front door across a sandy beach that was strewn with seaweed from the storms. And indeed, when we got there, it turned out to be true. I became so overcome with joy I raced around the house with arms stretched wide. I howled and burbled, dipping and wheeling like an airplane, and took off down the shore, scattering a flock of seagulls that strutted through the low-tide puddles. Some of my fondest early memories date back to what was no more than a destitute and pitiful existence.

This small lonely shack was eastward along the wild coast from Roundstone and Mum called it the Little Red House, as if it had fallen from the pages of Louisa May Alcott's *Little Women*. It consisted of a single room and had been located in that remote spot for the seasonal anglers who came to fish the inlets and rivers. Of course, like many other Roundstone dwellings it had no running water or electricity, but it did have stout stone walls and a secure corrugated-iron roof to resist the worst howling Atlantic storms.

The daily grind became an unmitigated drudgery for Mum. She tried to dry the hand-wrung nappies and ragged sheets by draping them across the scraggy hedgerows outside the back door. She chased frantically after these torn rags when they were blown away on a sudden squall, her wild blonde hair and polka-dot pinny flying before her.

For our daily needs Georgina and I would fetch a heavy pail of water from a farmhouse a mile or so away. By the time we had giggled and slopped our way back to the shack singing out "Jack and Jill went up the hill to fetch a pail of water," the pail's contents were reduced by half. In the shack's one draughty room, on the moldering concrete floor, Mum had laid a stained double mattress on which we all slept. At bedtime, as she told us a story, we peeped over the blankets and watched her as she used the increasing evening light to smock-stitch little dresses for Rosie and sew buttons on milkmaid bonnets for Georgina from an old gingham tablecloth. She never stopped making fond and diligent efforts to keep us smart.

Unlike Mum, we children could escape the baby wails and acrid smell of soggy nappies as we raced carefree across the inland moors chasing wild ponies. Mum arranged beach and birthday parties with Georgina's school friends from Roundstone. In fine weather she would set up our rickety old table outside the front door and on it, next to a large bowl of pink junket, she'd place a lucky-dip bucket full of hastily wrapped trinkets. The party would go on till the light faded and chill gusts started to blow in off the sea.

When on our own around the Little Red House we would spend long days picnicking and skinny-dipping in the nearby rock pools. To a four-year-old like me the Atlantic tide lapping right up to our doorstep was less amazing than the soggy mound of stewed nettles on my dinner plate that didn't sting when I swallowed them.

The recall of these days seems to stretch right through my earliest childhood memories, but it was after only three months, through the late sunny spring, that Mum tried to wriggle away from this poverty trap. Being too proud to ask for extra help from her mother, who imagined she was living in a well-stocked farmhouse with maids and child minders on every hand, it was Mum's sister Jane who told Louie of her plight. A check arrived for Mum's trip back to England forthwith, and Louie had found it in her heart to forgive Rosie's birth.

It was Jane, then living in New York, who was instrumental in our escape. She had met an English poet and art critic called Ruthven Todd, who had vacated a farmhouse at a place called Tilty, in Essex. As a present to her sister, Jane said she would pay the rent direct to Todd in dollars in New York. There was one condition. Mum was to parcel up the precious books that Todd had left neatly stacked around the many shelves and send them to him in the States.

It would have been a mammoth task for her and she couldn't afford the postage. I still have some of the books today, with his name and the

Mum, The George, 1949

date in black ink neatly claiming each one. He had foreseen that his work in New York might detain him longer than he at first expected, and in an attempt to safeguard his book collection, now moldering away in an unused house, renting his property to Jane's sister might solve his dilemma. Throughout our childhood we were to use the many scholarly and erudite tomes as drawing books, and we tore out the tissue-fronted illustrations for our nursery wall decorations, totally unaware of their value. Mum tried to keep a check on these barbarous habits of ours but must have thought that at least the books were being put to some use.

As high summer began and a warm June merged with a hot July, the morning sun burned off the collar of sea mist around the islands across Bertraghboy Bay. A new adventure was beginning, and with squeals of excitement at the prospect of a new home across the sea we tied up all our worldly goods into bundles of blankets, cramming our broken crockery into split cardboard suitcases. We pushed this ragbag collection into a pile on the foreshore outside our shack, and with Rosie safely in the old pram we hopped on top of our luggage and, not without a little sadness at leaving our Little Red House, sat cross-legged awaiting the arrival of the local taxi.

To help us on the trip across the Irish Sea and our onward journey to Essex, Mum enlisted the services of a jolly girl called Mary Prendergast in Roundstone, where, when the money would allow, she had occasionally been employed as a nanny. As we arrived she struggled out of the taxi with baby Rosie in her arms, and the three of us rushed out from behind her and raced up to the Mill House front door. Untended roses drooped in the heat around the white trellis entrance porch and when Mum finally managed to turn the rusty key in the lock, we burst through the door around her into the wide flagstoned hallway.

1951

✶

AFTER THREE CHAOTIC but wonderful years at Tilty, we moved
to London, although the Mill House was still maintained by Mum
and we were to move back there later. Mum had met the painter Augustus
John at Scarlet-sub-Edge during our wartime stay in Gloucestershire, and
now Mum was able to persuade his son, Caspar, to sublet a basement flat
he rented in Flood Street, off the Chelsea embankment. Here Mum could
be near us after her work in the West End and from where we were to go
to new schools in London.

Our new home was called Rossetti House and our new school, nearby,
was the Chelsea Froebel. We learned our multiplication tables and it was
here I also learned about national dress. One day a boy came into class
wearing the full Highlander outfit—pleated kilt, sporran, tartan socks with
tabs and a sheathed dagger he called a Skean Dhu stuck down the side.
He cut a dashing figure, so I said, Why not me too?

Mum looked doubtful but said we might have some Scottish blood
on her father's side.

"Blood? Why do you have to have any blood from Scotland in you?
Surely all blood's the same?" I asked her.

Georgina was quick to intervene.

"No you don't have to have Scottish blood, Mummy. It doesn't really
matter. All you really need is a kilt ... and I've got one."

So she ran off to get hers. I put it on and it looked a bit long to me and
it didn't have pleating, but Georgina said the real ones were like that. She
again disappeared and came back with a pair of her white ankle socks to go
with my black plimsolls. I was sent to the Froebel the next morning in my outfit with the top of a bone-handled kitchen knife protruding from my white
ankle sock and just touching the bottom hem of my dress. After registration

and the ridicule I spent most of the day in the lavatory, and all Georgina could say when I got home was "Oh really!" with a half smile.

The flat at Rossetti House wasn't the answer to our housing and living situation, and our stay couldn't last because Mum was violating the terms of the lease by having children there. Caspar John, who had been subletting illegally, was starting to get alarmed at the number of scribbles on the walls and the hoards of people staying, so he felt he had to ask Mum to leave.

During our time there, however, it meant we could visit Stanhope Gardens to see George's parents, Big Mumma and Pa. "Under the window where I often found her / Sitting as huge as Asia, seismic with laughter, / Gin and chicken helpless in her Irish hand," George wrote of his mother, and when I read it a vivid memory of her jolly presence immediately comes to mind. On entering the kitchen of their flat she could be made out through the cigarette smoke, wedged into a chair in the corner. She had a mischievous grin on her dimpled face and with a wheezy smoker's voice she called out for me to come over and, giving me a pencil and pad, she asked me:

"If you're so clever now you've been to a fancy school, show everyone in the room how to spell 'salmon.'"

Writing shyly behind my cupped hand, I laboriously spelled it out without the "l" and on looking at my answer she chuckled and told me I shouldn't think of leaving school just yet.

George went on to write: "She will not glance up at the bomber, or condescend / To drop her gin and scuttle to a cellar."

And I thought I could remember the wail of the air-raid siren masking the crump of a detonating bomb in the distance as the huge frosted sash window in the kitchen rattled from the blast. These were memories hammered together from many different visits to the flat and then intermingled with tales from Mum's knee. It couldn't have been true, I realize, because I was there only as a baby during the war and would have had no recollections of exploding bombs.

Mum had told me of her wartime experiences at 9 Hammersmith Terrace and I happily substituted that flat for Big Mumma's when I read George's sonnet "To My Mother." When we went round to the flat at Stanhope Gardens there were still many blackened bomb sites and craters around, as in much of London at the time, so it would certainly have been true to say those kitchen windowpanes had rattled in the blitz.

It was a large flat on the first floor and we all got very excited when we visited. We'd go chasing up the front steps to the portico entrance and ring the bell. We would hear the clattering of a glass door opening high up in the vestibule, followed by the patter of approaching footsteps down a narrow flight of stairs, and the door would be thrown open. The fresh young face of a relative or visiting friend would invite us in. Big Mumma rarely opened it herself. Tearing through the darkened and echoing hall as the front door banged closed, we would race up the stairs to wait at the top for Mum to catch us up. Like a mother duck with her brood, we waddled dutifully into the kitchen, where we would be enveloped by another planet.

Big Mumma ruled over this babbling world from her corner chair, the crockery stacked up behind her on a dresser. As we pushed shyly into the kitchen on arrival her beaming face would call us over to her knee, and hugging the four of us, often all at the same time, she'd chuckle and chide a happy welcome. The kitchen was really no more than a scullery, but it was a hotbed of gossip and socializing and it was packed with a large round table and with the extended Barker family and their friends, who made visits to it in a never-ending stream. Big Mumma and Pa had five children and their children now had children too, and they in their turn had friends and we all happily populated this kitchen at one time or another, often all at the same time. Chattering through the cigarette smoke, we sipped endless cups of tea. This was dispensed from a large brown teapot that sat imperiously in the middle of the table coddled by a scruffy tea cozy as sometimes bacon sizzled on the large cast-iron stove.

Big Mumma and Pa's marriage must have been one of some friction, although I never heard or saw any. There were profound differences between their backgrounds, but they had worked out a way of living together that provided a secure home life for their children. Pa—who was called either Bompa or Pa by his extended family—was known to have an explosive temper, which he must have inflicted on his wife many times as they developed their modus operandi. He was never seen in the kitchen, which is probably why I never witnessed any friction between them.

If the hubbub in the kitchen became incomprehensible to me, with chatter about people I didn't know or animated exchanges about writing, I filtered through the warren of the big flat to find Pa maintaining a stately existence in the front room. Here he survived, scorning the fripperies of the kitchen nattering, and for me the journey to the front room was a forbidding one. It entailed a dark passageway that led past the flight of stairs that led up to the bedrooms. Passing the glass entry-door that we had arrived through, I took a left turn along a vaulted corridor into lofty vestibule. It was known as the dining room, though we never dined there, and it had a huge and imposing painting depicting a vivid scene that we were told was the conquest of Mexico. It loomed at the far end and we inspected its weird symbolic animals with curiosity and bewilderment. Hurrying through the shadows of a darkened landing room, I carefully turned the large knob and slipped into the front room to join Pa. He'd be sitting at the far end of the room in a large armchair by a blazing fire in the wide grate, reading the paper as he smoked. His back would be to the three tall French windows that gave way to a narrow balcony overlooking the street below. Light from these windows polished his bald head as it flooded past onto the huge white pages of his broadsheet.

On entering the bright, high-ceilinged room my first concern was not for Pa but where the pigs were now.

"They're over there," he'd growl and without looking up from his paper he'd gesture to the line of shiny china pigs arranged in order by size along a low polished table. They were white and dotted all over with green shamrocks. The largest pig, the size of a beer barrel, stood at the front of the line. Our favorite, the little runt, brought up the rear. We revered these china dolls on our visits as Easter Islanders would their megaliths.

Although this was usually considered Pa's room, because he had inherited the contents from two wealthy American ladies for whom he had once been a butler, it was Big Mumma who we felt owned the pigs. She would carefully explain about the trinity of the shamrock leaves that in her Drogheda home were considered lucky. The rest of the room was very imposing, with tall chinoiserie vases girdled with snaking dragons, large oil paintings on the walls, polished furniture and two mantelpieces supporting mementoes of Pa's military campaigns. He was at that time serving as a butler at the ancient London legal center of Gray's Inn, where he was venerated as a straight-backed, punctilious majordomo with impeccable manners.

He once challenged me to a duel to see who could cut the thinnest slices of bread from a hot crumbling loaf. He won with ease. After I had gouged out my doorsteps he carved five thin wafers that fluttered from the loaf face. I imagined he had learned this skill not from his butlering, about which I knew nothing, but from his expert use of the sword he owned when he sliced up the enemy. I knew he had been a Coldstream Guard and Mum had explained to me that Pa was a retired warrior who sought order in the world from the correct way of doing things.

I was always a little wary when entering his room because we had been warned of his fiery temper, but it never flared at me. After I had fondled the runt china pig, he would put his paper aside and take a long look at me over his reading spectacles. Then, if I was lucky, his face would crack in a huge creased grin and he'd pat the side of his chair to summon me over. Pushing up against the chair, I would whisper to him from a lowered head and shyly ask if he could show me his medals. He would pull out a polished box, long and flat, from a nearby drawer. When he slowly opened the lid, I saw a line of ten glittering doubloons with a striped multicolored ribbon above each of them. He would take me round to the front-door lobby and there he'd point out, in the hat stand with the walking sticks and umbrellas, his ceremonial sword. When he let me try to unsheathe it, I hadn't got the height with my arm high above my head to clear the scabbard with the blade. We'd then pore over glossy black-and-white photos of him marching on the parade ground with his Coldstream Busby tilted down over his eyes and chinstrap obscuring his face. He gave me some of these photos and Mum had them framed and put on the wall behind my bunk in our new home. He whispered conspiratorially in my ear:

"Now, young man, the sword, the medals and more photos will all be yours if you decide to join the army."

And I felt we shared a daring secret. After the sword had been sheathed we returned to the front room and he would start on tales of his military career. In fascinating detail, embroidered with relics pulled down from the mantelpiece or drawn from the mahogany cupboards, he wove spellbinding stories of his campaigns in distant deserts. The stories were of the campaigns of the Royal Lincolnshire regiment in Sudan and South Africa. Sadly I later learnt that this was a well-rehearsed routine. All his grandsons had been mesmerized by these stories, with promises of ownership of the sword. Pa had long since abandoned any hope of interesting his sons in an army career, and his tales became taller and taller as he sought to impress his grandsons. He said his first campaign was in the Sudan, and he had stories of a strength-sapping 140-mile trek in the searing desert sun. He said he had been part of a detail entrusted with carrying Kitchener's grand piano as they were force-marched down the banks of the Nile to Atbara and on arrival at Omdurman had fought a ten-mile line of 50,000 Dervishes. At this battle, which took place in 1898, he would have been only twelve—far too young for recruitment. It's more likely that in 1897 his interest had been roused by the Royal Lincolnshires as they strutted past the gate of his home in Spilsby, Lincolnshire, on a recruiting march for their coming campaign. He would then have taken a close interest in them as he followed their exploits in Africa and, excited by the reports from the battles, he later took the Queen's shilling. The Royal Lincolnshires, however, were too close to home, so he first enlisted with the Coldstream Guards, whose headquarters were in London. The photos he showed me of himself on parade couldn't have been him either. As I remember them, they were glazed modern photos taken at Horse Guards Parade in London and at the time he gave them to me, although he had been a Class Z reservist for a time, he had been demobbed after the First World War for thirty-four years.

George (Pa) Barker was born in Spilsby, Lincolnshire, in October 1885. His great-grandfather Robert had been a miller just down the road at the Burgh-le-Marsh windmill, and his grandfather Frank had become a baker, using the flour from the mill for his bread. One day Frank took the train on a trip south from Burgh-le-Marsh to Skirbeck, in Boston, and lost his way. After imbibing a gallon or two of country ale in town he wandered around the streets calling out to all who would listen that he was lost. After being refused entry into several hostelries, he become befuddled and toppled headlong into a roadside sewage sluice, the Bargate Drain, and drowned.

Pa's father, my great-grandfather Walter, was an even wilder character. Often on a whim he abandoned his eight children for months with no explanation to his long-suffering wife, Elizabeth. She would continue to run the farm, of which he was foreman, while caring for their children. He once disappeared from home without a word, signing on with a ship as a deckhand bound for Australia, where he went to see a world-championship boxing match. Walter was a keen amateur boxer and it was said he tried to control his drunken rages by wrestling with the cattle in the night. At the age of forty-four he became consumptive, lost his job as farm foreman and had to move to a tied cottage in Swaby. This hovel could be found at the end of a muddy path colorfully called Shit Alley by the locals. It was all they could afford now he couldn't work. The family of eight children, Elizabeth and consumptive Walter lived a cramped existence. They had to climb a ladder to their quarters above the livestock, which were tethered on the packed earth of the ground floor. He lasted eighteen months under these reduced circumstances and then died. His third-eldest child, George, probably because he was the only one who could read and write, came up from the Chelsea barracks, where he was stationed, to register the death and bury him.

The fiercest action Pa saw in the Coldstream Guards as a batman or officers servant was boxing with the regiment, a skill he had inherited from Walter. He was in the magnificent uniform of the Coldstream Guards when Big Mumma first set eyes on him. If she had known her uniforms better, the meeting would probably never have taken place.

She was born in Mornington, Meath, Eire, in 1881 as Marion Frances Taaffe. Her father was the pilot for the port of Drogheda, on the north side of the river Boyne, where in 1690 the Catholic forces of James II were routed by the Protestants of William III of England. It's not surprising to learn, therefore, that she came from a line of staunchly Republican affiliations. In 1901 she had come to London to earn some money in service as a housemaid, intending soon to return to Mornington when she had saved.

Family lore had it that she first met Pa one sunny Sunday when she had taken a walk from the mansion in Kensington where she worked to admire the flowerbeds round Hyde Park Corner. George Barker too was strolling round the park in his Guards regalia. In its splendor, the uniform comprised a crimson swagger jacket over dark-blue drainpipe trousers with a broad crimson stripe down the side. On his head he wore a brass-braided forage cap, but the whole assemblage, unnoticed by him, was ruined by the loop of a pair of braces dangling down his back. As he rounded Hyde Park Corner he heard giggling and turned to see Marion Frances convulsed with laughter. He stopped to ask her what she found so funny, and after a brief courtship they were married in Our Lady of Victories, Kensington, on February 2, 1905.

This story, although probably not based on sound facts, presents the start of the confluence of their two disparate worlds. The Coldstream Guards were a direct descendent of Munck's Regiment of Foot, on which Cromwell's New Model Army was based, and, as such, mercilessly suppressed the Irish uprisings in 1650. Big Mumma came from a long line of Irish Republicans, the Taaffes. They had rallied to the Irish chieftains' cause in 1601 against the armies of Elizabeth I, and in 1649 the Taaffes had been put to the sword by none other than Munck's Regiment of Foot, soon to become the Coldstream Guards, as Cromwell subjugated Drogheda. She was to later join Sinn Fein, had many friends from the nationalist cause and of course was a devout and practicing Catholic. They settled in a house in Chelsea that was available to soldiers as regimental accommodation and here they started a family of two daughters, Olga and Eileen.

The wedding day of Kit and Ilse (nom de plume: Katherine Talbot) Barker, July 3, 1948, on the balcony of 23A Stanhope Gardens, London SW7. Left to right: Maurice Carpenter (poet friend of Kit and George), Monica Humble, Cass (Betty Pauline Cass), David Wright, Eileen Jackson, Kit and Ilse, Mumma (seated), George (with Maurice's clarinet), John Fairfax, Pa (George Barker Sr.), Wendy (Veronica) Humble.

Photo by Phil Jackson (Eileen's husband)

At the age of twenty-eight, three years after his marriage, Pa left the Guards to become a butler with two wealthy American sisters in Paddington, and while serving here they had their third girl, Monica, on October 17, 1910. When the American sisters died in 1913 he was left £5,000 in their will (then a considerable fortune) and felt financially secure enough to leave central London for Loughton, near Epping Forest, where he took up as a temporary police constable. My father George was born this year, on February 26, at 106 Forest Road. He was named after his father, with Big Mumma adding the middle name of Granville, which in later life George often encouraged people to think was after Harley Granville-Barker, who had been a glittering actor and won acclaim later as the writer of *Prefaces to Shakespeare*. He was making a name for himself as a director of theater at the time of George's birth. In fact Big Mumma named him after the Granville cinema chain, one of which she frequented in Loughton.

Three years later, after Pa had squandered his £5,000 bequest on unwise investments, the family moved back to Juer Street in Battersea, and my father George's brother, Albert Gordon, was born. Big Mumma wanted him christened Christopher Francis, but at the time of the birth Pa's brother was killed while serving as a soldier on the Somme and Pa insisted on his brother's names for his newborn son. His siblings immediately called him Kitten, because of his head of fluffy white hair, and when this was abbreviated to Kit—a short form of Christopher—Big Mumma felt marginally appeased, as she almost got her way.

These were threadbare years for the family and Pa's wages as a police constable were not enough to provide for his family, so eight years after he had left the Guards he returned to them. This must have been a move not without a little desperation and his re-enlistment coincided with the carnage on the Western Front. His 4th Battalion, made up of short-term enlistments, was sent straight to the Somme, where his younger brother Albert had been killed. He served for two years in the trenches, till the end of the war, and on his discharge he returned to his family and a London he had no qualifications or skills to offer. He sought out the cheapest living accommodation he could find for his family and went to look for work. The slum tenement block in Fulham that he moved his family into was owned by a trust set up to house the poor. By way of compensation to soldiers back from the Great War, the trust gave Pa a part-time job as a caretaker of the block. From here, after fulfilling his duties as a caretaker, Pa would set out and walk the streets looking for full-time work, while his sons ran ragged round the alleys scratching the bins for scraps.

Later, when George recalled these desperate days, he maintained that Pa clung resolutely to his brittle dignity, and to the grim solace of a possible last resort, by clutching his service revolver under his pillow at night. (Although it's certain Pa was never an officer, the sword, revolver and Sam-Browne belt were also given to RSMs, highest-ranking NCOs). George enjoyed embroidering Pa's fanciful military tales, but that he felt his father kept the gun for grimmer purposes demonstrates his sympathy for his father's despair at that time. Pa was to struggle for eight years under these conditions before he found satisfactory and regular employment.

Big Mumma had made a pact with Pa when they married that their children should be educated as Catholics, but Pa, a lapsed Methodist and an agnostic, insisted his sons go to the local council school and Big Mumma, who now had all her girls in the local Catholic Oratory School, relented. It was here that George, at the age of nine and after being introduced to poetry by his teacher Miss Christie, wrote ten pages of an ambitious jousting saga, having first been seduced by the cadences of Edmund Spenser's *The Faerie Queen*. In a later poem, *The True Confessions of George Barker*, he was to write:

The sulking and son-loving Muse
Grabbed me when I was nine. She saw
It was a question of self-abuse
Or verses. I tossed off reams before
I cared to recognize their purpose.

Pa had no time for any of this frippery and must have been appalled
to see his sons turning to the arts and away from a steady job in an office
or perhaps a career in the army. He was even more appalled when George
annotated a ledger of his (he was now working as an insurance agent).
George's flowery signature emblazoned the solemn pages everywhere the
young George felt the ledger was grand enough to house his fair copy, now
being mastered from the Italian scholars of the Renaissance. The boys were,
however, enthusiastically encouraged in a creative direction by Big Mumma.
She was moved to pawn her wedding ring to buy George his first typewriter. She was always a loving and spiritual influence on her sons, with Pa
the remote provider. On Sundays she would take them all to the London
Oratory in the Brompton Road, where George became familiar with the
chapels, shrines and statues of the church. Pa, now being agnostic, had no
input into his sons' religious welfare and as they grew George formed a
close spiritual bond with Big Mumma, shying further and further away
from his father.

When George was thirteen, Big Mumma put him under the religious
instruction of the Roman Catholic visitors to their housing block, Father
Kenneth Dale-Roberts and Father Phillip Francis Oddy. They gave him
extra lessons twice a week in the fundamentals of the faith at The Oratory
on Brompton Road. From Dale-Roberts and Oddy George formed a complicated set of beliefs that was based on Cardinal Newman's theology of original sin but from which he felt the church offered atonement through God.
From Oddy he learnt that faith can be fun, and, with a touch of Falstaff in
his deportment and attitude, Oddy brought a contrasting witty iconoclasm
to George's learning. The influence of these two fathers remained with
him the rest of his life and defined his Catholicism, which can best be
described as an unsolvable paradox in him, an affirmation of a belief through
being a renegade believer.

By 1927 his sisters were all out at work and George, at the age of
fourteen, moved school from the Marlborough Road Primary to a secondary attached to the Regent Street Polytechnic, which had been set up as an
education for the socially deprived. He was in love with English literature

but lacked the background of a detailed formal education and certainly felt he wasn't getting one at the Poly. After four terms there he discharged himself to continue his education by himself. He rather pompously and preemptively noted in his journals at the time that "consecutive thinking, syllogism, or any concatenation of logically inter-dependent parts is one of the ornaments I shall never wear."[1] Rejecting academia, he was later to write many acclaimed critiques, but for now he set out to fill his reading with those authors he liked, living at home.

It's hard to imagine how appalled Pa must have been by this move, but since it had Big Mumma's blessing he labored on gamely as the family provider, finding work wherever he could. His increasing income was steadily giving the family a secure home life and they moved to the top floor of a Victorian building in Ladbroke Grove. When he left school and went to live at home, George was doted on by his sisters as the precocious young poet and worshipped by his younger brother Kit, with whom he shared his boyhood dreams. Now fifteen, George came to bond closely with his sister Monica, who was the sister nearest to him in age. The typewriter given to George by Big Mumma was a gift to Monica too, so she could practice her typing skills for her work as a secretary, so she regularly typed out his first immature manuscripts.

The girls would come home at weekends and then glamorously and mysteriously dash away on exciting dates. One afternoon, as part of this traffic of glamour, Monica walked in with two Irish sisters, Kit and Jessie Woodward. They had been classmates of hers at the Oratory School and their father was a builder with a house in Parson's Green, their mother a devout Catholic from County Cork in Eire. Of the two, George's eye fell on Jessica, who was the younger and more serious of the two but, at nineteen, four years older than he. Contemporary descriptions of her depict a clear pale skin, sad eyes and dark hair. She had a stooped and martyred beauty that captured George's heart. So smitten was he at first that he bought her a fluffy white puppy, screwed up his courage to travel down to Parson's Green and thrust the dog at her through her door. Although entranced by the gesture of the puppy as much as by George's intentions, she could hardly entertain him as a suitor from the glory of her nineteen years. He was happy enough that he could be near her as they hung out together in Monica's circle of friends, but eventually they broke away as a pair. As their relationship intensified George became more confident and dominant, realizing she had a vulnerable, neurotic streak that led her into a moods of distracted self-censure. That she was able to soothe these moods by her pious belief and Catholic devotion had a fundamental appeal for George that he could never resist. Reciprocally, she revered his vocation and, like Monica, encouraged him, which increased his confidence in his work.

Growing through his teenage years, his greatest companion and confidante was his brother Kit. Together they formed an abiding addiction to motoring and its mechanics, journeying down to the Brooklands circuit at weekends to watch the racing. The noise and excitement at the racetrack sparked a lifelong fascination and preoccupation with motor mechanics that meant the two of them usually had a dilapidated wreck in their backyard that they would slowly dismantle and, just as slowly, reassemble.

In a gesture of generosity that demonstrated the family's improving prosperity, Pa bought George a 300cc Zenith motorcycle for his sixteenth birthday. George roared off into Ladbroke Grove to try it out and promptly ran under a lorry, from where he was carried home and laid in bed. These were the days before the National Health, so hospitalization was never a consideration and he was tended by a local doctor. In order to dislodge the embedded road tar and grit, the doctor prescribed a painful treatment of copper-sulphate solution to bathe the lacerations. As he languished in bed for some months he used the time wisely to continue his self-education as well as to try to improve his handwriting through diligently copying out examples from Renaissance calligraphy books.

A significant addition to the Barker household occurred at this point, as George surfaced from his recuperation. He had always been more interested in his Irish descendents than his English and when his grandmother, Big Mumma's mother, came from Mornington to stay with them in London, so impressed was he by her credentials that George started to reinvent himself as an Irishman. Grandma Taaffe brought with her a river pilot's certificate of competence that had once belonged to her deceased husband and that she framed and hung on the kitchen wall. From this certificate's associations dripped his Irish birthright, bringing with it the smell of the low-tide Boyne estuary, idiosyncratic syntax, sundry Gaelic endearments, and many Irish song lyrics. With these and other Erin trappings he started to hang an Irish persona over his English one, where, along with his newly acquired pose as a distracted poet, it stayed through his life.

By the time he was seventeen, and eager to be a poet, George had nonetheless attempted to support himself with a series of different jobs, including designing wallpaper, testing radio transformers and working in a garage. He had been writing letters of application to publishers in order to at least be in a literary working environment, and one application suddenly bore fruit. He was taken on as an errand boy at Janus Press, at that time an organ devoted largely to the publication of works by Percy Wyndham Lewis, the Vorticist (Vorticism being an English artistic and literary movement that was the antithesis of nineteenth-century sentimentality). The press was presided over by one Desmond Harmsworth, who according to George affected an accent with "so aristocratic an enunciation that I cannot easily follow his meaning."

Until then, George had spoken with the London argot of Marlborough Road Primary, but now he deemed it time for a change. Under the further peerless influence of Wyndham Lewis whirling through the office at Janus Press, George started to reinvent himself with twirling cape, black wide-brimmed hat and a cut-glass English modulation. His enthusiasms were short-lived, however, because one day he was called into Harmsworth's office and told that although senior members could exhibit an occasional eccentricity of deportment, for junior staff it was unacceptable and for tea boys, well, they would simply have to let him go. Later in life George joked about these immature boyhood affectations, but now he coupled them to his lapsed Catholicism and Irish roots and they formed the bedrock of his private and public persona.

For the next few years George feverishly cast about trying to establish in his mind and to the world that he was a poet. At nineteen and with no track record, it proved very hard. He was ably supported at this stage by his sister Monica, who typed out and sent a collection of his poems to Gollancz, the publisher, and when they were promptly returned she was there by his side to commiserate. He was also still enjoying a good relationship with Jessica and recalls frustrated passion on visits to Richmond Park in a later poem, "The True Confessions":

> O long-haired virgin by my tree,
> Among whose forks hung enraged
> A sexual passion not assuaged
> By you, its victim—knee to knee,
> Locked sweating in the muscled dark
> Lovers, as new as we were, spill
> The child on grass in Richmond Park,
> The cemetery of Richmond Hill.

He and the family were now enjoying a much fuller and more affluent lifestyle, and while his sisters paired off for marriage he was reading voraciously and presented his work to anyone who would read it. This bore fruit from a man called David Archer, who ran a bookshop in Bloomsbury. This bookshop not only contained radical books but introduced George to an underworld of literary subversives and political revolutionaries. Archer, a Cambridge graduate obtrusively besuited, tall and urbane, was often seen dispensing largess from his shop, in Parton Street off Red Lion Square. Characteristically he would wedge an evening paper under his elbow to camouflage a lamed-wing defect in the bones of his left arm. Camp and kind, he ran the shop with an urgent hap-handedness that creaked under the burden of his generosity, as penniless artists slept on the floors and made off with the books. It was here that George first came in touch with an invigorating wave of contemporary literary thinking and the society of like-minded poets; to him it was "an atmosphere of industrious conspiracy and illegal enthusiasms." Perhaps most significant of all, though, its influence was to give him an outlet for his opinions and verse. His poems and reviews were starting to appear in *New Verse, Twentieth Century* and *Adelphi*, all influential literary magazines to which he now had access. He was also perceptive enough to favorably review T.S. Eliot's *Sweeney Agonistes* at this time in *Adelphi*, a review that for him was politically astute and would repay him well later on.

These new influences led George, at the age of twenty, to find a new confidence and authority in his work, an authority he was to echo in his personal life. Pa had by now obtained the post at Gray's Inn as a butler and was able to move the family to a larger flat in Addison Gardens. George felt confident enough to leave home and set himself up in a loft in Westbourne Terrace. He was scraping together enough money from the reviews and odd-jobbing and, with a friend called Maurice Carpenter later coming in to share, was able to afford the rent. He was also able to interest a publisher in a work of fiction he had prepared from extracts from his journals, calling it *Alenna Autumnal*, following it shortly with verse in a slim volume entitled *Thirty Preliminary Poems*.

He was constructing a reputation that had to be ripped out of the literary establishment as he went along, since he never felt he was part of it, and in doing so he liked to think of himself as a maverick outsider and iconoclast. This stance came at a cost, and the emotional strain from his position was telling enough for him to worry his friends that he might be toying with suicide. He was very taken with the poet Thomas Chatterton, an outsider like himself who had come to London in 1770, who later, alone in his garret, poisoned himself in despair and poverty, and who was later found to have written much cogent and trenchant material under several *noms de plume*.

For George, suicide was not a subject of contemplation for long, because he found he was soon to be responsible for another life. In October 1933 Jessica told him that she was pregnant and so, because of her strong Catholicism and to conceal from her parents the time of conception, they decided to marry as soon as they could. On Saturday, November 18, they were married at the Holy Cross, Ashington Road, near her home at Parson's Green. Both the marriage and the pregnancy were kept secret from as many people as possible. He specifically asked his close friends, including Maurice Carpenter, who he hoped would spread the word among his Parton Street cronies, not to attend. He implied to Carpenter that because he was copping out to bourgeois respectability by marrying Jessica in white at the Brompton Oratory, the ceremony would be one they would hardly care to attend. Of course if they had turned up they would have found themselves at the wrong church anyway.

After the wedding and feeling unduly sensitive about turning his back on his London friends, he told only those he thought ought to know that he was retreating to the country to write, while to others he explained that Jessica had been suffering from consumption for some years and needed a change of air. He had by now developed a fine line in white lies. Later, Carpenter would take George to meet his latest girlfriend in suburban Wood Rising. His girlfriend's mother, normally a tolerant and patient woman, instantly took an unreasoning and instinctive dislike to George and refused him entry into the house. When pressed hard by Carpenter's girlfriend for a reason, her mother would only mumble that "She knew! He was immoral!"[2] So they picnicked in the woods behind the house with the girls.

Leaving a trail of dubious reasons and the publication of *Thirty Preliminary Poems* in David Archer's care, George borrowed a cottage from a chance acquaintance in the Parton Street bookshop and escaped London with his new wife to a cottage in Worth Matravers, Dorset. The move may have been wise in that it enabled him to avoid the censure of his in-laws, but it also allowed him to concentrate on his work, and in the following year he published two further works, one of prose and one of poetry—*Janus* and *Poems*. Having finished these, George set out on a work of prose that he titled *The Bacchant*, which borrowed heavily from the local turbulent and rocky shoreline. This, he decided, was to be his second novel. This Dorset coastline would inspire a further work, *The Dead Seagull*, some years later.

But for the moment the raging sea below him, as he walked the cliff tops, would move him to write a poem that he called "Daedalus."

As he continued with his prose work he sent this poem off for possible publication, and after it had gone through the hands of the Orkney-born poet, critic and novelist Edwin Muir (who sent it on to fellow poet Walter de la Mare) it ended up on T.S. Eliot's desk at Faber and Faber. Eliot had seen and remembered George's review of *Sweeney Agonistes* and now, aware of who George was, asked if he could use the poem for publication in *The Criterion*, the magazine of which Eliot was editor. George promptly shot off another poem to him, and the outcome of that action may have been even more beneficial, because Eliot asked him to drop by at their offices in Russell Square next time he was in London. So encouraged, George immediately followed up with further poems that Eliot liked, and when he received the tale *The Bacchant* Eliot decided to delay its publication until he could publish more of George's poetic works.

In 1934 T.S. Eliot was considered the illustrious high priest of English poetry. Not only was he editor of *The Criterion*, the highly acclaimed literary magazine, he controlled the poetry list of the most preeminent poetry publisher in the country, Faber and Faber. In April of that year George, who was coming to the end of his tenure of the cottage in Dorset, decided to call on Eliot at his office. The meeting was seminal and a great success, with Eliot offering immediate encouragement and patronage. He endorsed George's application to the Royal Literary Fund for a grant and urged him to complete enough work for a collection that Faber might publish.

Returning to Dorset with the good news, he and Jessica nonetheless had to vacate the cottage. The chance acquaintance from the Parton Street bookshop who had been instrumental in getting them the tenure of the cottage, the novelist Rosalind Wade, told them that her mother wanted it back now spring had arrived. They packed up and took off for Geldeston, in Suffolk, where they rented another cottage to await the arrival of the birth of their child. On June 2 the baby, a girl they named Clare, was born. George, with increasing anxiety about finances, wrote a letter to Eliot pleading for an advance on the coming work, which Eliot duly arranged. Still, all was not right. In fear of her mother finding out that the baby had been conceived before they were married, Jessica and George determined that the child be adopted, lest it be tainted in any way with illegitimacy.

The child was spirited away by Father John Owen of Gillingham Hall to be raised in the comfortable security of an adopted home, and Clare did not discover the truth of her birth until fifty-six years later. George and Jessica were never to forgive themselves. Although the baby would have been born after they married, Jessica feared her devout Roman Catholic mother would have soon calculated that the baby was conceived out of wedlock. George at first was less sure of the need for adoption but was easily persuaded by a fearful Jessica. Later, in Big Sur, when she found out of his infidelity with Mum, in her hysteria she cast the adoption back in his face as his doing.

When the tenure at Geldeston expired, George and Jessica returned to Dorset, renting a small cottage near Corfe Castle. Throughout the pregnancy George had kept the truth of Clare's birth and adoption from Eliot and others by pretending Jessica had a progressive neurological complaint. It elicited Eliot's care and concern to the extent that he was moved enough to organize a whip-round among a group of his wealthy friends, which Eliot was to collect and formally disburse on a quarterly basis. The checks started arriving early in 1935 and were to ease George's immediate cash-flow problems, and when both Kit and Maurice Carpenter joined him and Jessica in the cottage their immediate outgoings were reduced even further.

By Christmas 1935 the lease had expired and conditions in the small cottage were very cramped. George, Jessica and Kit moved back to Holland Park in London to stay with Big Mumma and Pa. This couldn't be anything more than a short stay, because the flat was too crowded for George to get any writing done. Once again he felt he needed the countryside for his work, so they moved again to Dorset, responding to a magazine advertisement. They moved into a cottage that had primitive utilities but had three bedrooms, which meant that Kit and Maurice Carpenter could go with them and share the rent. In late summer they set off in an old motor stacked to bursting with their belongings. They spluttered all the way down from London, only for the car to finally give out some miles before they reached the cottage. Freewheeling back down a hill and into local garage they had just passed, they left the car and their belongings to cover the last few miles on foot.

It was the autumn of 1935 and from this quiet retreat George was able to apply himself to his work as his reputation took hold. He was only twenty-two, but he gathered a second prestigious admirer in the form of the great Irish poet W.B. Yeats, who wanted to include him in his new *Oxford Book of Modern Verse*. George's reputation—or, perhaps more accurately in this case, his notoriety—spread farther when his sexually ambiguous prose monologue "The Bacchant," from *Janus*, was published, the reviews of which were to cause quite a literary stir.

The couple went through a period of relative contentment, with George able to apply his talents to his work in a quiet environment. It did, however, mean occasional trips up to London to meet Eliot, with whom he was now very close and who suggested he write a poem of greater length. It also meant he could enjoy a fuller social life, which he did as an apparently unattached single man. He usually left Jessica behind on these trips and set about developing his social acumen as he charmed the literary circles. In developing patrons who might be able to help his career, he ran across an American woman fifteen years his senior called Emily Holmes Coleman, who was a writer herself and the sometime mistress of a grand patron of the arts, Sir Alexander Hoare. She was wealthy and lived in fashionable Chelsea next to Sir Alexander with her teenage son. With a slightly scatty and irreverent character, she soon warmed to a similar iconoclasm in George. Flattered yet calculating, he had allowed himself to be seduced by her, later preposterously remarking to her that the guilt and nausea he felt after their first sexual encounter must be due to his bisexuality and Jessica's (invented) lesbianism.[3]

He had now found a base in London from where he could develop the other half of a double life, and through 1936, usually at weekends and also in the company of novelist and translator Antonia White, he was to spend many long hours at one or another of their Chelsea flats. In 1936 he also picked up another patron of the arts, Lady Ottoline Morrell, who singled him out by turning up at his Dorset retreat in her large Bentley, offering him a pair of bone-china teacups and a novel by Aldous Huxley.

While he worked on his new long poem, he sent extracts to Edwin Muir for approval. Muir, along with Walter de la Mare, was one of two new mentors and admirers of his work. Still enjoying trips to London as the ribald and outrageous young poet-elect, he would return to Jessica in Dorset to fill the role of protective and contented husband. When later he learned that Jessica had suffered a miscarriage, he became more committed to this role, but she grew ever more resentful that she had surrendered Clare to adoption. His epic poem, once again heavily influenced by his domestic rural setting, was accepted by Eliot at Faber under the title *Calamiterror*.

George had his allowance from Eliot's literary consortium extended from one year to three. Now they felt they could extend it no longer. Eliot, in an attempt to ease George's financial situation, helpfully suggested he turn his hand to more commercial writing. When that came to nothing, and perhaps because Eliot had been a bank clerk for eight years in an earlier life, he suggested to George that he seek gainful employment while continuing to write poetry. But this George felt he couldn't do, and he was reduced to begging letters to his better-heeled friends for funds. Emily Coleman wrote back after one such letter that he must stop thinking of himself as an unfortunate man; others were worse off than he. He should count his blessings, one of which she listed as his wife.

In the heat of that 1937 London summer, Mum stumbled across George's *Poems* in Better Books on Charing Cross Road and, entranced by the "complete juicy *sound* that runs bubbles over" of his words, she set her sights on meeting him. Although Coleman's rather sisterly advice may well have been true, his lack of a living, now that the stipend from his patrons had stopped, inexorably tightened its grip as his troubles mounted. Because many of his projects had been turned down by Faber, he was finally reduced to the point where he took on a series of lectures for extramural studies at Cambridge. Teaching, lecturing and professorships he considered cop-outs from the real work of a poet—a position he maintained all his life, though it was in direct contradiction to the advice offered by Eliot, and one that he preached enthusiastically to anyone who would listen, especially the young.

A temporary respite from his troubles occurred at this time, as the repercussions of his letter to Coleman suddenly reaped benefits. She said she was able to rent him a cottage in Sussex that his pocket could afford and she was able to persuade her friend Peggy Guggenheim, a wealthy gallery owner and patron of the arts, to provide a small subsistence allowance now that Eliot's friends had ceased their contributions.

George and Jessica moved into their new cottage in Sussex in May 1938, and in November he began his extramural lectures in Cambridge. Idyllic though this may have seemed to them, the threat of war drew ever nearer, as in September the British prime minister, Neville Chamberlain, ceded Sudetenland to Hitler in a futile attempt at appeasement. With the invasion of Poland the next year, all of Europe was thrown into turmoil as war was declared.

During the start of that year of 1939 George's peace was shattered when Emily Coleman asked him and Jessica to quit the cottage by April, because her father, who owned the property, wanted to sell it. Then Peggy Guggenheim wrote to say she would no longer be paying his allowance, and his creditors in Sussex started knocking on his door with increasing regularity, demanding payment of his bills. In despair with his indigence he felt compelled to travel up to London to buttonhole Guggenheim as she was setting up an exhibition in Cork Street, the home of London's most prestigious art galleries, and beg for a handout. When this plea was rejected he returned to Sussex and wrote to Coleman to explain that he could not comply with her instructions for vacant possession. Then, as his woes appeared to be closing in on every side, a gleam of hope suddenly appeared.

A letter arrived from a Mr. Pickering who was acting as an agent for the English Literary Society of Japan. When Pickering had left a lectureship at the Imperial Tohoku University at Sendai, in North Japan, the society asked him if he could make some discreet enquiries when he got back to England for the replacement of Mr. Ralph Hodgson, now retiring from the position of lecturer in English poetry at the university. The letter suggested they meet to discuss the matter. In fact Hodgson had suggested that Pickering approach Eliot for advice on possible candidates, and the offer was made first to the poet Stephen Spender. When Spender turned it down, Eliot suggested George.

Several things coalesced to make up George's mind. First, he desperately needed the money the position would pay. Second, although he saw the job as a professorship and therefore against his principles for the employment of poets, he had only just completed a course of lectures at Cambridge and this was, although half way round the world, no more than an extension of the Cambridge lectureship. Third, only a week after accepting the post from Pickering, war was declared in Europe, and George, at twenty-six and a prime candidate for conscription, felt fighting a war might "disturb my communication with Parnassus."[4] So, on August 26, 1939, and more in desperation than from an unencumbered act of free will, he decided to accept the position. A week later war was declared.

George's decision must have been particularly galling to Pa, who saw his son evading the call of his country in her hour of need. George, despite this, seemed only faintly aware that far from escaping a war zone he was going to a country that had been executing savage hostilities against China and whose fascist regime was becoming ever more sympathetic to Germany's.

Big Mumma and Kit went down to Sussex and helped him pack for the trip to Japan that, on November 18, was to take them from Tilbury docks, via stops in New York and Los Angeles, to Yokohama, where they would disembark on January 24.

1952

WE LEFT LONDON AND returned to Tilty and, for a short while at least, to our old school, Thaxted Primary School. In an attempt to improve our education, though, Mum decided to send all four of us to boarding school. When she told us I was heartbroken. The Victor Ludorum would now never be mine. I lost all appetite for playground races and tag, and watched the girls instead.

It was my last day at Thaxted. Jackie was at the head of a line waiting to skip. The long heavy skipping rope was turned at the ends by two girls who had defaulted in the game. It was now Jackie's turn and she approached the whirling rope, getting her body as near as possible by rocking her torso backward and forward as the rope whipped by her chest. She then expertly sprang into the vortex.

> As I was in the kitchen
> Doing a bit of knitting,
> In came a burglar
> And I ran out!

She sang prettily as she double-skipped. The whirling rope smacked and thrashed the tarmac, but it never caught her spotless white ankle socks. Then, on the word, she expertly sprang out. *She* never had to turn the rope. A stab of sadness overwhelmed me, as thought I would never see her again. She neither knew nor cared. She was now faster than me and that was all she needed to know. As I leaned against the low playground wall, sizzling in the roasting summer sun, I felt a lump come to my throat. Perhaps I could swap the blue paper twist of salt from the packet of crisps I was eating for one of the Kirby grips from her blonde hair sticking out on either side in sweet little plaits. Did I dare? In my memory this longing slowly fades as it meshes with the popping sound of a single-cylinder motorbike engine behind me. It gained speed as it came up the hill from central Thaxted to the divide in the road opposite the school playground. The high road led to Dunmow and London, the low road to the Thaxted council estate suburbs. The spluttering cough of the four-stroke quickly became a clear-throated howl as the bike gained speed. Instead of a gear change there came a squeal of demented rubber, a split second of ominous silence and a hollow boom. I vaulted the low playground wall and followed the tire marks freshly seared into the road. They pointed to a new gap in the hedgerow between the dividing highway. Burrowing through the undergrowth with increasing dread I stumbled onto the crash site.

The motorbike had slewed sideways into the vertical trunk of a huge fir tree and I couldn't make out the mangled man from his machine. The air was heavy with the stench of petrol and burning rubber. The sight of a perfectly clean white bone sticking through the side of a leather boot reminded me of one of our now more frequent half-carved Sunday joints. The last thing I remembered as I fainted was how the sun had blistered the tar in the road as it rushed up to meet my face.

I never did find out what happened to the unfortunate motorbike rider, but I do remember trying to fight my way out of the hands of the paramedics as they loaded me into the back of the ambulance. That acrid smell of blistering road tar in high summer still mingles with flashbacks of black motor oil rivulets curdling with blood and I shudder. If I eat plain crisps, I always get a headache.

Georgina and Rose went off to ballet school and Bashie and me were prepared for private preparatory school. The two Roberts helped us pack the trunks for our first term at Tyttenhanger Lodge in Seaford, probably knowing we were heading for a shock. MacBryde kept up the cheerful teasing as he crossed items off the endless clothes list. Valiant deeds on playing fields sprang readily to mind, colorfully informed by the Billy Bunter cartoon strip. I held the rough serge of the blue-and-yellow-checkered football shirts to my face in wonder. New football boots with toe caps and long white laces—refinements I had never enjoyed. And rugger and Latin and the cane. What were they? With horror I remembered Bunter's ample backside so often lashed with a bendy walking stick in the comic.

I carefully picked the stitches from my Thaxted County Council School blazer badge and put it in the top pocket of my new gray-flannel suit. This would really impress them. Mum took us to London and then on to Victoria Station, but she was crying as she whispered in my ear, "Don't worry, darling. If you don't like it you can come home at any time."

Why on earth was she crying and why wouldn't I like it? It all sounded such fun. On the crowded platform we joined a throng of schoolchildren with similar caps in blue and yellow and got into a train compartment with them. The corridor was packed with boys waving, larking about and with a few crying as the train began to move. Mum stood there, tears streaming down her face as she waved us goodbye. She was one of many on the platform. I sloped back to the carriage with the other pupils, convinced I'd never see my Mummy again but not sure why.

"You two new? Bros? Major and minor? What are your names?"

"Mine's Giffy 'n that's Bashie. 'N yourn?"

"No, you fool. Your surnames! Hey, Jenks! Do come and look at what I've found!"

This older boy called down the corridor. A rush of his mates tumbled into the compartment. They snatched a cap from a smaller boy and tossed it around to each other while the owner tearfully labored after it. They turned to inspect me. The first, an older boy, announced solemnly:

"I'm Voyce and I'm the train-duty monitor. If you're new you must be Barker Major and Minor. You'll be in Curlews House with me, so keep out of the conduct book or you'll be sent up for the cane."

None of this made the slightest sense to me, but with his air of authority I thought I ought to make friends. As they all leered at me, a friendly idea came to me.

"'Ere. D'you wanna see this. Came orf me old school blazer! Whatcha reckon?"

And with that I proudly pulled the badge out of my top pocket. Under the crossed swords and helmet was scrolled "Thaxted County Council School" in gold braid.

"Good lord," said Voyce. "The guttersnipe went to a council school!"

He snatched the badge from my sweaty palm. To my horror he tossed it out of the open window, where it fluttered and bucked in the train's slipstream and disappeared into the Sussex countryside. Enraged, I hit Voyce smack in the mouth and split his lower lip.

* * *

Tyttenhanger Lodge School, 1954. Col. Gossen is seated second from right, Arthur Cartwright fourth from right, Miss Dentine sixth from right, Mr. Moggeridge seventh from right. I'm standing, second from left, lower row.

Tyttenhanger Lodge School was a large Victorian mausoleum set in twenty acres of playing fields. At the front, amid carefully manicured hydrangea and rhododendron bushes, a scrunchy gravel driveway brought you to the imposing front door. I was in awe as we clambered off the bus from the station. This was a *school*?

Most of the boys seemed unconcerned at our arrival and chattered on about what "the Col" would expect from some Latin holiday work.

"You're for the high jump now, you know, Barker Major!" a voice squeaked from the back, adding to my apprehension.

Arthur and Mary Cartwright were pleased to extend scholarships to some special underprivileged children, and Mum had swung a deal with the headmaster, she had later told me, because we came from a family of writers. But Cartwright from the start looked down his nose at me as vermin. After I had walked endless corridors, with muffled squeaks coming through the thick pile carpets from the glazed floorboards, I finally arrived at a door with "Headmaster" emblazoned in brass lettering on it and an enamel plaque declared: "A.L. Cartwright, Esq., M.A." I knocked feebly.

"Come," yelled a voice inside.

I turned the highly polished doorknob and stepped into a large airy room that commanded fine views of the playing fields on both sides. I was confronted by a large man's hunched back.

"Ah-hah! Barker Major!"

The man peeled the spectacles off his sweating face and threw them on the desk, spinning round in a large swivel chair to face me. He stood up and, pinching his upper lip between thumb and forefinger, thoughtfully sucked air in through his whitening nostrils. He was a heavyweight in an immaculate double-breasted gray-flannel suit. His shoes sparkled and his slicked-back hair was graying at the temples. He adopted the demeanor of a man who had given what he was about to say the benefit of great wisdom. He flicked an imaginary speck from his lapel and leaned forward slightly as he undid his jacket button. The front swung open like a pair of barn doors.

"Well now, not a very auspicious start, young man. If you bring the antics of the farmyard to school you must be treated like an animal. Remove your trousers and bend over by the bookcase."

Animals? Farmyards? Was this about my home? Tilty? I was up to speed on some of it, though.

"'Ere, Mister.... Watcha mean? We wus on th' train. We wasn't even *at* school."

"You'd do well not to answer back, young man. Now, do as you're told."

He carefully took off his jacket and draped it over the back of the swivel chair. I gaped in horror as he opened a glass-fronted bookcase and, from a selection of canes and horn-handled whips, delicately picked out a riding crop with a hooped leather thong at the end. Greedily sniffing the air again, and confident he had the right implement, he test-whipped his leg for crop pliability. I turned round and nervously peered over my shoulder as I bent over. I slowly pulled my pants and trousers down. After dragging the thong slowly across my coccyx for range, he laid six murderous stokes onto my backside, one exactly on top of the other, with the thong whipping round my hip and lacerating my upper thigh.

"I hope that has taught you a lesson about the codes of behavior we at the Lodge expect of our pupils," he said, and smugly placed the whip back in the bookcase like a golfer replacing a divot.

Of course, it hurt like hell, but I never let him know it, and I even started to win some friends as they came to inspect the blood and bruising.

The dispensary was the epicenter of Miss Dentine's domain and she crackled with efficiency and moral rectitude. Tall, thin and without a microdot of forgiveness in her eye, she scraped her gray hair back from her face and lashed it down behind her head like a balled fist. As senior matron, the extent of her realm in the school should have been solely medical, but somehow she extended her sphere of influence much further. Her new-boy health inspections were legendary, and lurid rumors had already permeated us timid band of newcomers.

On the appointed day, before the central heating had been switched on, new boys were made to stand in a line up the staircase. Not to the dispensary on the second floor but, for some reason, the laundry room on the top floor. Presumably this was where the chilly air was thinnest. We stood for hours getting colder and colder, naked except for our voluminous Y-fronts. ("Don't worry about them darling, you'll grow into them.") We slowly inched our way up the stairs getting nearer to our appointment with Miss Dentine, with rumors flashing down the line concerning her surgical application of a long malt spoon. You couldn't confirm this with the outgoing victims—they were whisked off in a different direction. By the time we reached the door, our trepidation and humiliation were unbearable. I sidled in with my blue legs shivering from cold and fear as my Y-fronts drooped dismally about me. Miss Dentine was at the window looking out nonchalantly. Preemptively she half turned and with a withering look said:

"Bowel movements, Barker Major?"

"Er ... wot, Miss?"

"Have you passed any stools?"

Oh God, what could she possibly mean? I took a risk:

"Nah, Miss," and clenched my buttocks.

She noted this in a ledger and asked me to say "Ah" and put a raspy stick on my tongue. And then I saw it. The malt spoon! She reached behind her and picked it up. My loins started to shudder and an urgency to pass water became overwhelming. The panic quickly evaporated when, without appearing to notice any of this, she plunged the spoon into an adjacent big brown jar and came up with a trailing spoonful of syrup. This she deftly twirled to catch back the strands and handed it out to me. I seized it urgently in my fist, glad to have the spoon under my control, and as I was sucking on the sugary mouthful I was caught completely off guard. She whipped down my Y-fronts, felt for my testicles (which immediately raced to my throat) and left me standing with my mouth ajar, the sticky spoon gummed to my teeth. I reached pitifully down to my shaking knees and retrieved my pants. Making another note in her ledger, she pulled the spoon from my gluey mouth and filled it again with a viscous brown fluid. As I stood there with my dribbling mouth ajar she tipped the liquid down my throat.

"Next!"

At the end of one summer term and as a special concession, Bashie and me were given leave by the headmaster to go on a family outing with our American relatives. Aunt Jane and her son D'Arcy were over from the United States on holiday. D'Arcy was a year older than Georgina and looked very grown up. He was the son of D'Arcy Marsh, whom George had met in Ottawa during the war and with whom he had attempted to cross into US from Canada, only to be thrown in jail when they found his papers out of order. We had seen pictures of D'Arcy Jr. and had awaited his arrival with awe. George, who must have been trying to demonstrate to Mum that his relationship with her sister was entirely innocent, had suggested we all go for a picnic to Beachy Head at the Dover white cliffs. So Aunt Jane hired a car, we all packed in and set off.

There was much excited chatter among us children in the car about who would be the fastest runner now D'Arcy was here. He, of course, had Sioux blood too but was three years older than I and by the look of him had started to mature early. We drove the car as far as we could along the cliff top, got out and looked out to the sparkling sunlit sea. We were all peering across the water, trying to make out France on the horizon, when Georgina spread her arms and pretended to fly down the hill ahead of us. This immediately triggered a carefree race to the cliff edge. I remember looking out of the corner of my eye at D'Arcy as we bounded down the slope. We were line abreast, so I tried to increase my pace. He then took a tumble, came up at speed and continued on. So that's how you do it, I thought, and went into a flying forward roll. As I went down, my right knee made contact with what felt like a crumbling rotten tree stump and I looked down at my leg, intrigued to see the bony edge of my kneecap poking through a starburst of curled-back whitening skin. Blood spurted out and my trembling leg gave way under me.

The paramedics brought the ambulance along the cliff top to pick me up and as I was strapped to a stretcher I remember George taking the massive lump of concrete with its bloodied point out of the tall grasses and putting it in the middle of the path.

"So everybody can see and avoid it," he said.

As he got into the car to leave I saw a stranger roll it back into the grasses saying:

"That looks dangerous there. Somebody might get hurt!"

Mum accompanied me to hospital in the ambulance. Everybody else went to a hotel to begin the holiday. I had to be ferried fifty miles down the coast to the Princess Elizabeth Hospital in Eastbourne, because it was the nearest one with a children's ward. I had never been to hospital before, apart from visiting Granny, and was a little alarmed at the cacophony of crying babies that came from the surrounding cots. Mum blew kisses at me as she backed out of the ward and I was approached by the wary eye of Sister Pursehouse. She prepped me for the operation, and while I was under anesthetic they cleaned the wound, and for no apparent reason they put the whole leg in plaster.

Far from improving my condition, the operation increased the pain as the bruising spread. Finally I called out for Sister Pursehouse. After a long delay she came, angrily tutting down the ward, telling me as she primly tucked in the bedclothes not to make such a fuss. When the pain became excruciating and I could bear it no longer, she left the ward without a backward glance and went off duty.

A young night nurse finally came to my rescue when she could take my whimpering no longer. In the early hours, a paramedic illicitly cut the top off the length of the plaster cast and bound my leg to the lower half-cast with bandage. I caught a glimpse of my knee as the cast-top came off, and, apart from the sweetest sense of relief, I couldn't imagine who the leg belonged to. The yellow and blue bruising reddened with the surge of blood. The fifty large black stitches strained to hold the wound together, and the next day sister shook her head in disapproval—not at the state of the wound but at the night nurse's departure from "hospital procedure." The botched job had left a jagged three-pronged scar with torn stitch holes which I can feel as I run my fingers over it today, nearly fifty years later.

The two-week confinement was made much worse when I had family visits. They couldn't wait to tell me of the fun they were having. Once, even George came to visit. He was on his own—it was the first time I can remember being alone with him—so I was guaranteed his full attention. He kept me spellbound for the whole visit with tales of grand prix motor racing and he drew me the perfect picture of a cornering Bugatti, front wheels biting the road and stones flying. When he left I had a fleeting and happy thought that perhaps he now wanted to be my real father.

As the time for my release neared, Sister Pursehouse did a strange and spiteful thing. She could see how much I hated being in the ward with the bawling babies. During my family's visits she had often overheard what I would be doing on holiday when I was released. So she sat down on the end of my bed and sympathetically told me to brace myself for a shock. My release had been postponed, and I still had another two weeks to go. I managed to fight back the tears, but I was wary. She had never been considerate before. I held my breath until the designated hour, and when Mum walked through the ward to pick me up, I hopped straight out into the sunlight still in my pajamas, with the physiotherapist trying to unravel the bandages.

I couldn't wait to get to the beach in northern France where we were to spend a few weeks together with Aunt Jane and D'Arcy. Because I was so white and tender from my hospital incarceration I was badly burned in the sun and in the beach racing I was the one nobody wanted on their team. I could hobble quite quickly, though, but if I ever caught the leg and involuntarily bent it I was in agony.

Getting back to school that Christmas term, I was in a frenzy of anticipation in case I wouldn't be well enough to play rugby. Miss Dentine came to the rescue. She worked in tandem with a physiotherapist at first, who massaged the knee and bent my leg at more and more of an angle to free the joint. It was very painful and slow progress, as the leg was matchstick-thin from wasted muscle. Eventually Miss Dentine took over alone. I spent many hours with her as she pressed me through my exercise regimen and I was amazed at her tenderness and care. She was firm with me every session, insisting I do all my straight-leg raises, but was always aware of the pain it might cause. She invented a simple weight for my ankle that was just a long football sock with two bricks in it. It was draped over my foot and secured in place by the laces of my plimsoll.

She worked me through the regimen that Christmas term in the dispensary until the muscles in my right thigh were the same size as the left leg and when she finally gave me the nod I raced out onto the rugger pitch in time for the last game of the season. I had come to know her quite well and we started to share a lot as she insisted on another fifty leg raises. I had rolled so many bandages during this time that I had devised a novel way of doing this by using the back of my forearm. It impressed her, and I often caught her using the technique when I popped in to the dispensary unexpectedly. I also once rushed in and caught her combing her long gray hair, the only time I ever saw her without the bun, and it occurred to me how pretty she once had been before the scowl lines set in. Catching her in such an intimate moment I thought she would be furious. Instead, I think she blushed.

In the early years Leave Sundays were a nightmare for Mum to arrange. Always short of cash, she would catch the Green Line bus from Victoria and turn up at Tyttenhanger to take us out for the drizzly afternoon. When she asked us what we would like to do, we'd jump up and down and invariably squeal: "Oooh, Mummy! Can we go on the pier?" and her heart would sink.

The school called a taxi and we'd go down to the station and catch the local chuffer along the coast to Brighton. The leaden skies would close in round the cheerful plume of smoke billowing from the engine funnel. With us jumping up and down on either side as she kept us from running into the road, she'd walk us to the front, pushing through a relentless and dismal drizzle. For once Bashie and me were not excited by the seaside and beach. Clutching columns of grubby pennies, we'd dash about the amusements in the arcade, trying to grab a cheap trinket with a toy claw crane or shoot a Ping-Pong ball through the articulating jaws of a ventriloquist's dummy. Mum stood shivering in this drafty barn, her shoes leaking and the rain hammering on the roof. There wouldn't be another soul in sight to join us in this forlorn neon-lit purgatory.

Mum would fill our pockets with as many chocolate bars and sweets as we could cram in and, fingering through her purse, she sometimes declared that we would be able to go all the way back to school in a taxi. The farewells were sad for Bashie and me, but for Mum, her heartache must have been mixed with desperation.

* * *

Me, Brighton Pier, 1956

The annual school play at Tyttenhanger at the end of the Christmas term raised dormant thespian passions in those of us chosen to perform and was often quite a sophisticated affair. Mr. Moggeridge, the director, ran a disciplined show. In the normal course of schooling he maintained order in many cunning ways, and his quelling of schoolboy free-for-alls was a wonder to behold. He never raised his voice but would walk into a rioting room and simply start writing names on the back of a packet of twenty Piccadilly with a silver propelling-pencil. A fearful quiet permeated the mob, except in one hooligan corner, often with me in it, which the message didn't reach, and the rampage continued there while everybody else stood with heads bowed and looking guilty. Moggeridge quietly read out the list of names and, at the end, announced: "My room. In break." He rarely caned, but his tongue-lashings were almost worse.

I was often selected for the school play by Moggeridge and usually for an in-character role. I got a cameo as the Postman, who was supposed to have a heavy Gloucestershire burr in *A Murder Mystery*. Moggeridge felt I could do accents because I had arrived at the school with an unintelligible estuary slang. Actually, you couldn't get a fag paper between my Gloucestershire and Essex accents. Another one I landed was the March Hare in *The Mad Hatter's Tea Party*. Buck teeth, see.

Rehearsals started in the gym, and then came the exciting time of putting the stage up. The main hall of the school was usually divided into three classrooms by two great vertically hinged wooden dividers that ran on rails across the parquet flooring. Both of these dividers were folded back while we put up the stage at one end. The classes that were normally taken in those rooms were removed to the gym. The stage was a complicated set of interlocking trestle tables and boarding, which was great fun to figure out and erect. We often disappeared from sight during rehearsal amid gales of laughter as the boarding came adrift. There were even stage lights and a heavy swish curtain.

Now, *The Mad Hatter's Tea Party* is fine for a school play, but you have to successfully negotiate putting the Dormouse into the teapot. There are lots of vehicles for doing this, but we used Big Pot/Little Boy. The first night was a full house. The parents stayed awake and laughed at the right moments. I caught sight of Mum near the front and beamed at her. We had picked up Jockleson Minor (the smallest boy in the school) and safely put him in the teapot and were sweeping through the last few lines of the play. With the final curtain about to descend, disaster struck. My memory banks crashed and I dried. I looked in panic at the Mad Hatter, who looked at Alice, and we all swung round to the prompt, who was fast asleep in the wings on his upturned edition of the play.

A few sniggers started up from the audience, but still no words came to me. Then suddenly they came in a flash. We started racing through the lines again. But something was *still* wrong. Then it dawned on us. I had restarted from a point earlier in the script than where I had stopped and we were repeating our words. Worse, we felt as though we were in a barrel heading for the falls. The words sped on with a life of their own. Right up to putting the Dormouse in the pot. We stopped again. Backed up a few lines, and took another rush. So where was he? Well, he was still in the teapot, of course, and he should have been at the table.

Jockleson Minor had been stewing in the cardboard pot while we cocked things up, but nonetheless he had followed every word. After the second rush of lines, he stood up in the teapot with the lid still on his head, took a round of applause with a stiff bow (catching the falling lid as he did so), stepped down from the table and allowed himself to be put straight back in. For some reason it brought the house down. The whistling and cheering continued through to the curtain and we were given a standing ovation. I saw Mum helpless with laughter.

Of all the annual events at Tyttenhanger, my favorite was Sports Day and I had three there. They were all drenched in sunshine, and the smell of new-mown grass permeated every crevice of our mausoleum for a week or so before the day. It wafted in through the windows, which that had been thrown open to relieve the drowsy summer heat and let lost cabbage whites and bobbing airborne seeds distract the afternoon classes. My eyes were torn away from the blackboard to where the groundsman, with a little trolley of white chalk fluid, was marking the hundred-yard lanes. A shudder of excitement ran through my tummy. He also rigged up little string fences down these lines to prevent competitor crossover.

Cartwright wanted everything manicured to perfection for the arrival of the parents and families. The mothers came in their patterned cotton frocks with flared skirts and tight white belts matching white wide-brimmed hats. The fathers often wouldn't compromise their dress code for the informality of the day, and their pinstripe suits told of important jobs in the city. They would even run the fathers' race in them. With much jocular banter belying a deadly determination, some fathers, who had themselves been excellent athletes, came back to try to take a few scalps from athletes they once admired. One year in this race, much to my amazement, I saw three fathers leap into the air and limp to a halt, one after the other, with something I later learned was called a pulled muscle. When you got old, we were told, you had to stretch and jog about to warm up your muscles, but if you were seen doing this it betrayed a cocky professionalism. Winning under these circumstances in those days would have meant huge loss of face.

Their Rollers and Rovers lined up on the bank overlooking the grounds and, after extravagant hamper lunches from the boots of their cars, the fun began.

"Hey, Barker, your mater and pater coming?"

I had narrowly beaten Leahy to the tape in our first year in the blue-ribbon 100 yards, and he was hoping for a similar match, but I knew different. Leahy was my close companion through the years at Tyttenhanger. His father was a commissioner of police in Kenya and his family staunchly middle-class. He was not a great intellect, but he was great schemer and, like me, sports mad. For a boy so young he had put on a lot of weight in the last two years and he would be lucky to come second.

"Dad won't, but Mum might," I said, knowing for sure that George would never show. I don't remember him appearing once at the school for any function except to pick us up when we went to Beachy Head. Picturing him slapping backs and exchanging banter with his defeated rivals in the Fathers' Race was an image so completely incongruous to me at the time as to be absurd.

"But Mum might." Only now can I appreciate what a trial these days must have been for her. She was always uneasy with the braying English middle-class but had chosen nonetheless to send us right into the breeding ground of the "mothah countrih" she had ridiculed as a young girl. She felt she had to make sacrifices for a good education for her children. Our schooling was, after all, almost identical to the one she had undergone, except hers was in Canada.

When she arrived for the day she was conventionally dressed for a regular day at her office in London. We greeted her already kitted out for the races in shorts, plimsolls and vests under our school blazers. She looked hot and uneasy when she kicked off her high heels at the start of the Mothers' Race. But there was a devil in her eye. The other mothers giggled a lot and pretended not to know what to do. Mum did. On the word, she was off like a speeding arrow, blonde hair flying, and I stayed quiet as whispers

Sports Day, Summer, 1955

went round wanting to know who that wild woman was who had won the Mothers' Race. I was secretly proud of her.

Georgina duly cleaned up in the Sisters' Race, Bashie took the junior two-twenty, and it was down to me to do my bit. I managed it, but that hoary old chestnut the Victor Ludorum popped up again. I now knew enough Latin to translate it as "the overall winner," and since I had never lost an event in three sports days, winning six each year, I was quietly confident. At the victory ceremony after the races we marched backward and forward in front of the sports pavilion and received our fountain-pen prizes.

Then Cartwright got up, tugged his suit jacket down, and after slowly scrutinizing the assembled company over the top of his glasses he pompously proclaimed:

"My lords, ladies and gentlemen, I think we can all agree we have seen a day of sporting excellence. Yet again the weather has been very kind to our athletes and can I say to you ladies, I have never seen a more comely display ... of hats? Ha, ha, ha. Now to the Victor Ludorum. Some of you, over the years, have witnessed great individual performances and this year is no exception, which is why I am going to make one. I hope you will all join me in showing your appreciation for the bravest competitor I think I have ever witnessed on the playing fields of Tyttenhanger Lodge. For his never-say-die British-bulldog spirit, who has never stopped trying ... this year's Victor Ludorum ... Brian Leahy!'

Ah well, we Sioux ran away with just about everything else.

I knew we lived a different home life than the families and friends on the Duton Hill housing estates, but the stories of the home lives from our friends at Tyttenhanger were unrecognizable. Leahy's policeman father sent him occasional photos from home. Most of them were glossy black-and-white enlargements of beheaded Mau Mau insurgents slaughtered in dusty village compounds or peering terrified from a hiding place in the hollowed-out carcass of a cow. It never occurred to me that it was strange for a father to send pictures such as these to his eleven-year-old son. They certainly shocked me, but even more shocking was the size and splendor of his bungalow in its setting of manicured flowers and shrubs.

I determined that no one should ever know of our ramshackle house or of our wild and peculiar guardians. Gone was the excitement and gratitude for our big enamel bath and the novelty of hot running water when we first arrived at Tilty. The shame of not having electricity, and of a dusty old miller who came in to pump up our house every day to make it work, was hidden away as a dark secret. It was still a mystery to me that we never really saw our father, despite that our parents were man and wife. Mum had attempted to protect us from victimization by never explaining our background and we never sought to query it. She, after all, had come from a similar schooling in the colonies and knew how her peers would have reacted.

Returning home in the holidays was like being set free from prison. I naturally felt that my old friends from Thaxted had been left way behind now I knew Latin and French. I couldn't wait to show off my new learning. My smugness was short-lived.

One day I was strolling back through the meadows from the village shop at the start of the summer holidays. I was about to start on my bag of bull's-eyes, which for the first time I had bought without needing a ration book. Girls' voices drifted to me on the back of the warm breeze. They seemed to come from the edge of the wood about a hundred yards ahead. I stopped in my tracks with a bull's-eye halfway to my mouth and cocked my ear. Crouching down behind a line of bushes, I stalked along until the speakers came into view. As I gazed from my hiding place my heart lurched and then almost stopped. A girl was sitting in the curved end of a long branch, as if she were in the tree's cupped hand. She was gently riding the branch up and down as she chatted languidly to a girlfriend who was sitting by the bole of the tree. Every time she reached the apex of the branch swing she rode into a beam of sunlight and her tousled blonde hair flared into a halo round her face. There could be no mistake. As she gently landed on the downward swing, I watched with slackening jaw as Jackie's creamy stilts flashed beneath her fluttering summer frock.

This time I would not miss my chance. I broke cover and slunk out from the bushes. I marched over, arm thrust stiffly out in front of me holding the bag of bull's-eyes like a battering ram. I was astonished. She had recognized me! But again the words weren't there. My offering went mute.

"Nah," she said, shaking her head and tossing her curls. "You wanna bit of gum?"

Hugely flattered, I took a silver sliver, unwrapped it and without thinking popped it in my mouth with the bull's-eye that was already there.

"Now, I 'eard you just run off to a posh school, didn't even say cheerio."

And she went soaring into the blue.

I was trying to suck and chew at the same time so the garbled explanation tumbled out in an incoherent stream. Completely lost on her was my story of how others arriving on the accident scene had thought I was part of it and had tried to bundle me into the ambulance. This was the first time I had seen her since then. Anyway, fainting was sissy. This was going to be tricky. Suddenly she was back down from the heavens. She paused in the bounce and helped herself to a bull's-eye from the open paper bag in my sticky fingers. As I leaned forward her hot spearmint breath overpowered me and I went dizzy with her proximity as her hair brushed my face.

"You're a toff now, 'n oh so clever. That right?"

She shot off back to the sunlight. This time when she flared golden at the zenith she tossed the bull's-eye down to her friend below her. She reminded me of a colored drawing in a book I had just been reading of Montgolfier, the balloonist, shedding ballast to go ever nearer the sun. Or was that Icarus with his wax wings? My head was spinning. I blurted out:

"Well, no, actually. I just know more than you.... No! No! More than I *did*, I mean!"

It was too late, though. Nothing on God's earth could take it back now.

She came hurtling down from her golden throne in the sky and, spitting the gob of chewing gum in my face, snarled:

"All right, Mister Smarty-Pants, if you're so bleeding clever, how many pounds in a ton?"

My thinking systems whirred briefly then shut down altogether. With that, she jumped clear of the branch and brushed the front of her frock as I stood gawping. The branch, released now to its upper resting place, slapped my face as it swept by. Jackie turned to her friend and, with her nose in the air, said:

"Come on, Doris. Time for tea." And they skipped off arm in arm.

I was approaching the Common Entrance exams and some of my teachers started to voice concerns about my standard of work. Mum hired extra tutoring for me in the holidays to bring me to the required level to gain entrance to King's School, Canterbury, the school on which I had set my heart.

In the winter of 1955 we finally left Tilty, and with lorry loads of Todd's books we moved to Westbourne Terrace in Paddington. Todd had come back once or twice but didn't collect his books. For the most part the heavier ones were scholastic studies of William Blake, John Martin and other visionary artists, so he either changed his subject matter or realized it was too late to rescue the books from our sticky paws.

Mum never told us why we had to leave Tilty. At first we were traumatized. It had been muddy and ramshackle, but we loved it as the only secure home we could really remember. In the same way she did at the Little Red House in Ireland, Mum spiced up the mental picture of our new flat in Paddington, London, where we were heading. We'd still all be together and Mum said we would give lots of parties. We moved and waved our childhood goodbye.

The street was a picture of decaying Victorian elegance, with two avenues of trees shielding access terraces to rows of imposing classical porticos. But there the grandeur stopped. The facade of our building was shabby, with peeling paintwork and crumbling stucco masonry. Our bell had no intercom or lock release, so we had to lean out of the window to check the caller then toss the keys to them. But to us, coming from Tilty, the flat was the height of luxury, especially as we managed to talk Mum into wall-to-wall carpeting in every room, including stairs. There were two lavatories and, luxuriously, mains electricity at the flick of a switch. In the large front living room were three windows looking out over the trees in the terrace and, with the walls of the room lined with Mum's books, it soon became very cozy.

Bashie and me lost no time in exploring the local shops that littered the grimy corners on Praed Street and Edgware Road. As we passed by the high stained walls of St. Mary's Hospital, we gazed through the smudged plate glass at the faded offerings. Approaching the hospital environs, the sad and dingy window displays changed from secondhand suitcases, old electric razors and cracked plastic Kodaks to browning trusses, support hose and perished surgical rubber-ware. The sunny fields of Essex had never seemed farther away.

Mum sent us out one drizzling February afternoon to get an icing piper to apply the decoration on a cake for Rosie's birthday. Not yet understanding the narrow range of appliance these shops could offer, we strayed far and wide in unsuccessful inquiry as the evening closed around us. We realized our mistake only when, in the last open-all-hours grocer store, the assistant asked us if we wanted the *paper* with a plain or decorative edging.

Although we considered our home almost presentable to our straitlaced and well-heeled school friends, there was always an innate and ingrained shame about the unprepossessing milieu of exotic friends that Mum continually trawled from her forays into the pubs and bars in the West End. She worked diligently and frantically during the day, going to her offices at *House and Garden* in Golden Square in the center of Soho. As Soho had always been her favorite haunt, so often in the holidays she telephoned us, a little squiffy on her first drink, to say she would be back late and we should cook our own supper. Later, Mum would come crashing up the stairs with a rabble of swearing revelers well past midnight and the party raved on into the night in her front room. Sensing that this was an unusual way of behaving compared with the demur background of some of our school friends, we never dared invite them to stay in the holidays.

Back at school I kept my head down for fear of exacting punishment, which seemed to lurk on every corner. I simply pretended to myself that no one could see me and scurried round wincing in advance of the next blow. When I was a new boy and no more than a lowly fag and therefore the lowest form of sentient being, I heard from my English master that George had been invited to address the sixth-form English class. This, of course, filled me with dread and panic and I became almost paralyzed with fear as I anticipated what was sure to be an excruciatingly embarrassing visit.

He came down and, without a word to me, addressed the sixth-form boys and a few masters (apparently none of them could understand any-

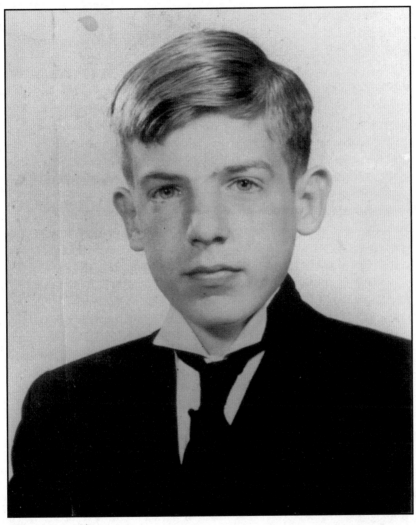

Me as school fag, 1958

thing he was driving at), pocketed the fee and returned to London. In fact, although I waited for him to call round and make contact and was bewildered when he didn't, I was secretly relieved. Nobody connected his name with mine and at least he had turned up sober. I was a little disappointed not to be even acknowledged by him. Mr. Medill, my English master, did know of the connection and was thrilled with the lecture.

* * *

In 1960 a painter called Paddy Swift and his wife, Oonagh, moved into the basement at Westbourne Terrace. Later that year, in collaboration with the formidable deaf South African poet David Wright, Paddy set up a magazine called X. It was beautifully designed and produced, with contributions from the artistic and literary worlds. Artwork by painters such as Giacometti, Aitchison, Auerbach, Colquhoun, MacBryde and Andrews appeared in their pages along with poems and articles from the likes of George, Paddy Kavanagh, McGahern, Gascoyne, Beckett, MacDiarmid, Anthony Cronin and others. Mum offered them the use of our large living room for their editorial meetings and would run around as waitress and factotum for them. I don't think she was ever asked to contribute. George, who was a good friend of Paddy and David's, had a say in most of the production, influencing its literary input. It had a short lifespan, lasting only seven quarterly issues, but between them the editors hatched quite a few rising talents on the scene.

David Wright had been deaf all his life but had been to a special deaf school as a boy and could lip-read incredibly quickly. He was a great lugubrious hulk of a man with a shock of unkempt white hair. He had a brain that was very quick and could anticipate the direction of a conversation, often saving himself unnecessary lip-reading. But to do so, he had to have a clear view of the speaker's face. People often thought it helpful if they stressed their speech by puckering their lips around words to make them clearer. If it slowed down the delivery of their thoughts, it did nothing but confuse David. George was ready-made for this kind of exchange, because he naturally spoke with punctuated animation, chopping the air with his hand and spitting out words for emphasis. He and David had been friends for years and George was therefore clearly understood. To hear them leapfrog each other's thoughts and arrive with gleeful chuckles at some unimagined conversational goal was a joy to be part of (if you could keep up). They enjoyed a similar brand of humor and when a little light literary dueling was upon them, the riposte in repartee was not necessarily George's to deliver. If David got the touché, and he often did with his uncanny ability to predict where a subject was heading, he sounded his delight with a patent foghorn blast of laughter. Many of the editorial meetings were completed in The Archery, a pub round the corner from Westbourne Terrace, where the exchanges often got very animated and, while the sponsors' money lasted, George was in his element.

Coming home from school on those days was like being beamed down from another planet. After shedding our pinstriped suits, wing-collars and waistcoats and slipping into our jeans and sweaters we could melt more convincingly with the medieval and alien life-forms that followed Mum around. A lot of them were overspill from the *X* connection and many were the kind who naturally gravitated to a literary scene. Nobody typified this more than a poet called Brian Higgins. He was supposed to be typical of a new wave of young poets and, with as yet little work published, he arrived from Batley in West Yorkshire carrying a small but promising reputation. He was to appear in the June edition of *X* and later appeared posthumously in Philip Larkin's *Oxford Book of Twentieth Century English Verse*. He may have carried respect in the world of poetry, but not with me. He could spot a tender and charitable heart three chattering rooms away. He made full use of Mum's generous nature, which, in my pompous and perhaps protective way, made me angry with him.

Although only a little over thirty at this time, he was already balding, with the rest of his coarse wiry hair shooting straight out behind him as if he'd emerged from a wind tunnel. He wore conventional but shabby clothes, layered with many tank tops and sweaters. He was quite unrepentant about this situation and took alms wherever he could find them. He came to Westbourne Terrace for tea once and among the others there was Henrietta Law (who became Henrietta Moraes when later she married the Indian poet Dom Moraes, another contributor to *X* and an editorial assistant for the magazine). She was foulmouthed but beautiful and totally uncompromising in her attitude. She had a cripplingly sardonic humor, which she embellished with casual profanity. Higgins asked Mum, "Hey, luv, d'yer mind if I take a bath?" The roomful of chattering people fell silent, and then everyone roared with laughter. ("Higgins" and "bath" in the same sentence was almost unimaginable.) When Henrietta finally stopped honking and hooting, she said fondly:

"Hey, cunty, mind you leave me some hot water. And if you piss in it, wipe the bath clean. I'm after you."

Higgins was a long time in the bathroom and returned looking scrubbed and polished. Up went Henrietta, but she came back down seconds later. She found Higgins sniffing round the kitchen and gave him a savage kick on the shins.

"You dirty [kick] lazy [kick] faggot [kick]. Go and clean the fucking bath. It's still full of your revolting pubic hairs, which are so fucking springy they refuse to go down the plughole!"

And she pushed him out the door as I squirmed in disbelief at her abuse. I made a mental note not to cross her. Higgins, who was used to being treated like this, leaned over and told me to close my mouth—it was only her convent education talking.

Mum would prepare marvelous stews for us kids that she put on the slow-cook hob for hours. This almost solved the problem of a continual food supply for us in the holidays when she couldn't get home from work and we all came in at different hours. Almost solved, but not quite. The pot, while cooking, was vulnerable to hostile raids. It was like a carcass left out on the veldt by a mother leopard for her cubs in the hope the hyenas wouldn't get it first. I once came in late, starving after a game of rugby, and asked Mum if there was any tea.

"On the stove," she told me. The stove in our kitchen was next to the kitchen door, and as I barged in I butted someone's back. I say "someone" only because identification was at first difficult. This person had an arm and his whole head inside Mum's largest stewing pot, and greedy snuffling and slurping noises came from inside. The slurping stopped abruptly and the head rose, scrofulous hair first. A figure turned to face me.

"Eh, Christophe. Um sorry! Um sorry! But my oh my, that were grand."

Higgins's mouth and nose dripped stew and gravy like a cathedral gargoyle after a rainstorm. He smiled and as his stained hand clutched the handle of the pan, he raised it above his head and let the last lumps of stew fall slowly into his mouth. Wiping it clean with the back of his jacket sleeve, he took me through to the living room, where a small party had started. I tossed my kit bag up the stairs as I went through.

"'Ere now, lad, yer should gie up t'Union rubbish'n take up League! They should pay you fr'all yer work!"

We had many heated discussions about Rugby League and Union, usually centered on my not getting money for playing. Unbelievably, he told me he had once played Rugby League and he was keen that I should take the game up professionally. He had different matters on his mind now and his eyes swung over to the fire at the other end of the room. (Mum continually lit our coal-fire grates despite the introduction of smokeless zones in London.) George was there, one foot on the fender and an elbow on the mantel. His other hand was slicing the air and he spat out words like poisonous pips. Higgins gazed longingly and lovingly for a while, then drooled:

"Ooooh, but aye, Christophe ... I love yer father!"

And with that he crawled across the floor on all fours and kissed George's shoe, which he had planted on the fender. George's eyes blazed in fury as he was interrupted in full flow. He stopped for a second and then, theatrically gritting his teeth, swung an exaggerated kick at Higgins, who rolled onto his back and burst into uninhibited wailing. It was, of course, a humorous pantomime they both enjoyed, but I was appalled at the time and felt increasingly sorry for Higgins. He died at the age of thirty-five. George announced that his heart broke in a morbid despair over the lack of recognition for his work. When I heard, I was upset but not surprised. I had grown fond of him.

My reaction to Higgins was similar to the one I had to another poet, Paul Potts. He had been an occasional visitor to Tilty. We liked him well enough, but there was something weird and remote about his self-pity that we children instinctively shied away from. He too was balding and had a stutter that he mixed with rapid blinking and an amused chuckle as he started a sentence. He had a sparse but effective output of poetry and prose centered on the publication in Dublin of a work entitled *Dante Called You Beatrice*.

When he had earlier stayed with us at Tilty, he cut a much tougher figure. He had once been in the Israeli army and we could see him gazing out of our family album from a set of black-and-white contact prints that Mum had rescued from a Deakin photo session for *Vogue* magazine. In an attempt to exaggerate this uncompromising attitude, he had turned his trench-coat collar up round his chiseled and granite face. Later he was to deteriorate into a sad figure and was barred from Soho pubs for incontinence as he bummed drinks. He survived until 1990, due to the offices of a good friend and social worker.

I went to see him in 1988 and found him housebound. He rarely got out of his bed, he told me. He had narrowly escaped death the night before after setting his blankets alight with a cigarette. His rank dressing gown flapped open to reveal glimpses of flaccid flesh. He was so much more vulnerable and pathetic than when I had seen him before. While we talked he rubbed his back against the wall from an itch that would not go away. Unwisely, I had brought him a takeaway curry and half a bottle of whiskey. He wolfed the curry down and was necking the bottle when he stopped and then, calm as you like, vomited a long column of Biriani onto the bed. He wittered on unabashed while I cleaned it up. Two years later he died from smoke inhalation. This time he had been too slow to escape a similar bedroom fire.

* * *

Mum could be very secretive—she had a "masked heart," as she put it—but I never knew her actually to lie to us about anything. She would keep her head down and hope that we would never ask her directly. I can remember, however, asking her directly once. It was a very confusing time for me at Westbourne Terrace. With a certain public schoolboy indignation I asked why George had never enlisted during the war. I said that he seemed to have draft-dodged his way around the world while his comrades enlisted and lost their lives. I half expected a curt reference to pacifism and conscientious objection, but she appeared startled and mumbled something about George feeling his poetry too valuable a commodity for him to risk losing as a soldier. It was a phrase I'm sure she had rehearsed in anticipation of the question and I thought this pretty damn lame, considering the number of his fellow poets who had died. My indignation was calmed when she added that George was as much in reaction to his father's starched military attitude as anything else.

I often became angry and ashamed of his disloyal, underhand and outrageous behavior, and Mum wouldn't really try to defend him. She just asked me to forgive him. It still left me feeling that even a poet or artist, be he the greatest that had ever lived, did not have the right to live outside society's rules while lying comfortably protected in its bosom (not always *so* comfortably with George). It made forgiveness difficult.

When we left Tilty and moved to Westbourne Terrace, the Roberts had to relocate too. For a while they largely disappeared from our lives, but we heard their careers had gained momentum and then faded. As their antics became wilder, stories abounded. I laughed when I heard that in a quiet London suburb one Christmas, the police were called by the neighbors to a party. A naked and livid Colquhoun brandishing an ax had been glimpsed chasing a naked and laughing MacBryde through the shrubbery.

Once, as a family group, we went for a night out from Westbourne Terrace to a private viewing of a Colquhoun retrospective at the Establishment Club. This was a members-only venue in Soho that frequently put on small theatrical shows downstairs (the comedian Lenny Bruce, among others, would appear there) and often mounted art shows upstairs. As we circled the paintings and drawings, Georgina came over, tugged my sleeve and with a flushed face told me to look at the large sketchbook. I was horrified when, as I turned the pages, I found I was looking at a graphic cartoon sequence in black ink depicting two bodies in an act of buggery. I was

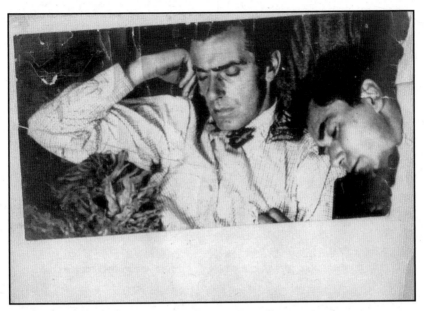

Robert Colquhoun and Robert MacBryde, spring, 1952

shocked to realize this is what our guardians had been doing to each other all these years and that the bodies in the drawings were theirs.

Sometimes the Roberts were invited to Westbourne Terrace for parties. More than once, as the evening wore on, Colquhoun's voice, thickened with whiskey, would rumble and explode, and this would be followed by the crash of a breaking bottle. For a few seconds panic seized me and I was back in my childhood bedroom, transfixed with horror and praying for a miracle to save me.

In 1962, when Colquhoun was forty-seven years old, he became ill and one day fell down clutching at rolls of paper laid out for a monotype he had been working on. Seconds later he died in MacBryde's arms from a heart attack. MacBryde was inconsolable. Mum let him have the small spare room on the mezzanine at Westbourne Terrace during his grieving, and when he finally left for a stay in Dublin we cleared it out. Under the bed among the dried excrement and crusty food we found dozens of empty liquor bottles, some still brimming with old and yellowing piss, even though a lavatory adjoined his room. We had often heard him sobbing into the small hours. We dubbed this little room the Wailing Room. Four years later MacBryde was killed by a Dublin taxi, hit as he staggered out of a pub.

Mum silently wept when, on a trip to Scotland later, we failed to find the Roberts' twinned graves as we combed a vast cemetery in Ayrshire under a gray and spitting sky.

Mum loved to throw a good party, something she did on a regular basis once we moved into Westbourne Terrace. The first thing she tackled was the guest list, and the more guests she could invite the better. I still have some of these lists today, scribbled out in her spidery scrawl in nervous anticipation of the coming fun. She made lists whenever she could, culminating periodically in an alphabetical one of all her friends at the time. Her children even got a mention in these. The striking thing about her party lists was the wide range of interests the guests represented. The next most important thing after the guest list was the booze. We emptied the local off-license of beer and wine, also hiring glasses. If I remember rightly, particularly at Westbourne Terrace, we never had a full complement of matching glasses at any of our homes. So many of Mum's guests through the years, when the drink was on them, would throw a glass to punctuate their conversation or, in a gesture of love or fury, sweep the tabletop to make a point. She secreted spirits around the flat in places only she knew, for those of her friends with "needy, nervous dispositions." Sebastian and Rosie operated our new Dansette gramophone. Georgina and Mum did the food. I'd be on the door and all of us helped to distribute drinks.

The core of the guest list was her friends from Soho, whom she endearingly termed (partly from the title of one of her books) her "rogues and rascals." They kept me on my toes as bouncer and a gentle enforcer at the top of the stairs.

Hetta Empson was one of Mum's fondest friends. She was originally from South Africa and retained a slight trace of Voortrekker in her accent, as Mum still had traces of Canadian. She was married to the revered poet and philosopher William Empson and she never missed one of Mum's parties, even if she hadn't been invited. At one of these, infused with Dutch courage, I was braying pompously concerning my readiness to fight for my country should we ever go to war. Nearby, Hetta, whom I hardly knew then, suddenly spun round without warning and slapped me hard across the face. She cried endearingly, "Oh, you foolish boy!" and hugged me. I was completely flummoxed and went scarlet in confusion. The times since then I wish I'd had the courage to do the same when overhearing a grating bore. She was in a beautiful gold dress that evening, and later on she

Elizabeth Smart's Copyshop 24 Peter Street London W1 Gerrard 5714 Elizabeth Smart's
Copyshop 24 Peter Street London W1 Gerrard 5714 Elizabeth Smart's Copyshop 24 Peter
Street London W1 Gerrard 5714 Elizabeth Smart's Copyshop 24 Peter Street London W1
Gerrard 5714 Elizabeth Smart's Copyshop 24 Peter Street London W1 Gerrard 5714 Eliz
abeth Smart's Copyshop 24 Peter Street London W1 Gerrard 5714 Elizabeth Smart's Cop
yshop 24 Peter Street London W1 Gerrard 5714 Elizabeth Smart's Copyshop 24 Peter St

Clare Rendlesham
Ruby Rae
Julie Reisz (+ Karel)
Frank Rudman
Isabel Rawsthorne
Henrietta Rous
Moray + Bobbie Reid
Glenys Randell
Gordon Ronan

Claude Virgin
Stephe Vicinzey
Sally Vincent

Alan + Olive Synge
John Smithwick
Marie Singes
Michael Summerskill
C. H Sisson
Helen + James Sutherland
Laurence Scott
Graham Spry
Penny + Percy Sher
Rebecca + John Starkey
Jane + Gavin (+ Kevin) Scott

Tom Wolsey
Denis Whelan
Paul Winstanley
Antonia White
Edward Williams
Hugo Williams,
Vivien + John White
Martin Wilde
Susan Ward
Francis Wyndham
Fay Weldon + Ron

Merilyn Thorold
Anne Trehearne
Ken Thompson

Mum's list of contemporary friends [front]

Hester Michael Asquith
Janet Allen
Craigie Aitchison
Sally Aitchison
Drusie Aitchison
Vivien Asquith
Henry Ashley
Patrick Alexander
Stephen + Carole Amor

John + Georgie Birtle
George + Elspeth Barker
Rose, Christopher, Clair John + Sebastian Barker
Sylvia Bruce
Rose Barnicoat (Cook)
Rita Biddulph
Muriel Belcher
Kit + Ilse Barker
Olivier, Bruce, Jeff Bernard
Leylord Bardwell
Francis + Grania Boylan
Brigid Brophy
Frank Bowling
George Begley
Cynthia Blyth
Marion Boyars
Tim + Olive Ball
Frank Bearland
Tim Behrens
Ann Barr

Denis Curtis
Dickie Chopping
Prunella Clough
Ann Chadwick
Jean Chambers
Patrick Carr
Colin Crawford
Alison Chitty

Harry Diamond
Marsh Dunbar
Hugo Davenport
Sally Ducks...
Nichette de Vas
Michael Dempsey

Hetta + William Empson
Moag Emerson
Noelle + Paul Edwards

Mary + Germano Facetti
Katie Fitzroy
Dan Farson
Fanny + Stephen Freud-Laton
Fenella Fielding
John Fairfax
Sandy Fawkes
Margaret + West de Wend Fenton
Eva Figes
Mike Farrell
Benny Fischer
Gary Farr

Anne Graham Bell
John Glashan
Martin + Fiona Green
Mary + Gordon Graves

Dennis Hackett
John Heath-Stubbs
Penelope Hare
Mary Hillard
Veronica Hull
Tristram Hull + 2 wife
Griell Hastings + Hermione
Tommy Hawkyard
Mrs Mathew Halton
David Hughes

Ruth Inglis

Mary, Casper, John + Caroline
Sara John
Paul Johnson
Hugh Johnson

Paddy Kitchen
Irma Kurtz
Katharine Kavanagh
Francis Kyle
Eddie Linden
Michael Law
Doris Lessing
Jay + Fran Landesman
Myra Loshak (Michael Sards)
David Leitch
Willy Landels
Sebastian + Rose Ann Lockwood
Sue Hynes
Juliet Hyson
Maria + Alec Kroll
Eleanor Moynihan
Nicholas Mosley
Dom Moraes
Henrietta Moraes
John + Dora Morley
Hedli MacNeice
Bimba MacNeice (Chris Shepherd)
Ross Maclaren
Olivia Manning
Andrey Sagal + David Mitchell
Christine McCausland
John MacDonald
John McGahern
John McNeill
Bryce McNab
Joe McCrae
Pippa Mellip
Graham Mason
Paul + Bobby Mason
Ann Murray

Geoffrey + Maris Nicholson
Jill Neville
Anne Nicholls
Frank + Geraldine Norman
Nigel Lewis

Peter Owen
Edna O'Brien
Charles Osborne
Philip Oakes

Alexander Plunket Greene
Paul Potts
Neal Pennitt

Mary Quant

Mum's list of contemporary friends [back]

let out a loud roar that was swiftly followed by the crunch of gristle as her fist found its home. I winced expecting it to be followed by shattering glass. But no, this time it was shredding cloth. She was having a frank exchange with her current boyfriend, Josh, and in frustration he had ripped the dress off her back. She simply tied the flapping remnants around her and with her bra and knickers on display carried on as if nothing had happened.

During that same party a colorful photojournalist called Dan Farson arrived. He swept in late to the party with a bodyguard of able seamen straight from the East End docks. Bibbed in smart blue and white, they stayed close to him, feeling perhaps a little out of their depth in this bohemian sea. But not close enough, as later became obvious, because I was called off the door to intervene in a scuffle that had broken out and arrived to find Dan lashing out at someone as blood bubbled from his nose. He was soft and squashy with alcohol when I grabbed him. As I held him to the floor in a half nelson, I remembered he wasn't alone. I looked up and there they were, encircling us, interlocked with outstretched arms to keep the party crowd back. One, with the build of a water buffalo, his muscles cocked and quivering, called:

"Okay, Dan, just say the word and I clear the room."

But Dan, although face down and with blood gushing from his nose into Mum's carpet, seemed to be quite enjoying himself as I rode his backside, holding his arm up his back.

"No, no. No problem! As you were, crew! Carry on, bosun!"

Very clever of Mum to have laid a red carpet in her party room when we first moved in.

George re-emerged into our life at Westbourne Terrace. He had been abandoned by Cass, his girlfriend for the last ten years, who had absconded in the night with Patrick Humble, George's nephew. George had also been devastated by the death of Big Mumma in May 1957, and went to Mum for consolation. As part of this consolation she had taken him on a trip to Paris and then, just as he and Mum appeared to be making an attempt to be more permanently reconciled, they had a nasty fight. They had returned from Paris, which hadn't been a great success, as he grew morose about Cass's departure and where he made embarrassing and persistent proposals of marriage to Mum.

He stormed out of Westbourne Terrace after a row with her, only to return that night of December 15. He was particularly surly after a drinking bout at the pub and had with him a pack of sycophants, eager to placate him. In the course of the evening he grew cantankerous and hit her. She flew at him in rage, but he pinioned her arms to her side. She relaxed and, pretending to kiss him in a gesture of conciliation, changed the kiss into a bite that severed his upper lip. More blood pumped out onto her red carpet, and George was taken to hospital and stitched up.

The next day, with a black eye patch over one eye, and looking battered, apologetic and very self-conscious, Mum arrived at King's School to take me home for the end of term. Georgina was full of hilarious stories of the morning's desperate hunt for the eye patch. Mum wanted a black one when every chemist they tried could offer only pink. At the time, George affected outrage, and let all know that he had been attacked by a fury from hell for no apparent reason and that she had clung to his upper lip with snarling fangs like a rabid bitch. Later, he said the whole thing was a jape and attempted to treat it as a love bite. He grew a grubby mustache to cover the scar and this accentuated his wounded look.

He started to visit the flat in the afternoons, knowing Mum was out at work. To see us, he said. At first I was happy and a little flattered. He had never come round to visit us there on a regular basis before. I'm not sure where he was staying at the time, but I remember we had to let him in the door at first until he managed to steal a set of keys for himself. He would come round, hug us all hello, and spend the afternoon reading in Mum's book-lined bedroom. I never saw him leave. There simply came a time in the course of an afternoon when he wasn't there any more. These visits, he insisted, should be kept from Mum. He mumbled some story about not wanting her to know, so soon after their fight, that he was spending time with us. It seemed almost plausible to me, but why, if he had come round to see us, didn't he spend more time actually in our company? And why did we never see him go?

Eventually the story of his visits did get through to Mum, who immediately rushed round to her bookshelves and quietly moaned, "Oh God, no." Many of her dearest and most cherished volumes had vanished. The ones that were missing were conspicuous by their absence and were a haul only he would have picked. Yet again, Mum never appeared especially angry. She was just resigned.

"He thinks all books are printed primarily for his benefit, so he always just helps himself. Especially if they are *by* him."

Many of her first editions of his work, lovingly collected since before she had met him, had gone. I was angry. Not least because the pilfering was systematic and carefully worked out to enlist our compliance while we were being duped.

At this point, as suddenly as he had reappeared in our lives, he vanished. We were perhaps too excited to notice, because at the beginning of the summer holidays of 1958 all four of us were due to leave for a trip to America. This trip was chaperoned by Aunt Jane, who had taken a holiday house near Provincetown on Cape Cod and where, with our cousin D'Arcy, we spent the whole summer at beach parties and surfing and sunbathing.

In the middle of our stay, and out of the blue, George came to see us. We hadn't the faintest idea he was in America. He stayed in the house with us for a few days and then left. Although at the time it was no more than we children expected, he seemed at first to be on very friendly terms with Aunt Jane, only to row furiously with her and then vanish.

He had in fact returned to New York, where he dropped in to see Jessica and the twins, about whom we of course knew nothing. On being pressed by Jessica for a more formal relationship with this part of his family, he swiftly left New York to take up an offer from the separated wife of a close friend of his, Dede Farrelly. She was from a wealthy Missouri background, and after her husband John left she could support herself alone in New York with her two children. Her means also allowed her to quit the city and holiday in Pennsylvania at the end of August when the heat became unbearable, and it was there that she invited George to come and stay. She and George enjoyed a peaceful few weeks there, as George sought sanctuary from the turmoil of his recent past.

Although only seven months after proposing marriage to Mum in Paris and three weeks after seeing his legal wife in New York, he felt emboldened enough to propose another marriage. This time the obstacles to this proposed new union proved insurmountable. Dede found that she would have to give up custody of her two children or remain domiciled in Nevada for a long period, should the quickie divorce be completed in Las Vegas. Also, Jessica continued to stand firm in her Catholic beliefs of marriage, as she had done seventeen years earlier, refusing to agree to a divorce.

George stayed in America for another year and a half, where, a year after their holiday together in Pennsylvania, Dede bore George his eighth child. Early in 1959 the extension to George's visa ran out and he and Dede decided to leave America and live in London, taking a large house in Chelsea. The next summer they took a holiday in Rome to attend the 1960

Olympic Games, and from there they never returned. They took a large flat in nearby Fregene and sent for Dede's children, who had been on holiday in Norway with a nanny. During these last two years, and despite the fact that only recently he'd been on a brief stay in London, we had very little communication with him.

He resurfaced in my life in the form of a stream of urbane correspondence that arrived on the letters table at school from this strange place called Fregene in Italy. George made this contact largely because of promptings by Mum, who was concerned about the standard of my handwriting, which, with important exams looming, was fast becoming illegible. Penmanship became an even more pressing matter when I was offered a provisional place at Oxford.

My housemaster at King's School had contacted a chum of his who was the principal at Corpus Christi College, Oxford. After the following letter and an interview with me clutching my best essays on E.M. Forster and a discreet mention of my rugby record, the college decided they would admit me with the very minimum of qualifications:

From the President.

Corpus Christi College,
Oxford
1st January, 1962

Dear Wilson,

I am glad you have thought of Corpus for your present Head of House, Christopher Barker. We give some of our Commoner places to boys who do well in Scholarship Examinations. But for the rest we like to pick out candidates who have something quite definite to offer over and above reasonable academic qualifications. We should certainly like to consider this boy for a place in 1963. It would not, of course, be easy for us at this stage to make room for him in 1962, but it seems clear from what you say that 1963 might be better and more convenient for him also. I hope he will get at least two A-Levels needed in the summer. As only one of them can be in science he will have to have O-Level Latin. I imagine that he already has an O-Level pass in French.

I enclose a form of application which he might complete and send me now. We can consider his plans in more detail later in the year.

With all good wishes for the New Year
Yours sincerely,
W.R. Hardie

King's Canterbury vs. Tonbridge School, Christmas 1960

I was ecstatic but a little concerned about the Latin. I had dropped Latin in the middle of the O-Level course. Since prep school and Colonel Gossen's unbending application of the declensions, I hadn't had the enthusiasm to master it. These exams were vital, with failure not an option, and to that end I had received the following letter, triple-spaced with address in red type, early in 1963 before my July exams:

Via Nemorense 72 Rome Italy 15 ii 62

My dear Christopher

I received from Mummy this morning a letter in which she tells me that there's a prospect, which we must turn into a good prospect, of a place at Corpus for you in 1963. First of all let me tell you how delighted I am to learn this, because both Mummy and I know only too well that three or so years you spend (as we hope) at the University may well be very very happy for you; and also because we both know that, whereas not all young men may be suited to the character of a University you, for all kinds of reasons, really are. It is, and I've just used the word, a matter of character. I believe that the time has just about come in your own affairs when the cultivation of the things of the mind may seem to you both valuable and good. They are. And in the process of the growth of one's character they may finally make the difference between a man constructed of nothing much, and a man constructed of that truly beautiful material, appreciation. But above everything else I don't want to bore you with a letter about abstract principles. One of my reasons for writing is to quote you the little sentence Mummy wrote on the back of the envelope of her letter: "C's handwriting is getting dangerously illegible. Could you influence in time for the exams? Most urgent for myopic examiners."

So that, quite simply, is what I'm writing you about. I have the "write" to do this because, when I was almost exactly your own age, I decided to turn my own handscript into something at least tolerably decent—for slipshod handscript is just as boorish to its correspondent as slapdash speech to a friend. It's not in the least difficult to work out a perfectly good handscript of ones own. All you need is a good model. When I decided to do so I went to the Italian scholars of the Renaissance, who employed a lovely script, and I did my best to copy them. My handwriting may not be the best in Europe, but it's by no means the worst. I've deliberately not written this letter by hand because that would seem to be TOO affected. What I suggest is that you get a large (not FAT) note book and give a few hours now and then to your own personal adaptation of the alphabets I send with this. They are, roughly, those of the old

Italian scholars. Don't ape them sedulously; just use them as a guide. In less than three weeks the whole horrible operation will be over. You will have a good hand. Now please forgive all this lecturing (but then, after all, I AM a Professor) and write me a letter (it don't matter how short) once a week for the next month. And again all my love.

 Your loving father

 George

The letter had an addenda sheet in ruled paper with an alphabet carefully copied out in pencil.

I sat the exams, never quite managing to redesign my handwriting. I didn't have time to master it before I had to take hurried notes in class when I would revert back to what had been little more than a sort of personalized shorthand. As soon as the exams were over and the holidays began I set out on a trip hitchhiking across France. Mum was taking a holiday house on a Greek island that summer and I had it in mind to travel through Italy and take the ferry through the Corinth Canal to join her.

With two friends I traveled through France and, crossing the border into Italy, we stayed at a youth hostel in Carrara for a few days. From Carrara I traveled alone to Fregene to find out how George passed his days. When I got there I found his house was, disappointingly, on a modern housing estate close by the sea, which struck me as very unlike George. I didn't know this was temporary accommodation lent by a friend. George was occupying it as a holiday home after he had moved out from Via Nemorense (the address on the last letter to me). A girl and three little boys and their mother lived with him, the youngest an eighteen-month-old toddler whom George doted on. I spent several pleasant days there and George was generous to a fault. This was an extraordinary about-turn from the mustachioed pilferer I remembered from two years before.

He prepared for our evenings out with great wit and charm, sipping a Campari-and-soda aperitif with me in the garden as the sun went down. The woman in the house, who circled round and made sure we had everything we needed, was the mother of the children and stayed tactfully in the background. We would then stroll out and George selected, from the many restaurants he knew, one that suited our mood for the night.

After a few evenings that followed this pattern I sensed he had something to say. After sitting down at a table one night and enthusing about the

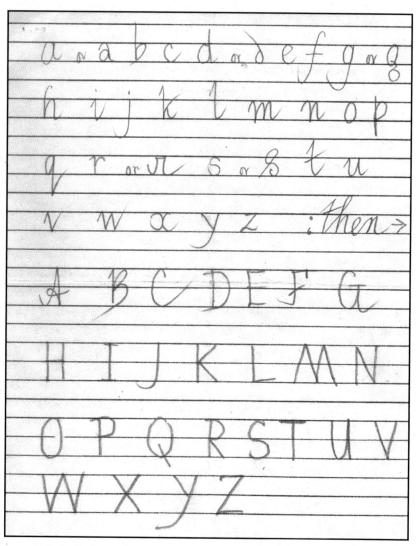

Alphabet by George Barker

Italians and their graciousness as they strolled by, he moved on to Mum. In words only a poet could get away with, he talked of his love for her. He recounted a time they were in the dining car on a train going through the Rocky Mountains at sunset. A shaft of light from the setting sun pierced the mountain crags and, passing through the train window, bounced off the jumbled disarray of empty glasses on their table. It sparkled into her face, lighting up her head of golden "coronals" and set her eyes on fire. She would forever be his sunrise over the Rockies. My eyes were stinging with tears as I fought back the emotion. Then, before I could recover, he told me he had asked her to marry him on more than one occasion and for reasons best known to herself she had turned him down each time. Without any noticeable animosity, he explained carefully that she had simply thrown him out and taken up with Michael Wickham. He picked up the tab, paid it, and we left. How I felt I had misjudged him.

But something was not quite right. Was it in the way he dandled the youngest boy on his knee the next day and called him "soooh brave a little heart" that had a ring of familiarity about it?

When I explained my itinerary to him, he asked if I could hold on for few days. He was about to buy a new Mercedes and, if I wanted, he would take me across Italy to Brindisi to catch the ferry to Greece. I said I would be honored and agreed to hang on for the lift. The intended purchase was delayed, so he said we'd take his little Ford and go anyway.

The whole stay had been a dream to me. I had come to terms with my father and readjusted my view of his past. Our trip across Italy was such fun. George slipped into the Ford driving seat and pulled on his string-backed driving gloves and we were off on the rally. We fairly skipped along the Appian Way. As he made every cog in the gearbox count, he didn't let one classical reference slip until all the countryside was alive with myth, lore and legend.

I didn't want the journey to end, but a bewildering incident occurred at the point of arriving in Brindisi. At his suggestion we were taking a dip in the Adriatic, as if in a biblical baptism, and I referred to "the plebs of ancient Rome," hoping he would spot my nod to the classics. It had rather the opposite effect, as he exploded with rage, forbidding me ever to use the word "plebs" again and denouncing my privileged education compared with his schooling of miserable poverty. His reaction left me completely dumbfounded and hurt, but then, as suddenly as it had appeared, the cloud passed and we carried on as if nothing had happened. Despite this out-burst, we parted as friends and I resumed my trip to Greece. I had been utterly charmed and treasured my days with him.

When I reached Hydra, I couldn't wait to tell the story to Mum. Despite the enthusiasm with which I retold the details of the last few days, I thought she was being somewhat circumspect in her reaction. Then, slowly at first, and with great gentleness, she started to put me right on a few things. I suppose she felt she should have done so a long time ago.

The woman with an American accent who had behaved as an impeccable handmaiden to George and me was indeed his partner, Dede Farrelly. The little girl I had met, and an absent boy, were Dede's children by her marriage to John Farrelly, but the two youngest were George's children by Dede and, therefore, my half brothers. It was true that he had asked Mum to marry him several times, but it was true too that when he asked he was married already. To a Roman Catholic, Mum explained, who was now living in the US and called Jessica and who would not divorce him. He had three children by her, one who had been given up for adoption, older than I, and two twins, a boy and a girl, some five weeks younger than I. But she stressed that even if he hadn't been married, she wouldn't have married him. And yes, she had taken up with Michael Wickham, but only after George had absconded from Tilty, with his goods and his gear, and left her alone with four children and run off to the south of France with a girl called Cass. She told me I mustn't be angry with him, because she still loved him very much, and the most important thing was that I had been able to have this precious time with him. She would do nothing but speak well of him.

I sat dumbfounded, unable to speak. It was far too much to take in. My father and mother not married? I was appalled. Maybe I had known intuitively all along but had just never spelled it out to myself. Half brothers and half sisters? Why had nobody told me before? I felt betrayed and hurt. Surely it couldn't have been Mum's fault. And George had lied. Or had he? Wasn't it just omission?

This explanation Mum had given made the situation ten times worse. It just begged more questions. But there was an important difference now. I had always assumed that even though George may have been a rogue, we four were his only children and therefore special. But we weren't. He had not just another family but two more. Nonetheless it was a fact that, by five weeks, I was his eldest son. All I wanted was a piece of him all my own, however small, and as I retraced my steps back to England that summer I clung to that fact.

When I arrived back from Hydra I had a nasty shock. I had failed my exams. In the same bundle of letters as the exam results was a postcard from George: "Got it. Magnificent. 110 m.p.h. Please let me know how your voyage on the Agamemnon went etc. Love to all, muchly. Geo."

A week later a letter arrived:

Via Scauri
7, Fregene,
Rome.

22 ix 62

Dear Christopher

The day before yesterday I had a card from Mummy (sent when she was between planes at Fiumincine airport—I was also there reading a paper) in which she mentioned in passing the wretched business of yr examinations.

I send this very brief word to hope that you won't let the disappointment (if there is any) get too deep under the skin. Do you have another opportunity? (I mean as regards Oxford?) Certainly if it's just Oxford then its not a matter of absolutely unparallelable importance. There are other Universities.

I'd like to hear how you enjoyed Greece & how the voyage on the Agamemnon went & what you found earth quakes like &c. I got back to Fregene in one day—we'd taken a route [?] as long again as the normal one, which is up through Bari. But I certainly don't regret that & hope you don't either. The Mercedes is, of course, marvelous. All I have to do now is to get the money to keep it on the road. And to finance the trip I would so much like us to take either later in the autumn or next spring. I can't tell you how much I enjoyed seeing you here, and I only wish you had received gentler hospitality: nor shall I easily forget the drive to the Adriatic. There is no better navigator than you, no matter what the examiners may think of yr applied trigonometry. Please write.

Love,
George.

Handwritten up the right hand side of page one was: "Nota bene: I hate to say this, but there are worse things in human life than not attending Oxford University."

This letter, looking at it now, seems nothing but love and concern. It was only two days after his good friend Robert Colquhoun had died. At the time it made my blood boil. Since her shattering revelations, and despite Mum's attempt to exonerate his behavior, a seed of anger had been germinating inside me. As I was growing up, although my family history was different from that of my peers, never knowing the truth about it always led me to believe this was just the way things were, for everybody.

I'd seen my father behaving badly and heard disturbing stories, but now I could allocate blame. Every word in this letter screamed treachery to me, and my reaction was made worse by my frustration from my exam failure. I remained confused by his N.B. Had not his earlier letter to me concerning my handwriting urged that I construct myself "of that truly beautiful material, appreciation" at Oxford? To him they were just words and he really knew how to use them. I became angry at his apparent sudden concern over my future. Where had he been all my life, anyway? It was only Mum's telling him to write to me that had produced this letter, and here he was with more empty promises about more trips we might take. I felt duped and heaped more scorn on his words as I remembered the cunning book thief lurking at Mum's bookshelves while we children were delighted each day by his arrival. Perhaps because of my low ebb at the time, and this sense of betrayal, I laid down a layer of mistrust in him that never left me.

These disappointments were carefully bottled away and I diligently and quickly set about repairing the damage. I took up plan B and immediately set about applying to Princeton University, New Jersey, in the US. I knew from Mum that we had cousins in the States and wrote to one of them that I knew to be the president of the Canadian branch of the Princeton alumni association. My old headmaster from King's School gave me a sparkling recommendation and, with these résumés, I applied to the college admissions office.

On returning from a trip to Denmark in the early spring of 1963, I climbed up the never-ending stairs to the flat at Westbourne Terrace to find a large white envelope from the director of admissions at Princeton. It had already been opened and scribbled on the front was:

"Christopher! Congratulations! & please forgive our opening it—we couldn't bear the suspense. Love Mummy & Geo." ... & Geo? Where the hell had he come from? I marched into the sitting room and there they were in bed together having a late breakfast. I was dumbfounded, yet again. Was he back with Mum or what?

Sex for me at this time was largely a guessing game. I hadn't had any instruction and certainly no practice. Did I need it? Who doesn't? But, for heaven's sake, I mused in my naïveté, when push comes to shove, surely it was only *natural*. Public school had been single-sex, so no joy there. Sex education at King's had amounted to learning quickly how to cope with the lascivious advances of some notorious senior boys when you were a fag. Further tempting nuggets of information were gleaned by scouring lines in our biology primer—over and over again, until the book would surrender and automatically fall open at this dog-eared page.

These nuggets left me with an unsatisfied feeling. Strange diagrams of an antlered reindeer's face next to what appeared to be the cross section of a coupling I took from a railway carriage only made the whole thing more complicated and mystifying. Voracious with curiosity, under these diagrams one read, "becomes longer and erect, and seeds which have been stored in the body of the male are introduced into the body of the female …" But where? When? How? This wasn't sex education, it was zoology and apart from sniggering street wisdom I had left school bewildered and none the wiser.

Mum was keen to enthuse about almost every eligible girl's comeliness to me. She had some obscure scale, which baffled me, for judging their suitability. I considered her choices far too dowdy. I watched with delight as the hemline raced up the thigh. Then miniskirts arrived and I would be instantly blinded to any personality charms by a luscious flash of leg. In an attempt to solve this problem in one cowardly and detached move, Mum left what she thought an appropriate book conspicuously under our noses. It was called *How Babies Are Born* and, as if in total logical explanation of the whole conundrum, the book had a photo of Michelangelo's *David* in it.

Although we talked for hours about everything that troubled us, sex was taboo with Mum and she soon abandoned any further attempts to enlighten her children. Ironically, she had been asked a year earlier to write a biography of Marie Stopes, a pioneer in the field of family planning, so she had more than enough information at her fingertips if she needed it. I am absolutely certain that if she had tried to explain the mystifying procedures of sexual love to me at that time, after excruciating embarrassment at the start, we would have been helpless with laughter.

I should not have worried about these mystifying procedures. In my first sexual encounter I was inexplicably spoiled by a gift from a stunning blonde called Lucia. I was loitering on the edge of the dance floor of the Establishment nightclub, musing over the disturbing images I had seen in Colquhoun's exhibition upstairs, when I was seized and pulled into the heaving throng. Long blonde hair fell across her face as she pressed me to a see-through dress whose hem seemed to stop just below a hip belt. As she hugged me to her curves, she parted her hair just enough for her tipsy eye to pinion me in a tangle of embarrassment and pleasure that brought a rush of blood to my cheeks. She, of course, was not overwhelmed by my good looks or lack of them but hell-bent on humiliating a boyfriend, who was lurking jealously nearby with belligerent intent. He stepped forward and without warning bludgeoned me in the face as I jiggled by. Every cell in my body went screeching into fight mode as he backed away. She cleverly and flatteringly caressed the aggression out of me as the bouncers moved her boyfriend away. Later that night, in my single bed, and under the blanket with toy soldiers marching round the edge, she rewarded me for my understudy part in her love life the best way she knew how. She rather spoiled the feeling of gratitude I felt for her, as I lay sated from this long-yearned-for experience, by suddenly sitting up and clapping her hands in delight like a happy sea lion. With great enthusiasm she hooted:

"Surely it's not. It can't be. Oh how *sweet*, Christopher. It's your first time!"

I had decided to go to Princeton University via Canada in the hope of seeing my Canadian relatives. I had never closely inspected our Canadian family background and wanted to find out more. I was aware only that we were Red Indians and it was from Canada that food parcels, Christmas presents and maple sugar came to us with strange stamps and exciting lists on custom declaration labels.

Georgina was in Canada, where she was working with a troupe of dancers called the Guilda Review in Montreal. Guilda was apparently a French-Canadian female impersonator surrounded by a troupe of high-kicking TV toppers of which Georgina was one. Georgina had been nervous about her grandmother's reaction to her dancing and had expected disapproval. She needn't have worried, because in an attempt to show how liberal-minded she was, Louie threw a party for the troupe at the Ottawa Country Club. The troupe turned up fully aware of what to expect and gave Louie their undivided attention. Louie, for her part, treated the encounter as an amusing novelty, circling round like a dowager duchess conferring *noblesse oblige* to one and all. I'm quite certain that if it had been her daughter's colleagues and not her granddaughter's the party would not have happened.

It was a time of late nights and post-show parties and by the end of it I was looking forward to arriving at the eponymous Grand Central Station at last, to try and imagine what Mum must have felt when she wrote her book. I had taken the train from Montreal, but before I reached the United States border I was approached down the carriage aisle by a conductor who checked my ticket and asked the purpose of my visit. I explained I hoped to be an undergraduate at university and was on my way to Princeton, New Jersey. He then asked for my student visa, and although I had managed to secure a Canadian passport, getting a visa had never occurred to me. The outcome was that I was escorted off the train at the next station, and as I watched the train lights fade into the night I didn't even know whether the platform I was standing on was in Canada or the US.

I managed to get back to Montreal and when I put through a call to Mum, back home, she told me not to worry, she would have me back at Princeton before the term started. This I doubted, since the term was to start two days later. The next day I got a letter by courier from the office of Lester Pearson, the Canadian prime minister, containing my student visa.

My stay at Princeton was not happy, and from the beginning I felt out of place. I was the only foreign undergraduate in the freshman year and, apart from a visiting lecturer, probably in the whole university. During my second term I started to make noises to Mum about my disillusionment with the whole idea when I received this letter from George:

> co Contessa Antonini,
> Villa Sole,
> Ariccia, Rome.
>
> Dearest Xtopher,
> Your letter, which reached me yesterday, conveys only too clearly why you should feel a little out of water at Princeton. (Incidentally I don't find in it any "failure to command the English language successfully." I think you write very clearly.) Part of the trouble, if it is a trouble, lies in that loveliest of illusions Canterbury: those years you spent there have done, I see, what, speaking for myself, I had always hoped they would do for you. That is to incline your mind towards what Syd [schoolboy friend], in his letter to you, calls "the poetry." This is a beautiful and shrewd remark of his, and better than shrewd: it is brave. For what your letter to me consists of is the love of that grace which Matthew Arnold saw when he wrote that only too famous description of Oxford about dreaming spires and the home of lost causes. America has many many marvelous things, but she ain't got a place like that. Nor, now, do I need to point this out to you.

Just as the self-absorption-obsession of the Princeton students you write me about really arises from an educational error in America: this is the over cultivation of the I or eye and an under cultivation of the ball that the eye is supposed to be kept on. For there the mere existence of the individual or person is regarded as somehow being a kind of miraculous and essentially inexplicable mystery, to be investigated at the expense of everything else. The fact that it is impossible to exist without being, in some degree or other, a person or individual, has been overlooked: it is no more remarkable than that one has also got a name. And this over cultivation of the ego leads to those diseases of the mind so prevalent in America. People who spend all day and most of the night fingering around among the machinery of the mind—"personality" in Shamerica—shouldn't be surprised if they sometimes upset its balance. The result is a society of psychiatrists. Americans are <u>surprised</u> to find that they exist; they are <u>surprised</u> to find that sex is with us; they are <u>surprised</u> to learn that there is a consensus of opinion as to what constitutes civilized conduct. For not only is anarchy the consequence of a religion of egomania; egomania is also the consequence of a religion of anarchy. Thus you get the dog chasing its tail which is American society.

But all this speculation about the nature of Americans and America is rather like juggling without the colored balls. The reason you hear so much about the American way of life is simply because there ain't no such animal. A soda fountain is not a way of life. Even a million dollars ain't a way of life. A way of life is what it takes a thousand years to evolve if your [*sic*] lucky, and if your [*sic*] not German.

And I think furthermore that you yourself are particularly given to the English style of things, which is so very gently put in a line of god-helpus William Shakespeare: "I will not praise that purpose not to sell." Which is precisely the opposite to the American style of things, etc. The friendship of America is a very precious thing, and, like all precious things, it can be bought at a price.

All this is very slaphappy. I think that you can be left to make this decision as to whether or not you stay in the States: for my own part I hope you do not: I say it quite simply because I think it more honorable to do so. But it is best that you should allow a little time to go by before you decide once and for all. It's remarkable how much of ones thinking can be changed by even such a simple matter as meeting one truly pleasant person. And after all, this contingency is not as remote as all that. Please write to me again about all this. And forgive all this abstract blathering. Here in Italy such matters went to the wall a long time ago. Here we believe that the sun shines, which it does, that people are human, which they often are, and that life is for pleasure, which it is. Personally I would give all the psychiatrists in America for half an hour with a glass of wine by the Tiber. Remember? I think I may be over in NY in the spring. I hope so, if only because I should like to see you.

All my love.

George

At the time this letter left me quite exasperated because I couldn't for the life of me figure out what the advice was. In the end I concluded that his conciliatory tone was based on the situation as it now was. He had never been in a position to know me or the way I felt and so when called upon to give advice, he gave it. Any advice. So long as it satisfied the need for telling me what he thought I wanted to hear and of course, as always, it read prettily. The Shakespearean quote had me flummoxed. Is that really a double negative? Also, I could not make sense of the line "I say it quite simply because I think it more honorable to do so," however many times I read it. Was it more honorable for me to stay in the States or for him to say it? Or for me *not* to stay? On balance I took it to mean that he thought it more honorable for him to *tell* me not to stay, which is what he knew I wanted to hear. As with his other letters, when reading them now all I can see is his concern, but at the time I read the letter with burning resentment and skepticism, yet for all that the outcome was the same:

Mr. Christopher Barker
9 Westbourne Terrace
London W.2, England
May 27, 1964

Dear Mr. Barker:

According to our information, you have simply left the University. For your information, I have taken action to the effect that you "withdrew, not in good standing, for personal reasons and for unsatisfactory progress in studies." I do hope that you will go on to a successful life in the future.

Sincerely yours,
R. Bayly Winder
Acting Assistant Dean of the College
cc: Mrs. Elizabeth Barker

I arrived back at Westbourne Terrace to find Mum working full time for *Queen* fashion magazine, where she had become the literary critic and book reviewer in a column she named "Queen's Counsel." She was also moonlighting from *Queen*, writing advertising copy for at least three different agencies to top up her salary, and I suspect mightily pleased to hear she no longer had to pay the crippling university fees for me.

She had been dashing around London with all these professional commitments even before I left school. In early 1961 she contracted hepatitis and had to be confined to bed. She had become totally exhausted and run down, but even then she couldn't afford to stop work and continued to do so from her bed. It was a year before she recovered and during the illness she rather lost track of Rose.

Rose, now fourteen, had been living with Mum. She was attending a local comprehensive, having left ballet school. Mum, incapacitated through illness and frightened enough by the experience to give up drinking, had no solution or energy to manage Rose's teenage rebelliousness. As a last resort she sometimes locked Rose in her room at night. I found this extraordinary. Any sort of confinement to whomever or whatever was totally anathema to Mum. It went against everything she believed in and was a sign of her desperation. Rose was enraged by this and often managed to escape. The next morning her room and bed would be empty, which made Mum ever more frantic.

Rose's "playgrounds" during these outings spread from Soho to Fulham. I remember her once being selected at random for a television broadcast from a smoky Café des Artistes off the Fulham Road. The subject under discussion was male heartthrobs and they asked some young girls in cafés and nightclubs for their comments. We all gathered round the black-and-white set at Westbourne Terrace and watched as Rose, looking as smoldering and beautiful as a young Juliette Greco, named her idol as Alain Delon. At that time the French actor was so hip he was almost unheard of, and they had to ask her to repeat her nomination. It was a mystery to us how she had managed to get on the program, let alone into the nightclub. She was fifteen.

Back in London after returning from Princeton, I talked to Mum about the possibility of photography as a profession and she said she might be able to help. These were the days of the emergence of working-class boys breaking into the photographic world and photographers such as Donovan, Duffy and David Bailey joined Norman Parkinson, flouting conventional approaches to fashion photography.

A new, exciting and sexy look that blew away the drab postwar mediocrity of the fifties swept in, and Mum's witty and original copy caught the mood and helped to launch the Swinging Sixties. She was partly responsible for promoting this new mood. She was by now one of the highest-paid fashion copywriters in London, and although competition for jobs in the photographic world was intense, I was soon being interviewed by a photographer in Belgravia only two days after my asking for her help.

Rose Emma Maximiliane Roberta. Rosie scooped all the leftover girls' names Mum and George loved. Mum had sorted through these when she was alone and deserted in the freezing Roundstone winter of 1947. She added Maximiliane after the woman who had been such a great friend and help when Georgina was born in Pender Harbour. In the misery of that winter, Mum had decided four children were enough.

Sadly, Rose was to be the sacrifice from the explosion of passion that was their relationship—perhaps a birth too far for their crumbling love affair. She slipped through the net of self-preservation that the other three of us had carefully rigged up. When Mum was preoccupied, Rose went into freefall.

By the time she was born she already had the seeds buried in her that were her undoing. When Mum first set out into the world with her uncompromising search for an ideal lover she stated she wanted someone who would, hand in hand with her, "leap bellowing with jungfreud into the arms of the infinite," but she had no idea who he might be. When she found George she never doubted that this was her man, but such was the uncompromising passion that she left a trail of complication and trauma. Rose was one of the victims.

George didn't see Rose until she was six and a half months old. By the time she was going to her first school she had no personal memories whatsoever of that strange thing called a father. It was during these formative years, when she was only three and a half, that she was packed off to weekly board at Pinewood School, Hertfordshire.

Yet when she was young it was never apparent that Rose would be anything other than perfectly well adjusted. After Pinewood, at the age of six, she was sent off to board at Legat Ballet School and came back with excellent reports. She joined in with us at home in everything we did and with her lovely sense of humor seemed buoyant and exuberant. Somewhere, deep down inside her, restlessness was growing, and the first signs of rebellion started to appear after seven years at Legat, when she lost interest in ballet and wanted to leave.

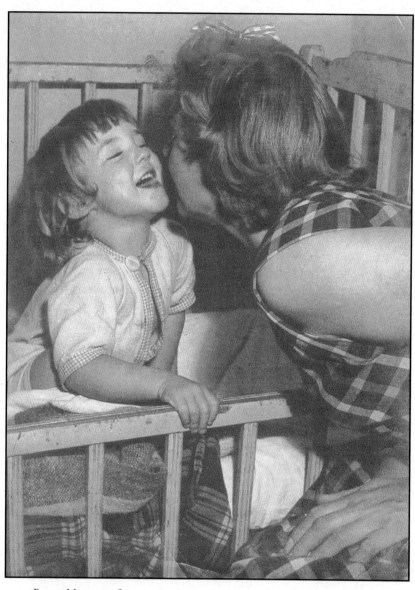

Rose & Mum, 1948

Photo by Michael Wickham

Mum took her away at the age of thirteen and she came to live at home in London, where she enrolled in a local comprehensive school in Paddington. Mum, so frantic to keep working, was unable to exert any leverage on her daughter and the decisions concerning Rose's future were made largely by either Rose or left to serendipity. She was the forgotten one at the end of the line.

Mum's freelance copywriting made huge demands on her as she struggled to keep the money rolling in for school fees. She was nothing less than a dervish in her pursuit of success in her working life. She raced about to meetings with important advertising and company directors and then would dash off an article for a magazine as she moonlighted for three copy agencies. At her work there were always support systems that enabled her to operate efficiently. These she was used to and knew how to apply. At home they were not there. She couldn't conceive of a way to rein Rose in.

Every time the telephone rang late at night or in the early hours of the morning Mum's heart missed a beat. She would pray it wouldn't be another grotesque emergency for which she would have to leap out of bed and go flying off to some awful fix that Rose had got herself into. Her drug addiction had taken her into a world of violence, homelessness and poverty. The calls for help didn't stop coming.

Rose's rage for self-destruction took a heavy toll on Mum and, combined with her workload, contributed to Mum's hepatitis. No one diagnosed it at first. so she staggered on, battling to keep her world together until eventually she became extremely ill.

In the meantime, Rose was becoming a problem at school and Mum was desperate enough to attempt any solution. At her sister Jane's suggestion, she sent Rose off to America to High Mowing School, in Wilton, New Hampshire. This was a Steiner school with no strict code of discipline. A year later the experiment was abandoned after Rose was expelled for pulling down the American flag in a graveyard prank. She returned to London in 1962 to be sent to private tutors. But by the age of sixteen, in 1963, she was beyond any sort of control from Mum, who even if she had been able to devote all her time to Rose and her problems, would have found the damage too excessive.

Ironically it was Soho that was the beginning of Rose's spiral into oblivion. In the locale that Mum had come to years earlier and sought out as the place where she could breathe and come alive, Rose found connections to score heavy drugs. It was here she picked up with a charming but often highly neurotic boyfriend.

Rose and Mum had gone out to Soho together after Mum recovered from hepatitis. They met a man called Jeff Bolger, who shared Rosie's wild and ironic sense of humor but was twice her age and suffered bouts of paranoia. He was tall and thin and with a stoop that gave him an apologetic air, belying the fact that he had been a middleweight boxing champion for the British Army. With horn-rimmed glasses, pursed lips and a slight stammer, he could have been mistaken for a visiting professor until his clipped cockney vowels and rhyming slang suggested a different background. Yet he fancied himself as intellectually informed and was one of several such Soho characters who crossed the line between "a bit of a geezer" and an opinionated bohemian. This was a reputation that he was happy to reinforce, with lurid tales of scrapes he had got into as he drove an unlicensed cab on the airport run from Heathrow.

In an attempt to help him now that he was involved with her daughter, Mum stood guarantor for him so he could buy a new vehicle for work. He defaulted on payment and the car was repossessed.

Later that year, when Mum had gone on a trip to Canada, Rose invited Jeff to stay and the two of them set up together in Westbourne Terrace. When Mum got back they were living there as man and wife, with Rose only sixteen. Mum and Rose rowed and Rose stomped out, saying she was leaving home. She was pregnant by Jeff and in August the next year gave birth to their daughter, Claudia. Of course Mum rallied round and now, a grandmother at fifty, she offered the couple her bedroom and double bed. With a newborn baby to occupy her, Rose soon tired of Jeff's paranoid self-pity and ordered him out of the house.

Rose was nervous of his reaction and when we heard he had been seen loitering outside the house we became worried. Mum, Georgina, Rose and I watched him nervously from the upstairs windows as he paced the terrace below. We saw him suddenly dive into the boot of his car and seize his car starting handle. He turned and bounded up the entrance steps and through the front door, left open by other visitors.

"He's coming up," I shouted over my shoulder, and all of us doubled back to the kitchen.

I had taken the precaution of bolting the upper door to our flat. He had worked himself up into such a frenzy that I could hear his footsteps speeding up the flights of stairs to this door, five at a time. He banged loudly and called out for Rose. With Mum and Georgina in the kitchen holding their breath, Rose and I crouched behind the door and she put her finger to her lips. But Claudia, who Rose had in her other arm, cried out in alarm. On hearing his baby he was seized by a sudden fit of violence and began to smash down the door with the starting handle. He shook the whole flat with repeated blows until the nose of the handle broke through the wood of the door. Rose, Claudia and I retreated up the remaining flight of stairs inside the flat as he leapt through the hole in the splintered frame and, spitting expletives and a stream of saliva, sped up the last few steps and raised the handle over my skull. It was hard to believe that this towering wild-eyed madman was the same man who had so amused us with his gentle and ironic philosophy. As wild panic clutched my stomach, a phrase about soft answers and wrath ran through my mind. It seemed little protection at the time. But I managed to stretch out a trembling hand to his chest and asked him to leave. Surprisingly, he began to back down the stairs, as he lambasted an unjust world, and with the starting handle still whirling, he exited the shattered door.

When at last the turmoil abated, Mum and Georgina stuck their heads gingerly round the kitchen door and asked if he had gone. Mum hugged me and said we shouldn't think badly of him, he had only come to claim his baby. A sudden wave of pity swept over me. This was not too dissimilar to the feeling I had when, a little later, he was found dead on his kitchen floor, head next to the gas oven, his mouth frozen open in a cry for help that no one heard.

Rose had a continual struggle with addiction, sometimes almost ridding herself of it altogether only to relapse. I soon learned that in many heroin addicts this is a pattern often repeated, and as the addicts relapse they develop a fine line in subterfuge to get money for their next score. This was so unlike Rose's open and carefree nature that when she turned into a convincing liar, she could really make you believe she was going to go straight again. Helping her by giving her money for rent (if she wasn't squatting) when she said she was drug free was a tough call. You had to be absolutely sure you weren't about to fuel the habit.

She also got money for her habit by prostitution, and word went round the rugby club where I was playing that my sister had been hooked in the West End by one of the players. She was appalled and ashamed when she heard I knew. Not for herself, but for me and any fallout that may have occurred. For me it was deeply shocking. I had absolutely no idea that this was the way she got her money for drugs, and to find out from the smirked whispers in the club dressing room made me feel angry yet again as I burned with shame. Instead of feeling sympathetic and compassionate and taking some form of responsible action, I smoldered with fury and resentment that she was upsetting our lives, especially Mum's.

In the middle of all this excruciating worry about Rose, Mum was evicted from Westbourne Terrace in 1965. She had forgotten to renew the lease and the landlord wanted her out, since he felt she wasn't paying a reasonable rent. He sent in a gang of builders into the vacant flat below us. They drilled and hammered all day and often until well into the evening. We were deafened by the noise until in the end—and I could scarcely believe my eyes—they drilled right through the floorboards into Mum's bedroom. They walked out of the building below, leaving a huge hole in the floor and brick dust settling slowly on Mum's precious books.

In desperation Mum found us a flat near Marble Arch as the family base. For herself she found a little flat in the heart of Soho, where she would write her advertising copy. She also found herself an isolated cottage in Suffolk, from where she planned to restart her literary career, something that she had always intended when her children had left home. By now *By Grand Central Station I Sat Down and Wept* was building a certain reputation. It was republished in 1966 by Panther with a eulogistic foreword by Brigid Brophy.

Rose battered backward and forward between these two sanctuaries, leaving Mum no peace and bringing her turmoil and worry. Finally Mum decided to quit London altogether and retire to the cottage in Suffolk to concentrate on her writing.

It was not to be. Rose was found staggering around half comatose in Earl's Court with Claudia in tow and pregnant with a second. She was taken by a kindly soul to a nearby hotel, where Drugs Anonymous was called, and she was left in the care of a clergyman. She was charged with possession of drugs and an injunction was taken out against her latest boyfriend for supplying her. Her second daughter, Jane, was born a little later, and Rose, in a moment of total irresponsibility, fled the hospital, leaving her baby behind. Georgina and Mum had to go round and pick the baby up from the hospital and take her to the cottage in Suffolk.

When Mum finally tracked Rose down she was persuaded to attend a drug-addiction-cure center called Spelthorne St. Mary's, a rambling old building out in the Sussex commuter belt run by nuns. She stayed for a month. The national press had a field day, with "Abandoned baby weaned off drugs" appearing in the *Evening Standard*. Claudia and Jane, following the case concerning Rose's possession, were later made wards of the court under the care of their grandmother. Mum now had two grandchildren on her hands at a time when she thought she might have peace and tranquility enough to resume writing.

Rose wasn't finished yet, though. On her release from the hospital, where she had been under the care of a psychiatrist, she moved to the flat in Soho that Mum had obtained expressly as her private little bolt-hole and where she could write her copy uninterrupted. From the flat, and in a demonstration of positive intent, Rose enrolled in a course of shorthand typing and with a new resolve set about picking up her life. It couldn't last. She didn't have the resolution to learn a skill so demanding and soon the people and influences from her previous days caught up with her. Once more she was picked up for possession. She was sent to Holloway Prison on remand and later sent off to Spelthorne St. Mary's for a six-month rehabilitation term. She was again in the papers.

Mum, although now in her isolated cottage, wasn't immune to Rose's influence. Fearing the impact of yet another emergency, she would pull herself together and cope. Up to this point Mum seemed to have her own way of dealing with these problems and emergencies. She wouldn't involve the men of the family, particularly George. Similarly, Sebastian and I were rarely asked for help. As long as I can remember, I would perch on the end of her bed while she had her morning coffee and we would iron the world out. It was as if she were teaching me her philosophy of life, and no emotion or trauma were allowed to enter our ethereal atmosphere. Humor, sense and reason where allowed. For panic, alarms and emergencies she used Georgina. Not only was she the eldest but she had been groomed by Mum to take some of the burden of responsibility and hardship off her shoulders. It was a role that was more fitting to a father. To Georgina she unburdened emotion, so even as a young girl Georgina would run around holding her hand, trying to sort out this ever more turbulent world.

Rose's situation was as bad as ever, and she felt she could take it no longer. She went to Mum and carefully explained that she wanted to kill herself. It was only her baby's need for a mother that was stopping her. Mum knew she meant it. Going out of her mind with worry and not knowing what to do, she sought Georgina and stated categorically that if Rose were to do this then she too would kill herself. Georgina was terrified that an imminent double suicide appeared to be approaching and she had no way of stopping it.

When the initial drama of the situation had calmed a little, Mum, still despondent, took Sebastian and me aside to ask for advice on how to handle Rose. Not being party to how forlorn the situation had become and now exasperated with Rose's behavior and the appalling effect it was having on Mum, we naïvely and primly told Mum what we thought she wanted to hear. We had absolutely no experience in these matters (and in the mid-sixties coping with drug addiction had not yet emerged as a widespread family problem). We told her we thought she had always been too soft on Rose and must leave her to her own fate. Mum nodded sagely, took our advice on board and did the opposite. Although she knew we were only trying to help with our adolescent recommendation, it seemed to crystallize her mind. She could never abandon her daughter, whatever the advice.

After this rehabilitation Rose once more determined to stay drug-free and indeed she even got married. Marriage, however, was never going to solve her problems. Her husband couldn't have been more unsuitable. He was a half-Turkish half-English commercial metallurgist who had been introduced to Rose by Mary John, the wife of Mum's old friend Caspar John. This new boyfriend told us he often invested in the stock market. After a successful day with his investments he would take us all out for expensive meals. He seemed lonely and even more so when he told us he lived by himself in a little suburban flat. We later learned that this was far from the truth, as his "lonely flat" was in fact a terraced house where he had a partner and two daughters. Before we could find this out, though, Rose had rushed to marry him. After the marriage ceremony, Mum was asked to look after her grandchildren a little longer while Rose and her husband motored off on their honeymoon. As they were making their way to the Folkestone port in her new husband's sports car, they had a blazing row before they reached the outskirts of London and Rose leaped out at a set of traffic lights. The marriage ended before it was consummated.

Rose returned and took her children back. Mum dared to think she might have some time for her own life. So often she looked out of the Dell window to see Rose and a tribe of friends straggling up the path to the cottage, babies on hips and hordes of children running ahead squabbling. They often had their blind collie-cross Rolly on a knotted string tugging on ahead of them, and they would all be coming for an indefinite stay. Mum would be briefly mollified because at least the middle-of-the-night horror calls would stop.

1964

COMING BACK FROM AMERICA I was beginning to feel perhaps I had misjudged George. I reread his letter to me at Princeton over and over again and could see less and less to worry about, although I was still smoldering with resentment from the discoveries of my lineage.

George's new girlfriend, Elspeth Langlands, had invited me to their flat in Islington. She was a year older than Georgina. Tall, dark-haired and with a pale complexion that accentuated her shy nature, Elspeth had come down from Oxford, having read modern languages, and was in London on a break from working as a teacher in Scotland, where her family lived. I had met her briefly in a pub in Chelsea with her fiancé before I left for a holiday in Denmark. After I had left for this holiday she had gone to a party at Westbourne Terrace. She was invited because her fiancé had been an acquaintance of George's from Rome, and the party was given in the fiancé's honor by Mum to welcome him to England on a brief visit. George had left Italy and his wife, Dede, now pregnant with her third child by him, was hoping that he might be able to return to Rome in time for the birth. When Elspeth and he met at the party, he duly outraged and insulted her, as was his ploy when meeting pretty girls. Elspeth, who had a determined and witty streak in her, had matched his repartee, despite her shyness and his bombast. As the exchange continued he got more irritated and in the end they had to be forcibly parted. At their next meeting in the same pub I had first met her, he forgave her behavior with a condescending kiss of benediction.

George returned to Rome and witnessed the birth of Francis, his tenth child, in July 1963. His relationship with Dede was deteriorating rapidly, because he appeared increasingly unprepared for domestication with their family. At times, when coming back late, the door was bolted. He often found himself homeless, waking up in the back of his car, where Dede had banished him, until she finally cut him adrift.

Wandering about in this largely homeless state, he was rescued by some friends and ended up in a small cottage by Lake Nemi in Ariccia, east of Rome. Here, although housed, he missed his English friends and to one of them, a painter called Tony Kingsmill, he sent an invitation to spend some of his summer there. Tony had been industriously trying to win Elspeth's hand and had asked her to accompany him on the trip and she had agreed, more in an attempt to avoid her humdrum life in London than for the prospect of romance in the Mediterranean. The three of them had met before, so when Tony told George he would have "Elspeth of Drumtochty" with him, George said he would be delighted to accommodate both of them.

Mum made good friends with Elspeth. The two had a similar love of the English language and had the shared experience of the thrilling discovery of George's work while browsing through a bookshop's poetry shelves. The two spent the last few minutes at Westbourne Terrace preparing Elspeth for her departure to Italy and Mum had joked, as she had pressed on Elpbeth some spare clothing, including Georgina's rather ornate Legat School cape, to take the clothes as a trousseau for her nuptials. They were both aware what the eventual outcome of the trip might be.

Tony was unwittingly imperiling his relationship with his girlfriend. As yet another triangular love match in George's life played itself out, Tony quit the field, defeated, by the time February arrived. Elspeth stayed on and enjoyed a few idyllic months with George, and by March she was pregnant with his eleventh child.

They decided to return to England for the birth of the baby and, tactlessly, George took Elspeth and his carload of worldly goods to Westbourne Terrace. There they proceeded to unpack and settle in as if they were home at last. While they were in distant Rome, Mum could bless the relationship and delight in her new friend's happiness, but when it was brought into her home, she was not pleased. The atmosphere became very strained and after a few awkward weeks they moved on. By August they had finally settled in a basement flat in Islington.

It was to this basement flat I was now heading, at Elspeth's invitation, to meet my father, who I had now learned had not just four children (my siblings and me) but eleven. As the evening wore on, everything proceeded in a civilized fashion, with Elspeth playing gracious hostess as the other guests arrived and George held forth, elbow propping up a mantelpiece. After a particularly witty exchange, which had obviously pleased him, he offered his packet of Consulate cigarettes around, to which at first I shook my head. At Princeton I had dabbled in smoking but just couldn't get on with it. As he was taking the packet away, I said:

"No, actually, do you mind if I do?"

I cannot imagine what was in his mind the next moment, when with one of his trademark vicious snarls he grabbed it back. Perhaps he imagined I was the arrogant young public schoolboy who took it for granted that everyone could be nonchalant and liberal with other peoples' cigarettes. He and his father had rowed furiously and continually, often exchanging blows, when he was younger, and perhaps he thought it was a natural exchange between father and son. Anyway, whatever it was, it enraged him and as he snatched the cigarette back in one hand, he very ineffectively tried to cuff my ears with the other. I was incredulous. He was well into his fifties now and I was a fit young man in my twenties. I had a sudden flashback to Tilty and his high-handed attempt to spank me. My blood began to boil. Here he was, at it again, and he had no right. As he attempted to hit me I reached over and picked him up by the throat and carried him backward down the corridor to the next room as he flailed about, trying to get a piece of me. There I banged him down among his latest baby's toys and carry-cot, stapling his neck to the floor, and watched him squirm about, helplessly trying to right himself. At that point I so dearly wanted to bash his brains out for all those wrongs and treachery. I stared down at him, my eyes loaded with accusations and fury. But then I imagined Mum's quiet voice coming to me:

"Please don't hurt him. He doesn't mean it."

The little soiree of guests fluttered and flapped around, horrified. I released him and he got up. Free again, but now humiliated as well, he convulsed into greater anger. He screamed at me to leave his house and never darken his door again.

George and Elspeth spent two more years in the basement flat in Islington—apart, that is, from times spent living-in at the universities of Buffalo and York as George fulfilled his duties as writer-in-residence. As their third baby's birth approached, though, they realized they would have to move.

Luckily, through a National Trust ad in the property columns of *The Times*, they were able to secure the tenancy of a seventeenth-century farmhouse in north Norfolk and left London for good.

Mum heard about my quarrel with George and was keen to see us reconciled. Not long after George and Elspeth moved to Bintry House in north Norfolk, Mum organized a meeting between us and I made a trip down from London. I was with a girlfriend and picked Mum up from her cottage in Suffolk on the way. My girlfriend, Clare, who had heard many lurid tales of George's outrageous behavior, was nervous about the meeting.

When we arrived he was in what he termed his Drinking Room, the main feature of which was a mantelpiece over an open fire, now roaring in the grate. As we timidly edged round the door, he glared at us and Mum introduced Clare to him. One hand held a drink and the other a cigarette, and an elbow was as usual locked onto the mantelpiece. Suddenly he smiled and, placing the cigarette into an ashtray on the mantelpiece, he hunched his shoulders and extended his freed hand wide in a gesture of welcome to Clare:

"Now, my beautiful wild creature, come over here and talk to me about love."

As she approached him warily with her hand extended to meet his, he caught her around the back of the head and, pulling her forehead to his, whispered:

"There is only one thing I have to ask you, young woman. When are you going to have babies with my noble son?"

Realizing he was perhaps a couple of drinks ahead of us and squirming with embarrassment, she replied:

"Er ... well ... I have no immediate plans."

He then thrust her head away from his and turning his back on her spat out:

"Then what you are doing together is masturbating and you are nothing but a whore!"

This was now a common trial by fire for pretty young girls, and the trick was to pretend you hadn't heard and flirtingly patronize him. Elspeth, at their first meeting, had treated him like an equal and so incurred his wrath. Clare, later to become my wife, did not indulge him for a second. She bridled like a filly full of hay and tossing her head, grabbed my hand and hissed in my ear that she would not stay a moment longer. As we left I realized, not without a little disappointment, that reconciliation would have to wait.

* * *

Over the next few years, despite that we lived in the same county, George and I rarely met. Once, he rushed to my bedside after I had a serious road traffic accident. I was lying in my hospital bed when, without warning, he appeared striding down the ward, strangely formal in a tie and light-brown herringbone suit. For a moment he stared at me, appalled. I thought he was stricken by the sight of his son as mangled roadkill (which I very nearly had been). Struggling to communicate and lying there with my head swathed in bandages, I suddenly realized the inherent irony of the situation for him.

In 1935, at the age of twenty-two, he had been at the family flat in Upper Addison Gardens with his brother and his friend Maurice Carpenter. They were taking a break from printing their work on a printing press they had set up in a garden shed. Back in the house, they strayed to the basement and Kit found an old fencing foil leaning against the wall. George seized a walking stick next to it. They began a mock sword fight and as Kit backed up the basement stairs in Douglas Fairbanks Jr. style, George thrust forward with the walking stick. At that exact moment Kit tripped and, lurching forward, took the thrust of the walking stick on his spectacle lens. The stick scooped out his eyeball and the shattering glass penetrated his eye socket. The embedded glass prevented the surgeons from replacing his eyeball, so it was removed. George gazed down on me in stunned disbelief. He was a great believer in omens and auguries and had even written a poem that had won the 1962 Guinness Poetry Prize "The View from a Blind I."

My accident happened when I was coming back from London to my home in Norfolk on a damp, drizzling Friday evening in November. I had the seats down in the back of my estate car to accommodate a mountain of photographic equipment for a shoot in France on the Sunday. The rain had stopped and the wipers were off as I crested a ridge on a B road I had taken as a shortcut round Bury St. Edmunds. Immediately I was confronted by two sets of headlights, one set to my right and the other in front of me. I had time to jerk the steering wheel to the left and to deviate marginally from a head-on collision. In the ensuing impact the off-side bonnet hinge snapped, leaving only one hinge to hold the heavy metal plate of the lid, which then swung in through the windscreen. As I catapulted forward, my head met the lid as it swung in through the shattering windscreen. It sliced past my left eye and came to a stop as it splintered the bridge of my nose. The car, meanwhile, glided graceful through a parabola into an adjoining field with me restrained tightly under the dashboard by a tangle of straps, seats and wires. I lay there, trussed in a fetal crouch, unable to move, pumping several pints of blood onto the dashboard from the head wound and dipping in and out of consciousness.

Minutes later, firefighters arrived and started cutting me free. As I slowly recovered consciousness I could smell petrol vapor all round and my main concern was that this fuel shouldn't ignite from the cutting-gear sparks and toast me as I was being freed. After being reassured that the cutting gear worked spark-free it occurred to me how little pain I was in. In hospital, as I was being prepped for a tidy-up operation, I asked a passing nurse if she could wipe the blood from my left eye so I could see properly. She made no reply and disappeared. I heard urgent and hushed voices and then a man in a white coat approached and told me, much to my amazement, that I would never see through my left eye again. I had lost it in the accident. When the shock passed, I experienced a sudden wave of tortuous pain in my forehead that left me roaring for a painkiller.

The marvelous nursing staff had me out of the hospital in two weeks and I spent time trying to adapt to my new one-eyed vision of the world, where you never know how far the bottle neck is from the glass rim. When I think of the minutia of unfolding circumstances during impact, I shudder. If I hadn't been wearing a seat belt I would have catapulted through two windscreens into the oncoming car, ending up as a shredded torso in its front seat. If the amount of play in the seat belt had been two centimeters more my head would have traveled that much farther into the bonnet top and I would have lost both eyes. Three more centimeters and I would have been lobotomized. But a tighter belt and I would still be binocular.

Rose would often have periods of clear introspection, and some of these she wrote down. They appear today as lucid and self-aware as you could wish. At thirteen she wrote in her diary:

> July 17, 1960. I wish my father would be like a father. He never pays
> for anything, he doesn't seem to realize he has a wife and four children
> who need money to live. I don't see how he can expect us to love him
> although I still do, but I can't say I always speak highly of him. I hope
> I see him next holidays. Oh I wish he didn't drink. I love Mummy so
> much, I hope I'm like her when I grow up, I mean the way she is so gen-
> tle and loving & kind, not in the way of jobs though, because I want to
> be an actress, and I know Mommy will let me be one if I really want to.

In 1971 Rose was arrested again for procuring drugs and, a year later, for possession. Then a real chance came along that we believed might, just might, save her. She came into a substantial amount of money from a legacy. Donald Buchanan, curator of the National Gallery of Canada, had been a very old friend of Mum's from her debutante days in Ottawa, and when he saw Rosie as a baby he was captivated and promised Mum he would include her in his estate, which would have been substantial.

Over the years it became a family joke with which we would often tease Rose. When he died we held our collective breath and waited for the apples to fall from the tree. We waited and waited and nothing happened. Donald Buchanan's brother had been changed to the main beneficiary, which, along with other complications, meant a long delay in its distribution. Suddenly it did come through and was, for Rose, quite a fortune. The £18,000 she inherited meant Rose, Claudia and her second child, Jane, were able to buy a terraced house and move to Cambridge to a place they could call home. Over the next few months, Rose made a game attempt to put her life back in order, but to do so required routine and discipline and those were things she didn't have. Within a year and a half she had galloped through the money and was in debt and had to sell up and move out.

We all became exhausted by Rose's antics. For Mum and Georgina, who were closely involved in the day-to-day emotional turmoil, in was particularly exasperating. For them the continual resurrection of hope was exhausting. We all prayed for her recovery. She would go tearing up to the brink and then fall back, only to start the procedure again. The back-and-forth seemed to be done with such willfulness that it was beyond anything anyone could do to help her. Her life was really a long suicide note that, even from the beginning, was impossible to decipher. Mum had spoken prophetically at Rose's birth that her weight distribution in the womb had been wrong. Nothing based on medical science, but literally a gut feeling. The first real indication had come at Legat School, when a scandalized Madam Legat came to Georgina with a shocking report of Rosie kissing the boys in the bushes. At the time she was only eight. Ironically, when she was taken ill for the last time she was free from her drug-taking but the years of damage to her body had taken their toll. She wrote in a letter to her brother Sebastian:

"There are times when I feel as though I'm insane but only because of my innate sanity. A high price to pay. I don't know where I belong: probably not even on this unendingly square-rooted globe. Still I'm here."

* * *

When Rose fell ill for the last time, I had a mind-chilling telephone conversation with a voice so distracted I hardly recognized it as Mum's. She
asked me to inform George and ferry him down to London to be at Rose's
bedside. I picked him up in my car and at first he seemed unconcerned
and full of banter at my little Citroën's quirky design. I suppose he was
finding it hard to confront the situation, as his voice slowly tapered away
to serious introspection. He knew his daughter had been dying for some
time with the slow collapse of her liver from her drinking and drug-taking.
It was apparent that this visit could be to witness her death. When we got
to the hospital, we joined a group outside the operating theater. Sebastian
and a little huddle of family and friends had been waiting anxiously all day
and he was beginning to talk in terms of a recovery when his voice trailed
away. There was a white coat among us.

"Rose is dead. Would you like to see her?"

As we shuffled into the operating theatre, a strange division took place.
I went in with the women and soon the corridors of King's College Hospital echoed with their cries. But my father could not bring himself to view
the corpse. He wasn't present at her birth and neither could he be present
at her death.

As we left the hospital that bleak day I came through the hospital
doors to the car park and saw Mum ahead of me, a fragile stooped figure
blown before an icy March wind, her thinning hair trailing across her face.
I ran to her and put an arm round her. She was ashen and was mumbling
"Oh, God ... oh, God ...," as if in a trance. She would not be mollified.

At that instant, Mum reminded me of the bent and sobbing figure of
my sister, now dead on a hospital trolley behind us, from some years earlier. I had just moved into a room in a friend's flat in Victoria, London.
One evening I answered the doorbell to find Rose at the door. She stood
hunched and shivering on the front step as the rain swept about her. To my
dismay, I saw she was shielding a baby in her arms. She was gaunt, pale,
and her clothes were threadbare. I had heard she was back on heroin again,
and because she had baby Claudia with her this visit could mean only one
thing. She hurried into the hall out of the rain and I took her to the kitchen
and gave her a cup of tea. When I was out of the room for a minute she asked
my friend Jake if she could stay the night. When I returned he whispered
to me her request, hissing that if I didn't show her out of the house before
she was sick on the carpet, I would have to go too. Incensed that Rose had
once again threatened to disrupt our lives, I angrily told her to leave. She
bundled Claudia up into her arms and I watched as the slanting rain flared

past the yellow streetlight and outlined her back before the darkness engulfed her. Remorse and pity swept over me in waves that night, and although Mum blamed only herself for Rose's death, I knew as I helped Mum to the car that bleak March day that we had probably all played a part in her death. Mum had brought her "hugs and kisses," but, of the four of us, Rose was the one who most needed discipline and a structure to her life from an early age. We too could have brought Rose an "explanation for her despair, her desperate why." "Biking through gales" just wasn't enough for what Rose needed, as Mum later confirmed in her poem "Rose Died":

> That my urgent live
> Message to you failed.
>
> Two sins will jostle forever, and humble me
> Beneath my masked heart:
> It was my job to explain the world;
> It was my job to get the words right.
>
> I tried, oh I tried, I did try,
> I biked through gales,
> Brought hugs, kisses,
>
> But no explanation for your
> despair, your
> desperate
> why.

She never really recovered from Rose's death. This anguished cry from Mum's despair and guilt was one of the last pieces she wrote. She did get a chance to go back and visit her beloved Canada, but the trip was not a great success. Her expectations and hopes were too high, and only served to take her mind off her mourning. Now, when I listen to the tapes of the many interviews she made, the thing that strikes me is how congested were her lungs. She was always a heavy smoker, but now she would suppress any cough for fear if she started she wouldn't be able to stop. The rattle and wheeze as she spoke was continually stifled and seemed to come from the bottom of a quagmire in which she was drowning.

When she returned from Canada, Georgina and I met her off the plane at Heathrow. She came shuffling down the endless concourse with sweat breaking out on her forehead. She was carrying bags of all shapes and

sizes and I felt an overwhelming pang of concern and affection as she waddled forward through the gates. Georgina gasped when she saw her pushing through the crowd and, furious with her mother's display of fragility,
gasped with a lowered brow:

"My God! That can't be her. She looks like an old bagwoman."

After settling back into her cottage she would occasionally come and
stay with me in my apartment in Soho. The apartment had a long climb
up endless stairs and I would open the door to find her doubled over and
gasping. By way of recuperation, she would flop onto the sofa and send
me out for forty Gauloises.

If we went out into Soho in the evening and we were separated she
would return on her own and several times, thinking she had finally made
the summit of the stair climb, she collapsed on the doormat of the flat on the
floor below. One morning I awoke and realized she hadn't made it home and
was starting to worry, only to find her asleep on the doormat outside of this
lower flat. She wouldn't compromise the chance of coming to London to see
her friends, for what I am sure she knew was her last time.

That night, in the small hours, having fallen into bed after a whirlwind
tour of parties and meetings, I heard her call out loudly and urgently in
her sleep:

"Mother! *Mother*! Oh ... *MOTHER!*"

It was so clear and anguished that when she began to angrily grind her
teeth moments later, I became alarmed and woke her up. She died the next
day, March 4, 1986.

We buried her next to Rose at St. Mary's Cross, South Elmham, and the
church was overflowing with people paying their last respects. I had hired
a charabanc to bring her "rogues and rascals" a hundred miles from London. A party raged at her Suffolk cottage after the funeral service. George
was stunned and bereft, and in a moment of despair at the wake scribbled
a note on the back of a piece of paper and handed it to Georgina:

> Ah most unreliable of all women of grace
> In the breathless hurry of your leave taking
> You forgot, you forgot forever, our last embrace.

Unknowing, he had written this on the back of Mum's last will and testament.

* * *

The side effects of smoking had killed Mum, and George too was suffering from its effects. He was, by now, becoming more and more debilitated by emphysema. One sunny Saturday afternoon not long after Mum died, I dropped in to see him. The house was empty save for a room at the back. The curtains were drawn and in among the collapsing furniture, by the pallid and flickering light of a black-and-white TV set, I could just make out a shriveled figure slumped low in an armchair. Lily, his youngest child, leaned lovingly on his shoulder as he coughed and wheezed at the television.

They were watching Saturday-afternoon wrestling and I felt a pang of betrayal. Had his love of the nobility of athletics been reduced to this? We had always shared a passion for true competition and particularly for middle-distance running. Whenever we met in the past and before the drink had started to take effect, we would endlessly discuss the merits of Coe, Ovett and Cram and compare them to earlier athletes such as Zátopek and Bannister. At the 1960 Rome Olympics he had been delighted as he watched the Italian sprinter Berruti scatter doves from the track on his way to a world record. He had spun me a picturesque scene of the high-jump competition there. Thousands in the stadium stayed on to watch Shavlakadze and Brumel inch the bar up as the sun went down over the stadium rim, both beating the world high-jump record. But here he was, watching what I felt wasn't even sport, just a sweaty Punch and Judy theater. It wasn't long before I too was laughing at the spectacle and sharing his delight through his wheezes and coughing. It was the last time I saw him.

Slowly and agonizingly the emphysema tightened its grip and he became more and more confined to the house. When he was administered medication he would petulantly spit his pills into the fire grate and light up an illicit cigarette. He defiantly shrugged off attempts to help him up the stairs to bed, bumping up alone on his backside. When this too became impossible he was carried up to his bedroom in his wheelchair, still barking out orders like Nebuchadnezzar building the hanging gardens from his palanquin.

In October 1991, when I was away in the United States, he died with Elspeth whispering Kipling into his ear.

* * *

As I write these lines fifteen years later I look out of my frosted window in north Norfolk over the icy waters of my garden pond. White flurries of snow start drifting toward me from the dark woods behind as the weak afternoon light fades. I gaze over the freezing landscape and some lines of his come back to me:

> And not far away the
> icy and paralyzed stream
> has found it also, that day the
> flesh became glass and a dream
> with no where to go.
>
> Haunting the December
> fields their bitter lives
> entreat us to remember
> the lost spirit that grieves
> over these fields like a scarecrow.

I am reminded that although my father always denounced and battled with *his* father, he dedicated this poem to his memory. When, on May 2, 1965, Pa died, my father had set out to attend the funeral, but on the way there he changed his mind and returned. In his poem "At Thurgarten Church," feeling he had "forfeited all" in the rightness of his beliefs, he came to terms with, and acknowledged, his father's uncompromising and faithless stance. Having spent his own life wrestling with his Catholicism and its offers of redemption, he saw his brittle and proud father, who lived "as though the soul were stone," usurp his own vacillating feelings. From this I now know that to understand another's life is to begin to forgive, as he did with his father. The poem finishes:

> And there in the livid dust
> and bones of death we search
> until we find as we must
> outside Thurgarten Church
> only wild grasses blow.
>
> I hear the old bone in me cry
> and the dying spirit call:
> I have forfeited all
> and once and for all must die
> and this is all that I know.

For now in a wild way we
know that Justice is served
and that we die in the clay we
dread, desired, and deserved,
awaiting no Judgment Day.

Not a mile from where I now sit, across those "December fields" and buried
in Itteringham churchyard, his "old bones" lie frozen in the "clay he …
deserved." His eyeless skull is turned forever to keep vigilance on the pub
door across the road. It is now lunchtime on Christmas Eve and he checks
the revelers as the pub fills with his family and friends, most of whom have
had only to cross the road from the house in which he died. He smiles as
he sees the party sparkle with piercing blue eyes and bald heads. My son
Leo, so carefully reared by Clare and me to protect him from his grandfather's influence, hunches his shoulders, leans his elbow back on the mantelpiece and chops the air with his hand as he makes his point. My emotions
reel as I watch Georgina, in eerie déjà vu, tipsily reach over the table and
put one hand on mine. With the other she tugs her hair across her face
and asks:

"Christopher, would you come if I called?"

Rose with daughter Claudia, 1965
Photo by Christopher Barker

NOTES

NOTES FOR 1913

1 Elizabeth Smart, "Scenes One Never Forgets," *In the Meantime*, 11.

2 Rosemary Sullivan, *By Heart: Elizabeth Smart, a Life*, 23.

3 Elizabeth Smart, *Autobiographies*, 157.

4 Charles Ritchie, *My Grandfather's House*, 153–54.

5 Graham Spry Papers, Vol. 5, Correspondence 1933–35.

6 Elizabeth Smart, *Necessary Secrets*, 44.

7 *Necessary Secrets*, 86.

8 *Necessary Secrets* (June 17, 1933), 22.

9 *Necessary Secrets* (July 12, 1933), 38.

10 *Necessary Secrets* (July 25 1933), 43.

11 *Necessary Secrets* (July 1933), 43.

12 *Necessary Secrets*, 43.

13 *Necessary Secrets*, 57.

14 *Necessary Secrets*, 59.

15 *Necessary Secrets*, 65.

16 *Necessary Secrets*, 66.

17 *Necessary Secrets*, 68.

18 *Necessary Secrets*, 73.

19 Elizabeth Smart, "My Lover John," Graham Spry Papers, Vol. 42-18.

20 "My Lover John."

21 "My Lover John."

22 *Necessary Secrets*, 78.

23 *Necessary Secrets*, 144.

24 *Necessary Secrets*, 136.

25 *Necessary Secrets*, 134.

26 *Necessary Secrets*, 147.

27 *Necessary Secrets*, 156.

28 *Necessary Secrets*, 155.

29 *Necessary Secrets*, 159.

30 *Necessary Secrets*, 154.

31 *Necessary Secrets*, 157.

32 *Necessary Secrets* (March 26, 1937), 163.

33 *Necessary Secrets*, 187.

34 *Necessary Secrets*, 188.

35 *Necessary Secrets*, 186.

36 *Necessary Secrets*, 191.

37 *Necessary Secrets*, 184.

38 *Necessary Secrets*, 180.

39 *Necessary Secrets*, 185.

40 *Necessary Secrets*, 195–96.

41 *Necessary Secrets*, 196.

42 *Necessary Secrets*, 197.

43 *Necessary Secrets*, 198.

44 *Necessary Secrets*, 198, 202.

45 *By Heart*, 135. Elizabeth Smart is quoting Anaïs Nin.

46 *Necessary Secrets*, 205.

47 *Necessary Secrets*, 232.

48 *Autobiographies*, 170–71.

49 *Necessary Secrets*, 226.

50 *Necessary Secrets*, 206.

51 *Necessary Secrets*, 207.

52 *Necessary Secrets*, 245.

53 *By Heart*, 149.

54 *Necessary Secrets*, 235.

55 Robert Fraser, *Chameleon Poet: A Life of George Barker*, 130.

56 *Necessary Secrets*, 243.

57 *Necessary Secrets*, 245.

58 *Autobiographies*, 126.

59 *Autobiographies*, 27.

60 Elizabeth Smart, *By Grand Central Station I Sat Down and Wept*, 17.

61 *By Grand Central Station*, 17.

62 George Barker, letter to Elizabeth Smart, March 4, 1941. This letter, along with other unpublished material quoted in the present volume, is housed in the Library and Archives Canada, Ottawa (henceforth LAC). Elizabeth Smart's papers and related documents reside there in the Elizabeth Smart fonds and several other collections. See www.collectionscanada.gc.ca.

63 *By Grand Central Station*, 20.

64 *Necessary Secrets*, 248.

65 *By Grand Central Station*, 26.

66 *By Grand Central Station*, 68.

67 Jessica Barker, letter to George Barker, LAC.

68 LAC.

69 *By Heart*, 170.

70 *Chameleon Poet*, 173.

71 Jessica Barker, letter to George Barker, LAC.
72 George Barker letter, Elizabeth Smart, February 21, 1940, LAC.
73 *Autobiographies*, 33.
74 *By Grand Central Station*, 91.
75 *Autobiographies*, 43.
76 George Barker, letter to Elizabeth Smart, May 5, 1940, LAC.
77 *Necessary Secrets*, 267–68.
78 George Barker, letter to Elizabeth Smart, LAC.
79 *Chameleon Poet*, 183.
80 George Barker, letter to Elizabeth Smart, July 31, 1941, LAC.
81 George Barker, letter to Elizabeth Smart, August 12, 1941, LAC.
82 *Chameleon Poet*, 184.
83 *By Heart*, 185.
84 *Chameleon Poet*, 191.
85 *Autobiographies*, 148.
85 Elizabeth Smart, *On the Side of the Angels*, 14.
87 *Autobiographies*, 31.
88 *Chameleon Poet*, 192.
89 *Chameleon Poet*, 193.
90 Jessica Barker, letter to Elizabeth Smart, April 4, 1942, LAC.
91 *By Heart*, 196.
92 Elizabeth Smart, *The Assumption of the Rogues and Rascals*, 29.
93 Willard Maas, letter to Elizabeth Smart, June 18, 1943, LAC.
94 *Autobiographies*, 79.
95 *Chameleon Poet*, 220.
96 *Autobiographies*, 103.
97 *By Heart*, 210.
98 *By Heart*, 214.
99 *By Heart*, 214.
100 *By Heart*, 220.
101 *Chameleon Poet*, 229.
102 *Chameleon Poet*, 229.
103 *By Heart*, 230.
104 *By Heart*, 234.
105 LAC.

NOTES FOR 1951

1 George Barker, *Journals* 1928–32, British Library archive.
2 Maurice Carpenter, *Rebel in the Thirties*, 49.
3 Emily Holmes Coleman diaries, March 22, 1936, University of Delaware Library.
4 George Barker, letter to Antonia White, quoted in Susan Chitty, *Now to My Mother: A Very Personal Memoir of Antonia White*, 1939.

BIBLIOGRAPHY

Barker, George. *Janus*. Comprises "The Documents of a Death" and "The Bacchant." London: Faber and Faber, 1935.

——. *Poems*. London: Faber and Faber, 1935.

——. *Calamiterror*. London: Faber and Faber, 1937.

——. *Lament and Triumph*. London: Faber and Faber, 1940.

——. *Selected Poems*. New York: Macmillan, 1941.

——. *Eros in Dogma*. London: Faber and Faber, 1944.

——. *First Cycle of Love Poems*. New York: Dial Press, 1947.

——. *The Dead Seagull*. London: MacGibbon & Kee, 1950.

——. *News of the World*. London: Faber and Faber, 1950.

——. *The True Confession of George Barker*. London: Fore Publications, 1950.

——. *A Vision of Beasts and Gods*. London: Faber and Faber, 1954.

——. *The Seraphina*. From *Two Plays:* The Seraphina *and* In the Shade of the Old Apple Tree. London: Faber and Faber, 1958.

——. *The View from a Blind Eye*. London: Faber and Faber, 1962.

——. *The True Confession of George Barker.* Augmented ed. London: MacGibbon & Kee, 1965.

——. *Dreams of a Summer Night*. London: Faber and Faber, 1966.

——. *The Golden Chains*. London: Faber and Faber, 1968.

——. *Poems of Places and People*. London: Faber and Faber, 1971.

——. *In Memory of David Archer*. London: Faber and Faber, 1973.

——. *Dialogues, Etc*. London: Faber and Faber, 1976.

——. *Villa Stellar*. London: Faber and Faber, 1978.

——. *Anno Domini*. London: Faber and Faber, 1983.

——. *Collected Poems*. Edited by Robert Fraser. London: Faber and Faber, 1987.

——. *Street Ballads*. London: Faber and Faber, 1992.

Carpenter, Maurice. *Rebel in the Thirties*. Essex: Paperbag Book Club, 1976.

Chitty, Susan. *Now to My Mother: A Very Personal Memoir of Antonia White*. London: Weidenfeld and Nicolson, 1985.

Coleman, Emily Holmes. The Emily Holmes Coleman Papers. Collection No. 105, Special Collections, University of Delaware Library, Newark, DE.

Fraser, Robert. *The Chameleon Poet: A Life of George Barker*. London: Jonathan Cape, 2001.

Ritchie, Charles. *My Grandfather's House: Scenes of Childhood and Youth*. Toronto: McClelland & Stewart, 2002.

Smart, Elizabeth. *By Grand Central Station I Sat Down and Wept*. London: Editions Poetry London, 1945.

———. *By Grand Central Station I Sat Down and Wept*. Reprint. Foreword by Brigid Brophy. London: Panther, 1966.

———. *The Assumption of the Rogues and Rascals*. London: Jonathan Cape/Polytantric Press, 1978.

———. *A Bonus*. London: Polytantric Press, 1977.

———. *Ten Poems*. Bath, UK: Bath Place Community Arts Press, 1981.

———. *Eleven Poems*. Bracknell, UK: Owen Kirton, 1982.

———. *In the Meantime*. Comprises "Scenes One Never Forgets" and "In the Meantime: Diary of a Blockage." Ottawa: Deneau, 1984.

———. *Necessary Secrets: The Journals of Elizabeth Smart*. Edited by Alice Van Wart. Toronto: Deneau, 1986.

———. *Juvenilia: Early Writings of Elizabeth Smart*. Edited by Alice Van Wart. Toronto: Coach House Press, 1987.

———. *Autobiographies*. Edited by Christina Burridge. Vancouver: William Hoffer/Tanks, 1987.

———. *Elizabeth's Garden: Elizabeth Smart on the Art of Gardening*. Edited by Alice Van Wart. Toronto: Coach House Press, 1989.

———. *On the Side of the Angels: The Second Volume of the Journals of Elizabeth Smart*. Edited by Alice Van Wart. London: HarperCollins, 1994.

Spry, Graham. Graham Spry Papers, Vol. 5, Correspondence 1933–3. Library and Archives Canada, Ottawa.

Sullivan, Rosemary. *By Heart: Elizabeth Smart, a Life*. Toronto: Viking, 1991.

Ustinov, Peter. *Dear Me*. London: Heinemann, 1977.

INDEX OF NAMES